DELAWARE

"Delaware's Enterprises" by Irene Prince

Published in cooperation with the
Delaware State Chamber of Commerce

Windsor Publications, Inc.
Chatsworth, California

DELAWARE

First Place

A CONTEMPORARY PORTRAIT BY
MARGO MCDONOUGH, JOE EMERSON, JUDITH PENNEBAKER, W. DOUGLAS RAINEY

Windsor Publications, Inc.—Book Division
Managing Editor: Karen Story
Design Director: Alexander D'Anca
Photo Director: Susan L. Wells
Executive Editor: Pamela Schroeder

Staff for *Delaware: First Place*
Manuscript Editor: Jeffrey Reeves
Photo Editor: Larry Molmud
Senior Editor, Corporate Profiles: Judith L. Hunter
Production Editor, Corporate Profiles: Albert Polito
Proofreader: Melissa Wells
Customer Service Manager: Phyllis Feldman-Schroeder
Editorial Assistants: Kim Kievman, Michael Nugwynne, Michele Oakley,
Kathy B. Peyser, Susan Schlanger, Theresa J. Solis
Publisher's Representative, Corporate Profiles: Marcia Cohen, Rob Ottenheimer
Layout Artist, Corporate Profiles: Michael Burg

Designer: Christina L. Rosepapa

Library of Congress Cataloging-in-Publication Data
Delaware first place : a contemporary portrait / by Margo McDonough
... [et al.] : "Delaware's enterprises" by Irene Prince.— 1st ed.
p. cm.
"Published in cooperation with the Delaware State Chamber of Commerce."
Includes bibliographical references.
ISBN 0-89781-415-0
1. Delaware—History. 2. Delaware—Description and travel—Views.
3. Delaware—Industries. I. McDonough, Margo. II. Prince, Irene.
III. Delaware State Chamber of Commerce.
F164.D393 1990   89-25004
975. 1—dc20   CIP

Windsor Publications, Inc.
Elliot Martin, Chairman of the Board
James L. Fish III, Chief Operating Officer
Michele Sylvestro, Vice President/Sales-Marketing

Fishermen wrap up a day's work at Cape Henlopen State Park. Photo by Brad Crooks

Contents

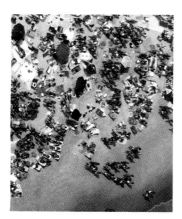   

Part

1

The Diamond State

Camp meetings converted thousands to Methodism in a wave of religious enthusiasm. This Red Lion Camp Meeting was like many others on the Delmarva Peninsula. Tents remained secluded in the woods, while wagons and carts surrounded the cleared preaching area. Courtesy, Historical Society of Delaware

When Henry Hudson sailed up what is known today as the Delaware Bay in 1609, he did not set foot on the land that now is part of the state of Delaware. Hudson, who was looking for a shortcut to China, feared that his ship would run aground in the shallow bay. Instead, he sailed north and discovered the Hudson River. It would be left to others to discover the true riches of an area that would live up to its later name, "the Diamond State."

An English captain, sailing into the bay in 1610, named it in honor of Lord de La Warre, the governor of Virginia.

In 1631 a group of Dutch fishermen had established a small settlement known as Zwaanandael (present-day Lewes) in Delaware. Its history proved to be brief and tragic. A misunderstanding over the taking of a metal item by the Lenni Lenape Indians resulted in the killing of all of the colony's inhabitants.

It was left up to Sweden, another growing power in Europe, to settle the new country. In 1637 two Swedish ships, the *Kalmar Nyckel* and the *Vogel Grip,* sailed up Delaware Bay and into a smaller river the Swedes named after their young queen, Christina.

The settlers, made up of citizens of Sweden and nearby Finland, adapted more easily than the Dutch to the new setting. The new country, like their native lands, was covered with trees that could be used for cabins. Log cabins, which would become a symbol of pioneer settlement in America, were first built in Delaware by the Swedes and Finns.

The Swedes, like the Dutch, saw the settlement, known as Fort Christina, as a source of profit, sending tobacco and furs back to Sweden. The settlers also raised livestock and grew crops, including corn, first cultivated by the native Americans.

While the Swedes established their settlement, the Dutch had not lost interest in the area and were, in fact, unwilling to share the fur trade. Peter Stuyvesant, governor of New Netherlands, ordered that a fort (Fort Casimir) be erected near present-day New Castle. After the governor of the Swedish colony ordered soldiers to take over the fort, Stuyvesant sent warships and soldiers and forced the surrender of the Swedes in 1655.

The First State

Left: In 1637 two Swedish ships, the **Kalmar Nyckel** *and the* **Vogel Grip,** *sailed up Delaware Bay and into a smaller river, the Christina, which the Swedes named for their young queen. With the settling of Fort Christina, the Swedes found a great profit in the export of tobacco, furs, livestock, and corn. Courtesy, Historical Society of Delaware*

Below: Henry Hudson was looking for a shortcut to China when, afraid that his now-famous ship, the **Half Moon,** *would run aground in the shallow Delaware Bay, he sailed north and discovered the Hudson River in 1609. Courtesy, Historical Society of Delaware*

The Swedish and Finnish settlers continued to reside near Fort Christina, while the Dutch founded a community near Fort Casimir and named it New Amstel. They also resettled the area near Cape Henlopen, naming the community Hoerkil. But despite the show of force against the Swedes, the Dutch were able to hold on to the Delaware Valley region for only nine years.

The English were becoming a far larger power on the Atlantic Seaboard, with settlements stretching from present-day New England down through Virginia. In a show of force in 1664, the English fleet sailed into the harbor at New Amsterdam, whose governor quickly surrendered to the far superior force. The Dutch also surrendered at the Delaware settlement of New Amstel. New Amsterdam was renamed New York, while New Amstel was renamed New Castle. The English, following the practice of the Dutch, allowed all settlers to stay in the newly acquired colony.

But the period of colonization by the Swedes and Dutch might have been only an interesting footnote in the history of Pennsylvania or Maryland had it not been for a dispute between the two English sponsors of the colonies.

The land that makes up present-day Maryland had been awarded to the Calvert family for settlement by Catholics who had been persecuted in England. Cecil Calvert, the second Lord Baltimore, claimed the area formerly held by the Dutch. However, the Duke of York, brother of King Charles II, would not turn over the territory, despite forays by Calvert's soldiers to Hoerkil that resulted in the burning of buildings and the killing of livestock. The duke cited a charter indicating that areas that had previously been settled by Europeans could not be part of Maryland.

The situation was further complicated by the duke's decision to award Wil-

liam Penn a colony along the Delaware River. Penn, a member of the Society of Friends, also known as the Quakers, founded the colony in part to allow members of the denomination to escape persecution.

Penn arrived in New Castle in 1682. From there he sailed farther up the river, resulting in the founding of Philadelphia. Penn went on to divide what was to become Delaware into the three counties that exist today: New Castle, which had already been in existence, Kent, and Sussex. Governmental activities were based in New Castle in New Castle County; Lewes in Sussex; and the newly founded community of Dover in Kent.

A small group of Nanticoke Indians preserves its heritage through membership in the Nanticoke Indian Association. Most members of the original tribe left Delaware in the 1750s, but a few remained. This unidentified Nanticoke from Millsboro was photographed around 1920. Courtesy, Delaware State Archives

William Penn, who was awarded a colony along the Delaware River, arrived in New Castle in 1682. In his ship, the **Welcome,** *he sailed further up the river and founded Philadelphia. Courtesy, Historical Society of Delaware*

Despite continuing claims by Cecil Calvert regarding Delaware, the region might have remained part of Pennsylvania had war not erupted in Europe between England and France. The two powerful navies of these countries fought in the New World, with French privateers and pirates raiding farms in Sussex County.

The raids upset residents of the lower counties. Penn, however, would not provide help because of the Quakers' antiwar beliefs. Residents of the lower counties also believed that Pennsylvania dismissed the threat from the sea because it was too far inland to be affected by pirates.

After it became apparent that a split had developed between the upper and lower counties of Pennsylvania over defense and other issues, Penn agreed in 1704 to give the lower counties their own assembly.

The Calverts still claimed ownership of the three counties and went to court in England to legitimize this claim.

They were so sure of their right to the land that they awarded grants for farms in Kent and Sussex counties that formed the basis of the agricultural economy in southern Delaware. The new settlers brought slaves with them and formed a tobacco- and farm products-based economy similar to the ones in Maryland and Virginia. Penn did nothing to stop the grants.

Among the Quaker colonists were merchants who would form the economic base of northern Delaware in the eighteenth and nineteenth centuries. One such merchant, William Shipley, moved to the new and struggling community of Wilmingtown, near Fort Christina, in 1735.

With the help of Shipley and the original namesake of the city, Thomas Willing, the village known as Willingtown began to grow, becoming a port that could ship out the farm goods that were grown in abundance in the area. In 1739, the city was renamed Wilmington in honor of the Earl of Wilmington, a prominent Englishman.

By the 1740s another Quaker merchant, Oliver Canby, had discovered that the fast-flowing waters of Brandywine Creek could be used to grind flour from the wheat that was being raised in the area. The availability of moving water brought other businessmen, including Joseph Tatnall, who owned a number of flour mills. The flour was sold to merchants, like Shipley, who owned ships that transported goods to other colonies.

As a result, to this day Kent and Sussex counties are often viewed as being part of the agricultural South, with New Castle County being thought of as part of the industrial North. This difference would continue to have a major impact on the political system and other facets of Delaware life.

The English courts later ruled against the Calverts, citing the previous colonization effort by the Dutch as the reason the territory could not become part of Maryland. That, along with Penn's decision to let the three counties form their own assembly, set the stage for Delaware's becoming a separate political entity.

While family feuds were taking place between individual colonies, the English were establishing their dominance over the new land. By 1763 the French and their Indian allies had been defeated in the French and Indian War, giving the English control over French holdings that extended from Quebec in Canada to the Mississippi River Valley.

While George Washington and other colonists had fought in the war, the English believed they should also help pay for the expensive undertaking. As a result, in 1765 the Stamp Act was

During the eighteenth and nineteenth centuries, the Brandywine River in northern Delaware supported a number of water-powered industries. Gilpin's Paper Mill operated until destroyed by a flood in 1822. Courtesy, Hagley Museum and Library

passed, requiring that colonists pay for the stamps on official documents, such as wills and deeds to land. Bad feeling toward England grew, with prominent Delawareans active in the protest, including Caesar Rodney and John Dickinson of Kent County.

The English later repealed the Stamp Act, but added duties to products from England used by the colonies, resulting in the Boston Tea Party.

Parliament retaliated by punishing Bostonians for their actions, leading to the formation of the Continental Congress that met in Philadelphia to protest the actions of the English. Caesar Rodney was sent to the Philadelphia meeting, joined by lawyers George Read of New Castle and Thomas McKean of New Castle County.

The heavy-handed actions of the English in Boston quickly turned the protests into an armed revolt. By 1775 English troops had battled militia at Lexington and Concord. When word of the battles reached Philadelphia, the Continental Congress decided to organize an army to fight the English.

Delaware, like many colonies, had mixed views on the revolution. Some colonists, particularly in Sussex County, opposed it, and two loyalists, Thomas Robinson and Cheney Clow, attempted to lead loyalist revolts that were quickly put down by the Delaware militia.

In 1776 the colonies declared their independence from England. Delaware declared itself independent from England and Pennsylvania on June 15, 1776. The event is still celebrated in Delaware as Separation Day.

In what may be the most celebrated event in Delaware history, Caesar Rodney, after receiving word that the Continental Congress would vote on independence, rode through a night filled with thunder and lightning from his Dover home to Philadelphia to cast his vote for freedom. Rodney's ride stands out as a central event in Delaware history, and today there is a dramatic statue commemorating the event on Rodney Square in the center of downtown Wilmington.

Two days after his dramatic ride, Rodney, along with Read and McKean, voted for the Declaration of Independence in Independence Hall. Delaware quickly raised an army that became known for its blue uniforms and its fighting skills. The army was also noted for the Blue hen chickens (today the state bird) it carried along for cockfights. The birds and the soldiers quickly won a reputation for bravery and fighting skills.

The battles of the war largely bypassed Delaware, the exception being in 1777 when the English sent a large army that landed near Elkton, Maryland, a community near the Delaware

Left: One of the best-known events in Delaware history is Caesar Rodney's ride from his farm in Kent County to Philadelphia on the night of July 1, 1776, to cast his vote for American independence from Great Britain. The tale has been embellished and romanticized by writers and artists. Rodney probably rode in a carriage instead of on horseback on that stormy evening. Courtesy, Historical Society of Delaware

Facing page: Colonel John Haslet's regiment joined the fight for American independence in 1776. The regiment distinguished itself for bravery and came to be known as the "Blue Hens Chickens" after game hens known for their fighting abilities. The regiment's motto, later adopted by the state of Delaware, was "liberty and independence." Courtesy, Historical Society of Delaware

Thomas McKean, a New Castle lawyer, was the first of Delaware's Revolutionary-era statesman to favor American independence from England. Courtesy, Historical Society of Delaware

border. Washington moved his force into northern Delaware, and the state's only battle took place at Cooch's Bridge near Newark, as Washington's troops harassed a numerically superior British force.

The British moved north and met Washington's army again at the Battle of Brandywine, one of the biggest battles of the Revolutionary War, near the Delaware line. The British defeated Washington's troops and occupied Wilmington for several weeks, but went on to spend the winter in Pennsylvania.

After many battles, Washington's troops, aided by French naval forces, forced the surrender of Lord Cornwallis' troops at Yorktown, Virginia, in 1781. By 1783 the English signed a treaty that formally ended the war.

The war left the Delaware economy in poor shape. In addition to runaway inflation and the English choking off Delaware ports, the state was affected in the postwar period by a weak national government and by the fact that it did not have a large ocean port that would allow it to control its own trade.

In the summer of 1787, Delaware and the other states sent delegates to Philadelphia to deal with the weaknesses of the Articles of Confederation, a document that did not provide the strong cen-

tral government that would ensure the autonomy of the state.

Working through the hot weather in Independence Hall, the articles were scrapped in favor of a new constitution. Naturally enough, the big states and small states debated on the makeup of the House and Senate. Large states wanted representation based on population, while small states wanted an equal number of representatives from all states.

The delegates finally worked out a compromise: membership in the House was based on the state's population; however, two senators represented each state in the Senate. Delaware was pleased with the compromise, and by December 1787 delegates had voted in Dover to approve the document, the first state to do so. Because of its quick action, Delaware became known as the "First State."

With the ratification of the constitution, the new nation elected George Washington, the leader of the Constitutional Convention, as its first president.

Delaware, along with the rest of the new nation, faced a Europe in turmoil, particularly in France, where a revolution had toppled the monarchy. In 1799 the du Ponts, a family with close ties to the monarchy, emigrated to America.

Eleuthere Irenee du Pont, a young member of the family searching for a way to continue the family's comfortable life-style in the new land, realized that American gunpowder was inferior to the gunpowder he had helped produce in France. Attracted by the abundant waterpower, he founded a mill in 1802 that produced gunpowder on the Brandywine River.

The du Ponts were not complete strangers in the new land. They had the good fortune to know the new president, Thomas Jefferson, who had spent a number of years in France and was

able to secure gunpowder contracts with the United States government.

Du Pont gunpowder proved to be useful to the young nation, which was attempting to stay out of the conflict between England and France, now under the rule of Napoleon Bonaparte. This became impossible because both France and England were attacking ships that they believed were involved in trade with their enemy.

After remaining neutral, and at one point refusing to trade with either France or England (a strategy that hurt Wilmington and other ports), the United States eventually found itself at odds with England, which continued to board ships and even forced American sailors to serve on English ships.

In 1812 war was declared on England, at the time the world's leading na-

val power. Two Delawareans, Commodore Thomas Mcdonough and Captain Jacob Jones, won important naval battles over the English that raised the morale of the new nation.

Delaware held its ground in battle with the English. When English ships formed a blockade on Delaware Bay and began bombarding Lewes in 1813, the small community did not surrender, because of the able leadership of Delaware militia leader Colonel Samuel Boyer Davis. The militia's small group of cannons returned fire, and the community was aided by the fact that the British cannon fire was inaccurate. No lives were lost and no homes were destroyed, and as far as anyone can tell only one house was hit with a cannon ball. Known as the Cannon Ball House, it is now one of the leading historic sites in Lewes.

In April 1813, the village of Lewes was bombarded by British warships demanding provisions. The townspeople held firm, and the English finally gave up the attempt. The cannons used in the defense of Lewes remained in place when this photograph was taken in the 1890s. Courtesy, Historical Society of Delaware

While Lewes was spared, the English continued to block Delaware Bay until the war formally ended with the signing of a treaty in 1815.

But war was not the only thing that concerned Delawareans. The state, like the rest of America in the late 1700s and early 1800s, was undergoing a religious awakening.

During the Revolutionary War Francis Asbury, a Methodist missionary, came to America to advocate good works and Bible study, rather than the drinking and parties that were favored at the time. Followers of Asbury and other ministers became members of the Methodist church. The denomination quickly became the largest religious group in Delaware, attracting both black and white members, and Barrett's Chapel, a landmark in Kent County, is called the "Cradle of Methodism" in the United States.

Two Delawareans served key roles in the founding of black Methodist de-nominations. Richard Allen, who was born a slave near Dover, bought his freedom from his Methodist owner and founded the African Methodist Episcopal church. When white members of Asbury Methodist church in Wilmington required black members to sit in another area, Peter Spencer led a walkout of black members that resulted in the founding of the African Union Methodist church.

While the area south of Wilmington remained an agricultural economy, industrial development continued along the Brandywine River throughout this period. With the notable exception of the du Ponts, this entrepreneurial energy came from the Quakers. In addition to the flour mills, Quakers Joshua and Thomas Gilpin built a paper mill in 1787. In 1824 another Quaker industrialist, Joseph Bancroft, built a textile mill that became one of the largest in the nation.

The Brandywine had become one of the new nation's leading industrial

centers, although transportation continued to present problems.

In an effort to improve a road system that became nearly unusable during wet periods, graded roads, known as turnpikes, were constructed. In return for paying tolls, goods could be brought overland more conveniently to Philadelphia and other areas.

Also aiding transportation was the completion of the Chesapeake and Delaware Canal in 1829. The canal, which cuts across the state, provided a shortcut between Chesapeake Bay and major markets. The canal also proved to be a dividing line between the two Delawares. To this day, the term "south of the canal" is still used to denote the differences between the industrial north of the state and more rural southern Delaware.

The invention of the steamboat also changed transportation and allowed peaches and other farm goods from the southern part of the state to be more quickly transported to major cities.

By the 1830s railroads were springing up on the East Coast, and Delaware was one of the first areas to see the "iron horse." A short railroad line was built across the state, allowing passengers to travel overland by train for a short distance on trips between Philadelphia and Baltimore or Washington, D.C. In 1838 a railroad passing through Wilmington connected Philadelphia and Baltimore. By the 1850s a north-south railroad was built, connecting the Wilmington area with Seaford.

The railroads also resulted in the growth of an industry in the Wilmington area that turned out passenger cars and other railroad equipment.

Despite these advances, however, Wilmington still lacked an ocean port that would allow its burgeoning manufacturing community to better compete with Baltimore, New York, Philadephia, and other growing coastal cities.

In 1837 a group largely made up of Quaker manufacturers formed a board of trade, the predecessor to the present-day Delaware State Chamber of Commerce. One of the first items discussed by the board was the dredging of the bed of the Christina River to allow use by larger vessels. Also discussed was improved mail service to Philadelphia. The Board of Trade became inactive in 1839, but was reorganized in 1849.

As the state entered the 1860s, it was caught in the increasingly bitter battle between pro-slavery and abolitionist elements. Its economy reflected the growing division between northern and southern Delaware. In the north, New Castle County remained an industrial center, while the southern counties were primarily agricultural, with a small slave population.

The Civil War further aggravated this division, though the state was never in danger of seceding. This was due in part because of its pride over being the first state in the nation to approve the

The Wilmington and Western Railroad first chugged through the hilly terrain of northern New Castle County in the 1870s. Company directors, local farmers, and industrialists hoped to connect Wilmington to new western markets, but the line only expanded 20 miles to nearby Landenberg in Pennsylvania. Courtesy, Delaware Historical Society

Constitution. Heavily industrialized New Castle County was a stronghold for the Union, while Southern sympathizers were more numerous in Kent and especially Sussex counties. The state never chose to outlaw slavery during the war, despite the fact that the institution was on the verge of disappearing, and trading in slaves had long since been outlawed.

As in the American Revolution, Delaware troops served valiantly in the war.

The industrial might of New Castle County also played a role in the Northern victory. The Du Pont mills were quick to align with the government of Abraham Lincoln and proved skillful in finding the raw materials for gunpowder that could only be obtained overseas.

In the late 1860s Wilmington businessmen led by Joshua T. Heald, a Quaker banker, revived the board of trade, which had once again become inactive. The organization once again was seeking a deep harbor for Wilmington, along with improved communications and train service to Philadelphia. This time the board reported some successes, including the establishment of a ship that traveled to New Jersey shore communities.

Despite the belief of board of trade members that Wilmington was being bypassed by ocean shippers, the city was thriving. Its steamships, railroad cars, and railroad wheels were being exported throughout the world, with local tanneries providing leather seats for the railcars. Other products included matches and of course Du Pont gunpowder, which was used in the westward expansion for mining and railroads.

Downstate, agriculture remained king. A peach boom developed as residents of big cities paid high prices for peaches shipped by rail and steamship from Delaware. The glory days of peaches ended during the 1870s, when a blight swept through the orchards, killing trees.

A race between two rival Wilmington fire companies was depicted by artist J.A. Morgan in 1880. The pumper of the Water Witch Steam Fire Company, pulled by a pair of white horses, tries to edge out the Delaware Fire Company engine. Courtesy, Historical Society of Delaware

Students of Georgetown High School learned tree planting and soil conservation techniques on the Tunnell Farm in 1948. Such progressive methods made the most of Sussex County land. Courtesy, National Archives

Delaware farmers proved resilient and found other crops that could be shipped to urban centers. That spirit of innovation would continue in the twentieth century, allowing many of the First State's farmers to escape the agricultural crisis of the 1980s.

The good times extended into the twentieth century, with Wilmington growing to 76,000 people, or nearly 40 percent of the total population of Delaware.

The board of trade still lobbied for a port in Wilmington to ease the congestion arising from the factories on the Christina River waterfront. The board also played a progressive role in improving the community by advocating the acquisition of parkland, road improvements, child labor laws, medical examinations for school children, and compulsory education laws.

In 1912 the board of trade became affiliated with the National Chamber of Commerce. Under Josiah Marvel, who served as president of the chamber, the board grew in influence and underwent a restructuring program to make it even more effective.

The early 1900s brought dramatic changes to Delaware, thanks in part to the Du Pont Company.

While du Pont family members had always exerted an influence on Delaware life, their gunpowder mills were not the largest employer in the state. Furthermore, the mills for many years were largely self-contained communities whose workers rarely mixed with Wilmington residents. Given the present-day size and influence of the company, it is hard to imagine that at the turn of the century Du Pont was on the verge of being sold, following the death of Eugene du Pont.

Instead, Alfred I. duPont purchased the company, joined by cousins T. Coleman du Pont and Pierre S. du Pont. The new management, led for much of the era by P.S. du Pont, transformed the company into a highly centralized concern housed in the building in downtown Wilmington that still contains the company's headquarters, along with the Hotel du Pont.

Du Pont successfully controlled two-thirds of the nation's explosives production—in the eyes of the government, too successfully. In 1912 the federal government ordered the company to halve its explosives holdings and spin off two new companies.

One company, Hercules Inc., now a diversified chemical and aerospace company, remains based in Wilmington with $3 billion in annual sales. The other, Atlas Powder Co., became part of Imperial Chemical Industries (ICI), a British company, in 1971.

The du Ponts were also busy transforming the state's education and transportation systems.

P.S. du Pont became concerned that the state's education system was inadequate. Through personal donations and by enlisting the support of Delaware citizens, he built new buildings and encouraged the formation of a tax structure that would allow adequate financing of public education. P.S. du Pont also helped create a women's college to assist in the training of teachers. In the 1940s that college was merged with Delaware College to form the University of Delaware.

T. Coleman du Pont, meanwhile, was busy on the transportation front, personally financing construction of the du Pont Highway, which runs the length of the state. The highway, along with others, aided the state's agricultrual community by reducing the amount of time needed to bring products to market.

World War I brought boom conditions to the state as Wilmington's plants turned out ships, ammunition, and other products. By the time of the First World War, Wilmington had grown to more than 100,000 residents, swelled by the immigration of Poles, Italians, and other European immigrants. The immigrants and others flocking to Wilmington found housing in short supply and efforts were made by the chamber and other groups to resolve the problem.

The city continued to prosper after the war as progress was made in establish-

ing a deepwater port. By 1923 the Wilmington Marine Terminal had opened, capping a nearly 90-year-long effort to improve harbor facilities.

By this time Wilmington was coping with the changes in its economy that would continue through the 1970s.

Du Pont shut down its now-obsolete powder mills as explosives became a smaller part of its business. At the same time, the chemical industry, led by the headquarters operations of Du Pont, Hercules, and Atlas, was thriving, while the traditional mainstays, such as textiles and shipbuilding, were on the decline. Wilmington was on its way to becoming a "corporate capital" rather than a manufacturing center.

Agriculture continued to be the backbone of southern Delaware's economy. With the help of the du Pont Highway and other improved roads, Delmarva Peninsula farmers turned to poultry production. The industry grew rapidly, in the process helping individual farmers and creating a number of nationally known poultry processors. Farmers were further aided by growing feed grains to supply the rapidly growing industry.

The strength of Delaware's economy

The Pierre S. du Pont High School in Wilmington boasted the most modern facilities, including a chemistry laboratory to train students for the state's leading industry. Courtesy, Historical Society of Delaware

Right: Toward making dangerous powder mill jobs more attractive, Du Pont paid good wages and took a paternal interest in its employees. Many men held their jobs for 40 or 50 years, and often their children would find work at the company. Courtesy, Delaware State Archives

*Below: The crew of the oyster schooner **Doris** posed for this group portrait in 1924 near the Delaware or Chesapeake bay. Oyster boats might be at sea for a week or more before returning to harbor, where the catch was shipped to distant markets. Courtesy, Delaware State Archives*

was not enough to allow it to remain unaffected by the Great Depression. Like all other states, Delaware saw its social services stretched to the limit by the growing numbers of unemployed people seeking relief. While the effects were severe, the state's largest employers were able to cushion the blow somewhat. There were also companies like Du Pont, that were willing to take risks.

A major breakthrough took place in the 1930s when Du Pont research scientists came up with a new synthetic material. The product, which was eventually named nylon, had a world of uses, and Du Pont moved quickly to bring it to production.

By now a company operating plants throughout the nation, Du Pont could have built the factory in a number of locations. Instead it chose Seaford, a small community in southern Delaware, as the site for a plant that would eventually employ thousands of people. With the addition of the Seaford plant and a pigments plant near Wilmington at Edgemoor, Du Pont was emerging as the state's largest employer.

While agriculture would remain the top industry in southern Delaware, the Du Pont plant represented the first large industry to move downstate. It would not be the last.

World War II brought the same challenges as World War I. Housing was in short supply for workers who labored in defense plants that turned out a variety of products. Soldiers and sailors from the state fought in both theaters of the war, including a group that served with distinction in the South Pacific.

Delaware's location also played a strategic role in the war. Air bases in New Castle and Dover played a major part in ferrying aircraft to the battlefronts of Europe. Another base on the state's seacoast was used in spotting the dreaded German U-boats.

But it was the period after World War II that brought the greatest changes to the state.

Companies were drawn by the fact that they could provide goods to major population centers on the Eastern Seaboard from Delaware, which was halfway between New York City and Washington, D.C. In New Castle County, General Motors and the Chrysler Corporation established assembly plants to serve the massive East Coast market. In addition, Getty Oil, now Star Enterprise, opened a massive refinery in Delaware City to handle oil shipments brought into the United States.

Agribusiness also moved into high gear, thanks to the broiler-chicken industry. A number of companies, including Delaware-based Townsend's and Allen Family Foods, along with nationally known Perdue, based in nearby Salisbury, Maryland, built large processing plants employing thousands of people.

The biggest postwar changes came to Delaware's cities. The decline in population in the city of Wilmington accelerated after the war, as mile after mile of new housing was built in Brandywine Hundred, north of the city, and in Pike Creek, Newark, and other surrounding areas.

Business also began to move to the new suburbs. While the Du Pont Company kept its headquarters downtown, new campus-style office and research areas were sprouting up at Barley Mill Plaza, Chestnut Run, and even Glasgow near the Maryland border.

Delaware remained a friendly place for big companies. Its incorporation laws were favorable to corporations, who enriched the state treasury by incorporating in Delaware.

Although often overlooked by the growth upstate, some of the most dramatic changes may have been taking place in Dover. Although the city of

5,000 or so was the state capital, the growth to the north had bypassed it. For many years the city held the dubious distinction of being the only state capital without a newspaper. That would change after the war.

Dover, like many communities, was near an airfield that closed after World War II. In the early 1950s, however, the military took another look at the facility and decided to reopen it as Dover Air Force Base, a major air transport base. Also moving into Dover was General Foods, which built a plant employing more than 1,000 people.

Pennsylvanian Jack Smyth moved to Dover, bought up two weekly newspapers, and in 1953 made the *Delaware State News* the state's first daily south of New Castle County. The state's two other dailies in Wilmington, the *Morning News* and *Evening Journal*, recently combined to form the *Morning News Journal*.

To the south, in Greenwood, John Mervine set up Nanticoke Homes, a manufacturer of prefabricated houses that is now one of the largest companies of its kind on the East Coast, employing in excess of 1,000 people.

The 1960s and 1970s were a time of growth and trouble for northern Delaware. I-95 was built, easing congestion and bringing growth to the Newark area south of Wilmington. It did little, however, to help the city of Wilmington.

Like many East Coast cities, Wilmington was in trouble. Left behind in the move to its suburban areas was an increasingly poor population that could not afford to pay the necessary taxes to support city services. There was talk that Wilmington was becoming another dying city ringed by affluent suburbs.

With the growth came concern about the environment, culminating in a successful effort to stop construction of a refinery by a major oil company. The Coastal Zone Act, a major piece of legisla-

tion in the 1970s, banned refineries and other types of heavy industry from coastal areas. The act—while now viewed by most Delawareans as necessary to protect the delicate environment area along Delaware Bay—left the impression that the state was hostile toward business.

Delaware was also hurt by one of the nation's highest state income taxes and continuing problems in balancing the state budget. Businesses were leaving and others were making noises that they might do so in the future.

With the support of the State Chamber of Commerce and other groups, Governor Pierre "Pete" du Pont and his successor, Michael Castle, forged a bipartisan effort to turn the Delaware economy around through reforms in state government and through incentives to draw business in the state. The state income tax was cut and a landmark piece of legislation, the Financial Center Development Act, became law. The law freed banks from restrictions on credit card interest rates and provided tax advantages for banks moving assets to the state. The legislation was a tribute to the ability of the First State to move quickly to solve problems by talking them out.

The Financial Center Development Act went on to draw many of the nation's largest banks to Delaware to set up credit card and other operations, in the process creating tens of thousands of new jobs. Existing banks in Delaware also expanded, although the consolidation of the industry resulted in the mergers of Delaware Trust Company and the Bank of Delaware with Pennsylvania holding companies. Wilmington Trust Company grew rapidly and remained fiercely independent, aided by the fact that it ranked among the top in the nation in financial performance.

In the 1980s no one talked about Wilmington's being a dying city. Homes and townhouses were being restored and new housing was going up. The city's impressive skyline now contained high-rise buildings carrying the names of nationally known banks such as Chase Manhattan and Manufacturers Hanover.

The boom also affected the suburbs as large office parks were built to house, among others, credit card operations of Maryland Bank, American Express, and the Sears Discovery Card.

Du Pont reduced its work force during the early 1980s, but did so with a generous early-retirement program that lessened its impact on the economy. By the end of the decade, the company was expanding and upgrading many of its research and development facilities in northern Delaware. Even the venerable Seaford plant was prospering, thanks in part to the invention of Stainmaster carpet fibers by Du Pont that allow the removal of stains that were once permanent.

ICI's acquisition of Delaware-based Atlas Chemical in the early 1970s proved to be a plus for the state. The British chemical and pharmaceutical giant made Wilmington the headquarters for its North and South American operations and embarked on an aggressive expansion program that included the acquisition of Glidden Paints and Stauffer Chemicals. By the late 1980s ICI's American employment had grown to 3,600.

Despite a wave of plant closings in the automobile industry, both Chrysler and General Motors chose their Delaware facilities to manufacture their new lines of automobiles.

The once massive railroad car industry also saw a small revival. Amtrak, the federally owned rail passenger system, operates two large operations in Delaware that build and modify railroad equipment.

Even Phoenix Steel, a massive mill north of Wilmington that failed to survive the brutal shakeout in the industry, was brought back to life as CITISTEEL USA, a venture owned by a Chinese company.

The long struggle to develop the Port of Wilmington was paying off in a big way. Throughout the 1980s the port was taking a large chunk of Delaware River port traffic.

The robust nature of Delaware's economy, described by Wilmington Trust Company chairman Bernard Taylor as "practically recession-proof" was reflected in the state's financial picture. While other states in the late 1980s were beginning to increase taxes, Delaware legislators were once again looking at lowering the state income tax. The state had also embarked on an ambitious improvement of its highway system, capped by a north-south route to Dover, adjacent to Coleman du Pont's highway.

As the state enters the 1990s, it faces the task of managing growth in a way that will preserve the quality of life and the vitality of the economy.

One example of the pleasures and perils of prosperity is housing. Housing prices—while far more reasonable than in many other areas of the East Coast—increased sharply in northern Delaware. At the same time, the supply of moderately priced housing has declined. By 1989 the State Chamber of Commerce had placed affordable housing at the top of its list of priorities.

Meanwhile, agricultural land is being lost to new development. Some say it is inevitable. Others believe zoning practices and poor planning are to blame.

The task of growth management, without throttling the economy, may be too much for other areas, but Delaware, a state that takes its "Small Wonder" slogan seriously, appears to be more than up to the task.

At Wilmington's annual Flower Market, **News-Journal** *photographer Fred Comegys gets some on-the-scene shots. The May festivities raise funds to benefit Delaware children's agencies. Photo by Kevin Fleming*

s Delaware Governor Michael N. Castle says frequently in speeches: "Quality of life is, after all, what sets us apart." The state's gem-like qualities—small, but of great value—were first noted by no less than Thomas Jefferson, who referred to it as "The Diamond State." The appraisal stuck, becoming the state nickname, which is proudly used even today.

Just what is this elusive "quality of life" of which Delaware residents boast? A pat definition doesn't easily come to mind; still, whatever you're looking for to enhance your life-style, Delaware probably has it and is glad to share.

A New York banker, one of thousands transferred to Wilmington to take advantage of favorable legislation passed in the early 1980s, grumbled all the way down I-95: "No one lives in Delaware." But a few weeks after his arrival he found Delaware's sparse population to be just one of its many assets. Today, he is a true ambassador of the state and wouldn't consider living anywhere else.

Much of what makes Delaware such a pleasant place to live is its prime location. The state occupies the eastern half of the upper Delmarva Peninsula—the finger of land between the Chesapeake Bay and the Atlantic Ocean that stretches down to North Carolina. Delaware is bordered picturesquely by the Delaware River estuary and the Atlantic to the east, bumps Pennsylvania on the north, and is wrapped in Maryland from the west and south.

The distinctive arc marking the northern border of the First State has a 12-mile radius (an average day's journey by horseback) from a point that is now the spire of the New Castle County Courthouse, built in 1732. The boundary, drawn by surveyors in 1701 with a simple compass, separated the Delaware River counties for which colonial governor William Penn was awarded a long-term lease from Pennsylvania in 1681.

"Small Wonder" is the third in the trinity of fond nicknames for Delaware. It's no wonder. Beauty and opportunity are all around. The transplanted banker and many others have found that big isn't always best. Delaware is the country's second smallest state, with a land area of about 2,000 square miles, and the fourth-least-populated, with approximately 660,000 residents—about the same number as live in Memphis, Tennessee. Rhode Island, half the size of Delaware, has half again the number of residents. Unlike many, more populous states, Delaware offers its residents—whether native or newly arrived—some of the country's most scenic surround-

Living Well

ings and recreational playgrounds, and a thoroughly tranquil life-style. Nonetheless, cultural life is surprisingly rich and educational opportunity excellent.

Five years ago Earl and Karen Cannon and their three daughters left their home in Ashland City, Tennessee, to take advantage of some of these opportunities. Today the Cannons live in Lewes. Karen is supervisor of personnel for the Cape Henelopen School District, while Earl is a middle school principal in the Seaford School District. Although they left family behind and sacrificed the teaching tenure they had earned in Tennessee, they are pleased with the move.

"Delaware has very high standards in its school system," says Karen. "Since the state is so small, the educators all know each other. We're cooperative, not competitive. I think it's a wonderful place to live."

The picturesque Brandywine Valley is the stuff landscape artists dream of. Here the Piedmont plateau rises from the coastal plain. Wooded country roads northwest of Wilmington follow the gentle Brandywine River on its winding trip over green and rolling countryside to the Delaware. In this setting is the picturesque Chateau Country, so called for its magnificent stone manors. Many, built by du Pont heirs, reflect their Gallic ancestry and are today inhabited by the eighth and ninth generations of the family.

Flowering plants and trees in Delaware are lush and abundant. It might shock Atlantans to know that the peach blossom is Delaware's state flower. Many flowering fruit trees, along with azalea, rhododendron, dogwood, magnolia, and redbud, contribute to a breathtaking spring with its sweet fragrance. Daffodils, tulips, roses, and forsythia are everywhere, brightening neighborhood gardens, city streets, and even occasional stretches of interstate highway.

Throughout the 1980s a large influx of white-collar newcomers discovered Delaware's relatively peaceful ambience. Compared to their counterparts in nearby states, executives in the Diamond State enjoy a "life in the fast lane" without quite so many bumps. Photo by Kevin Fleming

Right: Despite its location between Washington, DC, and New York City, Delaware is one of the most sparsely populated states in the nation. Much of its area stretches out as farms and state parks. Photo by Kevin Fleming

Facing page: The Wilmington area is a mecca for bird-watchers. From this great blue heron, to huge flocks of geese, they arrive to enjoy the abundance they find on Delaware's shores and fields. Photo by Kevin Fleming

Below: A heron is a picture of natural purity against a clear blue Delaware sky. A national wildlife refuge near Wilmington offers a haven for the variety of migratory species that pass by each spring. Photo by Kevin Fleming

Autumn's painted foliage is no less spectacular. The state tree, the distinctive American Holly—tall and conical like a Christmas evergreen—livens the landscape with its lush red berries and commanding shape. In summer, Delaware is a green, lush land where garden parties, ice cream socials, and outdoor concerts are still part of leisure life.

Sea birds, such as the egret, ibus, heron, tern, sandpiper, and seagull, are common inhabitants of the Delaware coast, while—farther to the north—Canada and snow geese, feeding in open fields or flying overhead in impressive formations, are a common sight. Hundreds of Canada geese make their home at Winterthur Museum and Gardens (a former du Pont estate), nesting in the decorative grasses that border

the many ponds surrounding the mansion.

The Delaware River is part of what ornithologists call the Atlantic Flyway—the path of migrating birds on their trip to the South. Bombay Hook National Wildlife Refuge, a quiet 15,122-acre haven for both migrating and resident waterfowl, lies 35 miles south of Wilmington. Each May, with astounding regularity, nearly one million migratory birds that have flown nonstop from as far away as South America descend on the beaches of the Delaware Bay to feed on the tens of millions of eggs laid in the sand by horseshoe crabs. This event attracts serious bird-watchers from around the world. Since winters are moderate here, many birds remain and their happy calls fill the air in spring and summer.

Above: A lifeguard signals to a colleague above a spirited throng on Bethany Beach. Delaware's summers are mildly warm, with plenty of sunshine. Photo by Kevin Fleming

Facing page: More than 150 years old, the Inner Harbor Lighthouse in Lewes is a historic treasure in a state well known for deep roots and beautiful landscapes. Photo by Kevin Fleming

Several endangered bald eagles nest at Bombay Hook, carefully protected by wildlife authorities and the Tri-State Bird Rescue and Research Center near Wilmington. Delaware's state bird is the Blue hen chicken, a fighting fowl whose reputation for aggression dates back to Revolutionary War times.

This naturally beautiful area has not only inspired three generations of the artistic Wyeth family, but has also encouraged an informal, though expanding colony of artists to reside in northern Delaware, drawing inspiration from the surrounding bucolic beauty and painting in a mode that has come to be known as the Brandywine School. Founded in 1900, Arden, in North Wilmington, is a small, tree-sheltered community of artists—painters, sculptors, writers, and actors—and listed on the National Register of Historic Places as a surviving

Utopian community.

Delaware's pleasant climate is another plus, with a daily mean temperature of a moderate 54 degrees. In July temperatures in the state average 76 degrees; in January the average temperature is 36 degrees. The sun shines frequently on Delaware. Even when it's cold, it's seldom gloomy. There are also four distinct seasons. Such considerations have attracted an increasing number of retirees and others seeking refuge from the Northeast winter's wrath. Farmers, too, are lured by the climate, with the advantage of double, and often triple, cropping.

Delaware's three counties are stacked on top of each other, and are so dissimilar in character and inhabitants that they might as well be different states. In fact, the state began as a confederacy of these counties—New Castle,

Kent, and Sussex—and sectionalism still runs deep. Parts of New Castle and all of Kent and Sussex counties lie "below the canal." The Chesapeake and the Delaware Canal, which accommodates ships from all over the world, has jokingly become known as the state's Mason-Dixon line. "Upstate" and "Downstate" residents—as they refer to each other—still have friendly, if heated, debates over which is the better place to reside.

A section of the Mason-Dixon line—designated by those English surveyors Charles Mason and Jeremiah Dixon—still separates Delaware and Maryland today at Delmar, which straddles the state line and is known as "The Little Town Too Big To Be in One State."

The northernmost, smallest, and most populated county is New Castle (county seat, Wilmington) with two-thirds of the state's residents. In central Delaware is Kent County, also ranking middle in size and population. Green farmland, the state capital, nature preserves, and picturesque little towns steeped in history and folklore are the delights this county yields. Dover, the state capital and county seat, has a population of 23,000, a figure almost doubled with military personnel, dependents, and civilian employees working at

The Lewes and Rehoboth Canal runs through the fertile farmlands of Sussex County, one of the largest agricultural areas in the East. Photo by Kevin Fleming

The Laurel Farmers' Auction Market is a highlight of the year for Sussex County farmers, as hundreds of wholesalers and brokers buy more than $2 million worth of melons. Photo by Kevin Fleming

Dover Air Force Base. The area also offers many historical and recreation sites.

To the south lies Sussex County (county seat, Georgetown), with the most land and the fewest permanent residents. While the county has a delightful blend of historical and recreational sites, it is largely agricultural, producing more broiler chickens than any other county in the nation. More than 20,000 year-round jobs are provided in the raising and processing of poultry, the largest business on the Delmarva peninsula. In 1988 poultry sales on the Peninsula amounted to more than $1 billion—

something to crow about.

Delaware boasts the largest percentage of farmland on the East Coast. Kent County, the central county, is rich in farmland, as is the western part of Sussex. In the eighteenth century Kent was a small grain-producing region, valued during the Revolution as the breadbasket of the Continental forces. Today Kent County farms raise primarily corn and other grains, soybeans, and dairy herds. In Sussex County watermelon is the largest fruit crop.

The French Huguenot ancestors of W. Charles Paradee, Sr., came to Kent County in 1692 and the family farmed that same land in Jones Neck for generations. In 1930 Paradee, now 83, formed the Paradee Oil Co., a petroleum company. He has since sold the company, but remains an active community leader. "They're special people here—very friendly," he attests.

The Dover Air Force Base is home to half the U.S. fleet of C-5 Galaxies, the world's largest airplane. Lieutenant Colonel George Findlay, deputy commander of the base, and his wife, Lucy, love it in Kent County, they say, although neither had Delaware ties before coming to the state in 1974.

The Findlays especially enjoy the

More than half of Delaware's Atlantic shoreline is state parkland, drawing tourism in the summer and falling nicely quiet in the off season. Photo by Margaret McCaule

warm relationship that exists between the city of Dover and the base. "The base is really a part of the community. That doesn't happen very often. No one feels like a stranger here very long," says Lucy, who has helped write a brochure for Air Force dependents that touts the state's assets.

Eastern Sussex County is noted for its beach towns stretching along 25 miles of coastal shore, from Lewes—where the Delaware flows into the Atlantic—to Fenwick Island. More than half of that area is state parkland, attracting more than 100,000 visiting sun-worshippers and summer residents on weekends during the season.

Consider the municipality of Rehoboth, which was established as a Methodist meeting ground and bears a Biblical name meaning, aptly, "room enough." A town of a mere 3,000 during winter, it swells to 50,000 residents in the summer. Many of these fair-weather residents are from out of state. So many visitors from Washington, D.C. flock to the Delaware shore during the season that Rehoboth has come to be known jokingly as "the nation's summer Capitol," the vacation home of great numbers of diplomats, politicians, and prestigious journalists.

"It's nothing to walk along the beach and hear six different languages being spoken," notes longtime Sussex County resident Milton Mitchell, vice president of marketing for Atlantic Publications, a chain of weekly newspapers from Delaware to South Carolina.

Actually, a lesson in diction is one of the first things newcomers to the state get—right after the hearty welcome. They learn that Newark, Delaware (population 24,000), 16 miles south of Wilmington and home of the University of Delaware, is clearly pronounced "New Ark." If you don't respect that colloquialism when asking directions, you'll

Beachfront homes offer vacationers a retreat from the hectic pace of their East Coast metropolises. Photo by Kevin Fleming

A fisherman hauls in a freezer-full of shark filets, an increasingly popular item. Four of the six species found off Delaware's seacoast are considered fine eating. Photo by Kevin Fleming

find yourself headed across the Commodore Barry Bridge into New Jersey. The tony Wilmington suburb of Hockessin ignores the "c" and calls itself "Ho-Kess-En" (accent on the Ho). Downstate, the town of Lewes—oldest in the state, where the Delaware River meets the Atlantic—is pronounced "Lewis" and Leipsic, a Kent County village of 200 on a river by the same name, is "Lip Sick," if you please.

Apart from life on the beach, sport fishing is another attraction of southern Sussex County. From the dock outside the Fisherman's Wharf Lighthouse Restaurant in Lewes, Marlin Longenecker has run his tourist fishing boat, the *Gravel Gertie,* for more than 10 years. Sharks are a frequent catch, but the ones "that aren't good eatin'," he tags and throws back. In Bowers Beach, just north of Lewes, bumper stickers read: "My wife says if I go fishing one more time, she'll leave me. Gee, I'll miss her."

The center of New Castle County is Wilmington. With more than 70,000 residents, the city is relatively small, but sophisticated, urbane in attitude, and the cultural center of the state. It even harbors some commuters to easily accessible surrounding states, who value the

property prices and lower cost of living they have discovered in friendly little Wilmington. (Nine percent of the state's work force, in fact, commutes across state lines to work.) Since one-third of the U.S. populace resides within a 350-mile radius of Wilmington—a day's drive—it is far from isolated. In Wilmington, where major corporations thrive, things are busy, but without the frantic pace of larger East Coast cities.

"This is the best of all places," says Mary Byrne, a retired librarian, who lives in North Wilmington with her husband, Jack, a retired Du Pont Company employee. "We're close to the water, the cities, the cultural advantages, and good schools—both public and private."

"Everything here," happily noted a Wilmingtonian, moved recently from Connecticut, "is less than 20 minutes away." Key metropolitan areas surround the city, making trips to Philadelphia, Washington, New York, and Baltimore all within a half-hour to two-hour drive from downtown Wilmington. Amtrak's Northeast Corridor, with hourly Metroliner service, connects Delaware with the major metropolitan areas surrounding it, putting the occasional commuter in the heart of Manhattan in a mere 90 minutes or at a desk in Center City Philadelphia within 30 minutes.

The Wilmington train station, built in 1905, is a fascinating brick structure with a clock tower, peaked red tile roof, old-fashioned ticket windows, and murals on the walls. It appears on the National Register of Historic Places.

Downstate, the Lewes-Cape May Ferry connects the northernmost Delaware coastal town of Lewes to Cape May, New Jersey, during a 70-minute ride.

International airports are accessible. The Philadelphia airport, just over the state line, is a 30-minute drive from downtown Wilmington, with shuttle service to pick up or drop off passengers at their doorsteps. The Newark, New Jersey, and Baltimore airports are also within easy commute.

There are 57 incorporated municipalities in Delaware—with populations ranging from 106 to more than 70,000—yet the state yields thousands of acres of rich, undeveloped land, where a person can be as private as he likes. Delaware is proud of its 11 carefully protected state parks and more than 50 lakes, which are testimony to the state's beauty.

"A Place To Be Somebody" touts a sign near the elaborate and historic Hotel du Pont, which celebrated its 75th anniversary in 1988. Indeed, being somebody rather than a number is refreshing to one frequently uprooted corporate wife, now living in Wilmington.

"I feel comfortable here," she explains. "It's big, yet it's small. It's friendly. The doctors and others know you personally. You're not just a file."

Because of the large chemical corporations headquartered in Wilmington, Delaware is home to more scientists and engineers—many Ph.D.s—per capita than any other state, according to *Who's Who in Technology*. The Wilmington

This ferry boat transports New Jersey tourists to and from historic Lewes. Photo by Brad Crooks

An Amish man transports a Christmas tree west of Dover. Photo by Kevin Fleming

chapter of the American Association of University Women is one of the largest in the nation. Wilmington Women in Business is an organization of more than 500 women executives with a diverse membership roll, from neurosurgeons to printers. Wilmington also boasts an abundance of private schools, surprising in a city of its size. Families find Delaware a fine place to settle, offering high-caliber public schools for their offspring. FBI statistics show that Delaware's incidence of violent crime is far lower than the national average, encouraging a sense of security among prospective residents.

Whether you're a gourmet or not, a broad array of restaurants presents a diverse and sophisticated menu—from haute cuisine to international fare. Don't forget the area specialties, Blue Crab, weakfish (an ocean trout), and mushrooms, served in infinite variety at eateries all over the state. Chicken salad

with fried oysters is a delightful, if unlikely, local dining duo concocted to celebrate two of the state's main resources—poultry farming and fishing.

Shopping, too, is tempting with high-quality retail stores, name discount shops, factory outlets—and no state sales tax, luring bargain hunters from across state lines. Other metropolitan amenities are within easy commute.

Offering one of the lowest costs of living on the East Coast, Delaware boasts average income levels quite high by national standards. During 1988 personal income increased by 7.7 percent per capita in the state and is 7.8 percent higher than the national average. Delaware's welfare rolls have dropped 30 percent since the beginning of the decade. Meanwhile, employment in the state has increased 20 percent since 1981. Today state unemployment is low, more than two percentage points below the U.S. average. The number of jobs in Delaware grew 2.9 percent last year, compared with growth of 2.0 percent for the region. More than 191,000 businesses are incorporated in Delaware, including more than half of the *Fortune* 500 companies and more than one-third of the companies listed on the New York Stock Exchange. In recent years Wilmington has often been referred to as the corporate capital of the world. Proximity to other metropolitan business capitals is also a consideration for businessmen locating in Delaware.

A series of cuts in Delaware's state income tax have bolstered its appeal in recent years, and property taxes are among the lowest of any state—ranking 43rd in the nation. Homeowner and auto insurance rates in the state are also considerably lower than those of many Mid-Atlantic metropolitan areas. Gas and electricity rates compare favorably.

In 1987 Wilmington ranked as the sixth-fastest-appreciating housing market in the country, with about 3,500 single-family homes constructed. In 1988 building permits for single-family homes were up nearly 22 percent, while comparable residential building in the rest of the nation declined nearly 3 percent. Beautiful homes are a point of pride in Delaware, and each year's social calendar contains a wealth of well-attended annual house and garden tours, especially in more historic areas during the spring and summer months. Wilmington Garden Day in 1989 included more than 30 impressive residences. Festivals in Dover, New Castle, Lewes, and other interesting Delaware cities include tours of homes rich with history. Proceeds go to charitable foundations or for historic preservation.

Delaware residents are generally generous with their time and energy, supporting their community through fundraising efforts and volunteerism—

helping others to help themselves.

A native of New York State, Mary Kennedy, a resident of North Wilmington married to an ICI executive, lived in seven states (one twice) by the time she'd been married 19 years, and was never too busy to do for others, wherever she lived. Currently, she is one of 175 Wilmingtonians involved with the Literacy Volunteers of America program. Her contribution is teaching an inmate of the Women's Correctional Institute to read, a commitment which involves a six-week training course and up to two

This young Delawarean and friend are decked out for the state fair. Photo by Kevin Fleming

hours tutoring time weekly for a year. Mary is also a volunteer at the gift shop of Rockwood Museum, a county historical site, and a Sunday School teacher at St. Nicholas Ukrainian Church.

Dolores Alfano, who recently became development director for Wilmington's majestic Grand Opera House, also has a history of volunteerism. "Delaware is a state where you can make a difference," she says. Some of the differences Alfano has sought to make include chairing the Heart Ball benefit two consecu-

Right: Visitors to Pea Patch Island ride back to the ferry after a day at Fort Delaware State Park. Photo by Brad Crooks

tive years and acting as state finance chairwoman for Pete du Pont's race for the Republican presidential candidacy, raising more than $1 million in Delaware.

History is everywhere in Delaware and the state vigorously protects it. The Historical Society of Delaware, a private nonprofit organization located in one of its many successful restorations, the Old Town Hall Museum in downtown Wilmington (built in 1798), celebrated its 125th anniversary in 1989. In 1975-1976

the society saved an enclave of eighteenth century houses from razing, moving them to a plaza across from Old Town Hall. The complex is called Willingtown Square for Thomas Willing, who in 1731 laid out the village that would become Wilmington. The extensive restoration of the George Read II House, a stylish Federal house built in 1804 in historic old New Castle, occupied much of the organization's efforts from 1978 to 1985 and is now open to the public.

"The continued preservation of such areas is key to the quality of life in Delaware," says Charles T. Lyle, executive director of the Historical Society of Delaware since 1980.

Religious and ethnic diversity are part of what makes Delaware an appealing place to live. The state is conscious of its varied immigrant ancestry, and in 1988, Wilmington celebrated the 350th anniversary of the founding of New Sweden by Swedish and Finnish settlers. In celebration of their heritage, the Kalmar Nyckel Foundation began that year to build a reproduction of one of the original ships that brought members' ancestors here to the shores of the Christina River. Spearheading the task is "Nick" du Pont.

Heritage events and ethnic celebrations abound. Most of the state's ethnic organizations hold a festival of song, dance, and food, making for a calendar of international celebrations that begins in April and ends with First State Carol Sings at three locations in December. Groups celebrating their roots on a regular basis include Swedes and Finns, Irish, Poles, Italians, Greeks, Germans, Hispanics, Jews, Blacks, and Nanticoke Indians. Chinese, Koreans, and Ukrainians are other ethnic groups with a growing population in Delaware. Near Dover more than 200 Amish families live and intermingle with other central Delaware residents.

The December holiday season is observed throughout the First State with candlelight tours, concerts, and special exhibits. Entire towns, such as Lewes, Odessa, and New Castle, celebrate the season by candlelight, and halls are decked at Rockwood, Hagley, and Winterthur museums and Longwood Gardens. A Farmer's Christmas can be found at the Delaware Agricultural Museum in Dover, where 200 years of farming history are documented, and a Victorian Christmas is celebrated at Rockwood Park in Wilmington.

The scope of religious faiths represented in Delaware is equally broad and its churches serve not only as places of worship, but also, in many cases, as monuments to history. Several small towns in Delaware were established as church meeting grounds.

Built in 1698 with stones from the Brandywine River and bricks from Sweden, Old Swedes Church (now called Holy Trinity) in east Wilmington is one of the oldest churches in the country still in use. Originally a Lutheran church, it has been Episcopal for more than 200 years. Immanuel Episcopal Church-on-the-Green in New Castle is a restoration of a 1723 church gutted by fire in 1980. Tombstones in the churchyard date to 1707.

Wilmington is a diocesan city of both the Roman Catholic and Episcopal churches. Today, the Episcopal Diocese of Delaware is relatively small with about 13,000 communicants in 40 parishes and missions. Catholicism developed slowly in Delaware, with the first church built just west of Wilmington in 1772. Established in 1868, the Catholic Diocese of Wilmington takes in not only all of Delaware but also Maryland's Eastern Shore with 56 parishes, 19 missions, and more than 132,000 parishioners.

The Delmarva Peninsula is known

The Old Swedes Church, or Holy Trinity as it is known today, is one of the oldest American churches still in use. Photo by Robert J. Bennet

Right: The losses and hopes of a by-gone day stand for all to read outside St. George's Church, near Lewes. Photo by Robert J. Bennet

Below: New Castle is the center of the Presbyterian faith in Delaware and home to one of its oldest churches, in use for almost three centuries. Photo by Kevin Fleming

as the "Cradle of Methodism." A society established at Lewes in 1739 did not survive, but at Barratt's Chapel, one mile north of Frederica in central Delaware, Methodists firmly established the New World chapter of their religion in 1784. Old Asbury Methodist Church in Wilmington dates to 1789, named for Francis Asbury, the first consecrated Methodist bishop in the Colonies. Methodist churches—about 500 with a total congregation of 100,000—are located in towns and sprinkled through the countryside of the Delmarva Peninsula. By 1685 Presbyterians were holding services in New Castle and in 1703 built a church on Second Street in Wilmington. Today there are 54 churches and 15,000 congregation members in the New Castle Presbytery, which governs the peninsula.

Baptist churches, most independent, are scattered throughout the peninsula. Some are affiliated with American Baptist churches and a movement dating to 1940 seeks to establish Southern Baptist affiliates. While there were some Jews in early Wilmington, congregations were not organized until a surge in immigration from 1870 to 1880. There are six Jewish congregations in the state today—

four in the Wilmington area and one each in Newark and Dover. The Quakers were influential in the development of Wilmington, building a meetinghouse before the Revolution, but today their numbers are small.

Justifiably proud of all their state has to offer, Delawareans are also passionate about preserving the quality of life they now enjoy.

Citizen awareness of environmental issues is high, for it is undeniable that vital resources such as land, urban housing, educational and recreational facilities, roads, water, and sewer systems are under pressure. Ironically, it is the growth of the 1980s—a goal high on the state's list of priorities—that brought the consequences that now are in conflict with the kind of life-style the state's citizens want.

These are issues that hit Delawareans where it hurts: how they live and how they will live in the future. The problems are not the same in each county, however, and reactions have varied. But the news is that citizens all over the state are becoming aware of and educated about the forces bringing change into their lives and are starting to work actively to shape them.

Pressure brought by the new prosperity has been felt everywhere in the state. Around Wilmington, in New Castle County, economic development has touched off a building boom that has increased traffic and brought an influx of new residents that is straining the county's infrastructure. A version of this scenario is operative around Dover—with the variation that more jobs and economic development are still wanted for the mid-state region. In other parts of Kent and Sussex counties, the facilities of small towns cannot absorb projected population increases; change is slower here, but inexorable. The beach areas of lower Sussex County face yet a differ-

ent challenge: the growing number of apartments and condos for vacationers—many from out of state—is threatening to outrun the capacity of the area's water and treatment facilities. Further large-scale development, it is feared, could damage the ecology of the streams and wetlands into which treated effluents now run.

The involvement of citizens can be highly organized, as in New Castle County which has experienced—to a greater extent than downstate—both the benefits and the drawbacks of Delaware's recent prosperity. The Council of Civic Organizations of Brandywine Hundred, known for short as the Brandywine Council, is an umbrella group of neighborhood associations in the prosperous suburbs northwest of Wilmington. To describe the council as concerned and active is an understatement. It is a new kind of activism that combines technical information, knowledge about how things work in the development process, and the capacity to use the legal system to obtain its ends.

Thus armed, the council has brought considerable weight to bear in countless hearings and local government meetings on development issues ranging from zoning variances to highway and road surveys. It has also begun to apply pressures on the sensitive points in the growth process—planning, zoning, transportation, and services—and the way public officials use their voting power when considering development proposals. The message for local elected officials and bureaucrats is a dual one: development decisions must take adequate consideration of existing facilities and the effect of future proposals on them. Further, the mechanism by which the community provides for its life-style, such as zoning and planning frameworks, must reflect the concerns of all citizens.

A painter climbs casually up to one of the highest vantage points in the state: the Delaware Memorial Bridge, joining the Wilmington area to New Jersey. The peak is 441 feet above the Delaware River. Photo by Kevin Fleming

In the words of one council official: "The future definitely looks bright for us." Unmanaged growth has been stopped and New Castle County officials are now keenly aware that the process has to be more open to citizen input. With a former council chair now leading the county government, the planning process is moving from being "a failure, to one that will truly reflect the needs and visions of all sectors," he notes.

In Kent County, the focus is different. Its northern neighbor may be rethinking the benefits of growth, but in Dover, Milford, and neighboring towns, jobs and new business are still wanted. Local government and business interests, aided by the state's Department of Devel-

opment, are eager to bring financial services companies and other white collar employers into the area. They are sympathetic to requests for zoning variances and financial incentives from municipal and county governments—all in the name of providing more jobs and boosting economic activity in the area.

Longtime residents look at the new office parks, shopping centers, and rehabilitated city buildings, and wonder. What is occurring in and around their cities could mean congestion, higher taxes, and overloaded municipal facilities. They wonder in which direction their best long-term interests lie.

Restricting development in the downstate area is not seen as equitable. Why should the opportunities of prosperity be denied to those citizens because they live where they do? This is the state government's view; and rightly so, since it governs for all Delawareans. So in Kent and Sussex counties, there is increasing interest in comprehensive planning—developing regional blueprints that will channel growth in directions that avoid the excesses feared by residents.

The more forward-thinking leaders in these areas see the planning process as a way to assure that all sectors of the communities get their say in deciding how much and what kind of growth they will get. The experience of New Castle County—and the success of citizen groups in bringing change to the way local officials deal with growth and the quality of life issues it brings—has not been lost on those watching from downstate.

Even more encouraging for the prospects of citizen-responsive planning for growth is the effect that the New Castle County groups have had on the state government: legislators, the executive branch, and the state agencies that play a large role in development through their regulatory powers.

Until 1987 the state's concern with the environment had been limited largely to highway development and 1971 legislation regulating industrialization along Delaware's coast. In fact, state government found itself more often promoting Delaware's growth than dealing with its effects.

Since then, however, citizen awareness and pressure has forced serious consideration of broader environmental concerns. The official response has not been halfhearted.

In 1986 both the executive and legislative branches began to deal with life-quality issues. The governor formed the Delaware Environmental Legacy Program, a citizens committee charged with making a broad study of environmental issues and reporting its conclusions and recommendations to the governor. The House of Representatives, also recognizing the level of citizen concern with the future quality of life in the state, formed a standing Committee on Land Use and Economic Development. Its immediate goal: a task force to take public testimony on land use and related issues.

Both committees sought the participation of Delawareans from all parts of the state, representing the broadest possible range of concerns. The areas of main focus were air and water resources, waste management, land use, the ecosystem of the state, environmental awareness, education, and beach preservation.

Throughout 1987 both committees held a series of public meetings and workshops to hear all sides of the land use issue and its ramifications. Resulting from this citizen input, a total of 17 bills were introduced in the House dealing with various aspects of this crucial growth issue. Nine of these were administration-sponsored—called the Quality of Life Initiatives by the governor, reflecting his emphasis and support for the findings of his Environmental Legacy committee.

The legislative proposals covered such diverse matters as funding future highway and road development, the powers of the state Department of Transportation over infrastructure modernization, and the setting of minimum requirements for ways in which the counties develop plans for land use, zoning, and the like.

Perhaps the number of competing proposals is the most convincing testimony to the depth of feeling on such issues throughout the state.

Delawareans take great pride in their state and will go far to protect it. With so much to offer combined with this progressive spirit, the future becomes brighter all the time.

A worker smoothes a steel pipe at the Deemer Steel Casting Company, which has cast metal parts in New Castle County since 1904. Manufacturing continues to play a large role in Delaware's diversified economy. Photo by Kevin Fleming

There are myriad reasons for the growth and prosperity of business and industry in Delaware, but the basis of the state's success is a public/private partnership that exists between business and industry and state government. It is this give-and-take relationship that helped create the economic success the state enjoyed through the 1980s. Americans, however, share an innate fear of such a partnership. It is a union that conjures images of Big Brother and Big Business against the little guy. Yet the partnership seems to work, and many economists in Delaware believe that the little guy, ultimately, is the beneficiary.

To understand why the partnership exists and why so many people advocate its survival, it is necessary to take a look at its beginnings, a time when the only thing rosy in Delaware was the rising sun.

A little more than a decade ago, then-Governor Pierre S. du Pont IV claimed that Delaware was on the verge of bankruptcy. A tax hike was not a viable solution. Delawareans were already paying the highest personal income tax rate in the nation. The two administrations preceding du Pont's (one Democratic and the other Republican) had seen state legislators vote in some 20 tax increases, pushing the maximum personal income tax rate up to 19.8 percent.

"The state had no controls on spending. If the budget didn't gibe, the answer was to raise taxes," said Jeff Welsh, Delaware Governor Michael N. Castle's press secretary.

Delaware's fiscal instability didn't sit well with the state's business leaders. Al Giacco, then chief executive officer of Hercules Inc., was considering Houston, Texas, as a site for the chemical giant's corporate headquarters, which since 1921 had been in Wilmington, Delaware. Giacco's primary grievance was the state's painfully high income tax

A Successful Partnership

Prosperity in Delaware results from cooperation between government and business. Many economists believe this partnership ultimately benefits the average citizen. Photo by Kevin Fleming

rate, but it was the overall business climate in Delaware that had the likes of Giacco sweating. Delaware, after all, was the state that had just failed—by a hair's breadth—in an attempt to put the proverbial screws to J. Paul Getty.

In January 1975, both houses of a Democratically controlled General Assembly, with the help of then-Governor Sherman W. Tribbitt, moved quickly to levy a penny per gallon tax on products of in-state petroleum refineries. Legislators needed tax dollars to help settle a teachers' strike. There was and still is only one refinery in the state, the Getty Refinery (now Star Enterprise) in Delaware City. J. Paul Getty was furious and threatened to close the refinery, but legislators stuck to their guns and the tax made it through both houses of the General Assembly. On February 10, 1975, Governor Tribbitt changed directions and vetoed the bill, but not before the business world had one more reason to hang an anti-business label on the state.

When Governor du Pont took office in 1977, the state had image and spending problems. "The first part of the solution for the du Pont administration was to get a handle on spending," Welsh said. Du Pont fought for and established a fiscally conservative government, a signal to the private sector that Delaware still was a fine place to do business.

Toward realizing fiscal stability, state expenditures were limited to 98 percent of annual revenue. A law was passed that forces the two houses of the General Assembly to muster a three-fifths vote to increase taxes. The state also established a "rainy day fund" that by law must equal 5 percent of estimated revenue for the coming fiscal year. Curbing the state checkbook benefitted taxpayers. As of April 1989 personal income tax rates had been reduced five times, dropping the maximum rate from 19.8 to 7.7 percent; further reductions had been proposed.

Nowadays, aside from fiscal stability, Delaware offers businesses favorable

Lumber from British Columbia waits at the Port of Wilmington for distribution throughout the Northeast. South American fruits are another specialty—the port handles a huge volume of bananas. Photo by Kevin Fleming

tax, trust, and corporation laws and a state Chancery Court (one of only three remaining chancery courts in the nation) that provides business and industry with a well-established body of case law. Pro-business incorporation laws, established before the turn of the century, give the state an added allure. Approximately 7,400 companies incorporated in Delaware in 1988, bringing the total to about 191,000, and more than half the *Fortune* 500 companies are incorporated in the First State.

State officials were convinced,

though, that more had to be done to draw business and industry to the state. In the early 1980s, hoping to broaden Delaware's economic base and enhance its appeal to businessmen, legislators established laws that created a favorable environment for banking—laws that are fast turning Delaware into a banking capital.

More recent pro-business legislation includes a law allowing Delaware corporations to limit or eliminate directors' liability in certain instances. And in 1988 the nation watched as a law was passed in Dover that has been described by

Right: An increase in construction is among the signs that the state's economy is on the rise. In 1988 housing starts were down elsewhere the nation, but up in Delaware. Photo by Kevin Fleming

Below: Nanticoke Homes fill a unique niche in the housing market. Photo by Kevin Fleming

Governor Castle as "probably the nation's best law governing hostile takeovers."

A booklet produced by the Delaware State Chamber of Commerce and developed by economist Eleanor D. Craig, former chairman of the Delaware Economic and Financial Advisory Council under the du Pont administration, claims that government red tape in Delaware is minimal: "Needed legislative initiatives can be defined, developed, and adopted quickly when a new plan benefits both business and the people of Delaware."

Making itself user-friendly has had a measurable impact on Delaware. Moody's Investor Service named Delaware and Alaska as the only two states

to improve their financial strength during the last recession. And, in the mid- to late 1980s, Delaware's bond ratings were upped five times by Standard and Poor's Corporation Records and Moody's Investor Service. As of April 1989, Delaware's Standard and Poor bond rating was "AA," and Moody's rating for Delaware was "Aa."

There are other, more tangible, barometers. In 1988 Delaware housing starts were up 4.2 percent while housing starts nationwide were down 5.4 percent. Delaware's unemployment rate for 1988 dropped to 3.2 percent, compared to a national average of 5.5 percent. What's more, Delawareans' per capita personal income in 1988 was above the national

norm. And, as if to justify the business world's renewed faith in the state, business failures in Delaware decreased by 34.8 percent in 1988, the fourth-largest decrease in the nation.

The pro-business attitude and legislation that have helped business and industry prosper in Delaware are intact. The state's goal of building a positive rather than adversarial relationship between the private and public sectors—the notion that evolved into an acknowledged public/private partnership between business and government—also is alive and well.

As for the small businessman, good business always has a bottom line that serves as a compass. Delaware's bottom line is its populace, according to Ruth L. Mankin, vice president of the Delaware State Chamber of Commerce.

Delaware's user-friendly attitude toward business and industry isn't the only reason for the First State's economic bounty. The state offers employers a large, available work force. Delaware is home to 660,000 people, over half of whom are in the job market, and nearby states offer an almost unlimited pool of additional employees. The Delaware Development Office provides figures on the number of workers available to Delaware's four major labor-market areas. Estimates of the number of potential workers within a 25-mile radius of Wilmington, in 1990, total almost 1.5 million. The same figures for Newark, Dover, and Georgetown, respectively, are 665,734, 108,085, and 124,847.

Delaware is part of the Eastern Megalopolis stretching from Boston to Washington, D.C. One-third of the nation's population lives within a 350-mile radius of Wilmington. That's more than 70 million consumers, all within a day's travel by either road, rail, river, or air. Tighten the circle drawn around Wilmington to one with a radius of 150 miles and it still contains New York, Philadelphia, Washington, and Baltimore, all within a few hours' drive on modern highways.

Interstate 95 runs north from Wilmington to Philadelphia and New York City and on to Boston. Follow Interstate 95 south from Wilmington and it hits Baltimore, Washington, Richmond, and eventually Miami. Delaware's major industrial centers tie into the interstate system through U.S. highways 13 and 113, routes that provide direct connections with the Chesapeake Bay Bridge Tunnel

to Norfolk and on to the southern states. From Sussex County, the southernmost of Delaware's three counties, New Jersey and the Garden State Parkway are easily accessible via the Cape May-Lewes Ferry.

Railroads run the length and breadth of the state. Amtrak, Maryland & Delaware Railroad, Octoraro Railway, Wilmington & Western Railroad, and Delaware Coast Line Railroad provide everything from speedy commuter service to direct connections to the Port of Wilmington for import/shipping. Piggyback service is also available to most

major U.S. industrial and distribution centers. Commuter rail service—conventional and Metroliner—is available to major cities up and down the Northeast Corridor. Amtrak Metroliner service from Wilmington to New York City takes only 90 minutes, and commuter trains to and from Wilmington and Philadelphia leave on an almost hourly basis.

Although (as of 1989) no airlines provide commercial passenger service in or out of Delaware, commercial and corporate aircraft can be accommodated in the north by the New Castle County Air-

port, which is said to offer worldwide cargo service with the fastest, most efficient ground delivery service in the four-state area—Delaware, New Jersey, Pennsylvania, and Maryland. In central Delaware, through an agreement with the U.S. Air Force, business aircraft may access the 9,600-foot-long runway of the Dover Air Force Base. In southern Delaware, the Sussex County Airport handles charter services and corporate traffic. In all, 15 public and private airports and airparks are scattered throughout the state, and two of the nation's largest airports—Baltimore/Washington International Air-

port and Philadelphia International Airport—are within a few hours' drive of any point in Delaware.

Air, road, and rail aren't the only means of transporting goods and people. In 1638 the Swedish sailing vessel *Kalmar Nyckel* crossed the Atlantic and sailed up the Delaware Bay and River to establish Fort Christina. Now, the same waterways are plied by ocean going freighters and tankers, and the Port of Wilmington handles a large piece of the cargo being transported by this traffic. The port's volume of imports in 1988 gave it seventh-place ranking among the

Above & Left: More than 70 million consumers live within a day's travel to Wilmington, either by road, rail, river, or air. Photos by Kevin Fleming

37 of the free world's largest cargo planes, C-5 Galaxies, operate out of Dover Air Force Base. Photo by Kevin Fleming

top 20 ports in the Northeast. The port, which is only 65 miles from Atlantic shipping lanes, annually handles 500,000 tons of waterborne cargo: import and export vehicles, frozen meat and seafood, fresh fruits, frozen juice concentrates, lumber, steel, aluminum ingots, newsprint, salt, gypsum, urea, coal silt, petrocoke, bulk ores and minerals, and liquid bulk such as petroleum products. The port is Volkswagen's primary port of entry to the United States; it also receives more bananas than any other U.S. port.

Foreign trade has gained enough momentum in Delaware to warrant Wilming-

ton's new World Trade Center. The Delaware Development Office has identified 125 in-state exporters, and others are being discovered every day. Exports range from poultry vaccines and cars to rebuilt car engines. A gentleman in southern Delaware rebuilds Ford's big-block 427 engines and exports them to England, where they are placed in Shelby auto bodies. Other exporters include Du Pont, ICI, General Foods, Intervet, and Sterwin Labs. The latter two manufacture poultry vaccines.

Foreign Trade Zone No. 99, established in the mid-1980s, is an attempt to expand Delaware exports and further en-

Children get a taste of the marvels of military engineering at a Dover Air Force Base open house. Photo by Brad Crooks

hance the state's desirability to business. As far as U.S. Customs Service is concerned, Delaware's two trade zones and three sub-zones are outside the country. Wyoming, Delaware, in Kent County, and the Port of Wilmington are the trade zones. The sub-zones are New Castle County's Chrysler and GM plants, and Wiltex, a clothing manufacturer and division of Cluett and Peabody. Companies may assemble, manufacture, or process goods for import or export in these zones without paying U.S. Customs duties or worrying about quota compliance. No duty is paid unless or until the raw materials or goods enter U.S. Cus-

toms territory. The zones encourage the passage of cargo through the state and the Port of Wilmington, and the sub-zone status given Wiltex and the auto plants has helped keep the operations in the area. General Motors, for instance, imports parts. Duties on the parts are deferred until they are used, at which time GM pays a duty rate on a percentage of the value of the finished product.

Manufacturing continues to comprise a large and important part of Delaware's economy, but thanks to moves made by legislators in the early 1980s, the state's economic base is broadening. In 1981 Delaware took its first step toward becoming a bankers' mecca with the passage of the Financial Center Development Act (FCDA). The FCDA made Delaware a haven for bank operations by removing artificial interest rate ceilings. The response has been excellent. Between 1981 and 1988, 29 major financial institutions established operations in Delaware, and six other institutions had either applied for or been granted charters to operate in Delaware. In all, 52 financial institutions, including state-chartered banks, national banks, and mutual and federal savings institutions, now operate in Delaware. The aforementioned have assets totaling more than $61 billion, generate more than $704 million in net income, and employ

Like many of Delaware's seafoods, clams are harvested both in small amounts by amateurs and en masse by pros like this Rehoboth Bay clammer. Clams have become the new catch from what used to be oyster beds; in the 1950s the oysters were devastated by a parasite and the clams moved in. Photo by Kevin Fleming

16,464 people. That's a sizable and still growing white-collar work force. The ability to supply such a large number of educated, low- and upper-grade white-collar workers is a testimony to the quality of the state's educational system.

To maintain the influx of financial institutions, other bank-friendly legislation followed the FCDA. These include the Consumer Credit Bank Act, the International Banking Development Act, the Export Trading Company Act, the Bank Securities Powers Act, the Delaware Interstate Banking Act, the Savings Bank Acquisition Act, and the Foreign Banking Development Act (FBDA).

As yet, the impact of the FBDA and related legislation can not be fully measured. The influx of banking and financial operations is ebbing but not complete. It's safe to say, though, that the shift away from lopsided dependence on manufacturing has made Delaware less vulnerable to fluctuations in the U.S. economy.

State officials think more can be done. By 1988 Delaware had chartered 185 insurance companies, few of which have their headquarters in Delaware. Efforts by the office of the state insurance

commissioner may have insurers establishing headquarters in Delaware. State Insurance Commissioner David N. Levinson wants to see to it that all Delaware-chartered insurance companies establish in-state headquarters. If carried out, Levinson's plan could have a significant impact. Dependence on the manufacturing sector would be further reduced, Delaware's job market would expand, and more cash would flow into state coffers.

The push for white-collar service sector jobs will have to be a long and hard one to diminish the importance of manufacturing to Delaware. In 1988 manufacturing accounted for 21 percent of jobs in the state; the national average for the same year was 18 percent. However, almost half of Delaware's manufacturing jobs in 1988 were with chemical companies, and nearly half of those 32,900 "chemical" jobs were positions in corporate headquarters and research facilities, which helps explain why Delawareans can claim more Ph.D.s per capita than residents of any other state.

The chemical industry employs 10 percent of Delaware's total work force, yet that 10 percent earns more than one-third of Delawareans' $6.6 billion in annual wages. While workers in the manufacturing sector make an average annual salary of about $20,000, workers in the chemical industry average more than double that—$41,800.

To Delawareans the word "chemical" is synonymous with the names of three companies: the Du Pont Company (officially E.I. du Pont de Nemours & Company), Hercules Incorporated, and ICI Americas Inc. As of 1988 Du Pont employed 140,000 people worldwide. The company's Delaware work force totaled 24,000, making Du Pont the state's top employer. ICI is the state's 10th leading employer, and Hercules ranks 11th. All three of these giants maintain manufacturing and research facilities in Delaware and corporate headquarters in Wilmington.

Du Pont is now the largest chemical company in the world. Hercules is the 14-largest chemical company in the United States, and Imperial Chemical Companies PLC ranks fourth in the world.

Research and development conducted by these companies has tiny Delaware making giant strides in a variety of sciences. Du Pont earmarked $1.4 billion for research and development in 1989, approximately 40 percent of which was slated for "new directions" research. The Experimental Station in Wilmington is the hub of Du Pont's research and development efforts. The station employs about 5,000 people, more than 1,800 of whom are specialists—physicists, biologists, chemists, and engineers.

The Genesis 2000 DNA sequencer, introduced in 1988, is a product of scientists working at the Experimental Station. Genesis 2000 is a machine that gives scientists a rapid means of reading the human genome. A person's genome is the DNA blueprint that determines his or her physical and mental characteristics, everything from hair color to the dis-

eases he or she is likely to display. Genesis 2000 is being used in government and academic labs to chart the genome, and the information being accumulated is helping scientists understand the complexities of the human body.

Prior to Genesis 2000, in the mid-1980s scientists at the Experimental Station managed to manually sequence the genome of the AIDS virus, a significant step toward understanding and treating AIDS. Du Pont scientists at a research facility in Glasgow, Delaware, continue to look for ways to detect and understand the AIDS virus.

ICI, too, is working to alleviate human suffering. In recent years the scope of ICI's product research and development has expanded significantly. Today the company is a recognized leader in the development of drugs to treat cardiovascular disease, infectious disease, and breast and prostate cancers. Major research accomplishments include the discovery of the first clinically effective

Du Pont's main think tank, employing some 5,000 people, is located in New Castle County. Part of the Experimental Station's work is research on DNA molecules, increasingly aided by computer imaging. New treatments for cancer and the common cold are among the possibilities explored. Photos by Kevin Fleming

beta-blocking drugs (blood pressure medication) and the development and marketing of Nolvadex, the most widely prescribed product for treatment of breast cancer. ICI Pharmaceuticals in Newark, Delaware, manufactures and distributes products such as Nolvadex and Tenormin, the latter being the world's leading treatment for hypertension.

Hundreds of highly skilled and educated personnel man the research and development facility, part of the company's Wilmington headquarters. The headquarters/research and developemnt center underwent a major expansion in 1979 with the addition of 100,000 square feet of laboratory space and support facilities, doubling the size of the research section. The research center was expanded again in 1987 when 160,000 square feet of space was added. More expansion was planned for 1989.

Hercules' center for new-product research is within a short drive of its corporate headquarters in Wilmington. Hercules' FreshHold packaging system was developed at the center, which is the company's major research site. Fresh-Hold is a patented name for a film, or wrap, that allows oxygen to pass through but keeps carbon dioxide out. Fresh-Hold could add weeks to the shelf-life of fruits and vegetables. Specialists at the center also conduct research aimed at upgrading established products such as paper chemicals, resins, synthetic fiber, and polypropylene film. Hercules manufactures the lion's share of the world's paper chemicals—products that, among other things, allow toilet paper to dissolve and make paper towels absorbent. Hercules is also the top producer of polypropylene fiber, natural citrus flavors, and carbon fiber.

Hercules, Du Pont, and ICI aren't the only chemical companies operating in the state. There are 14 others, including American Hoecsht-Celanese Corp.,

CIBA-GEIGY Corp., and Occidental Chemical. These companies produce a wide range of products, from pharmaceuticals to pigment for paint.

Companies such as Du Pont, ICI, and Hercules have traditionally been pioneers in their fields. These companies know that research pays dividends. Du Pont's willingness to invest billions on research and development affirms this—so does the Delaware Research Partnership Program, which involves the University of Delaware, industry, and the state. The university contributes researchers and facilities, and the state and industry provide matching funds used to solve problems and either create or sharpen Delaware industry's technological edge. Millions in state and private funds have poured into the university since the program began, and almost every college within the university has been tapped. For example, in 1988 Delmarva Power contributed funds to research being conducted within the College of Marine Studies; Du Pont was working with the Department of Chemical Engineering (along with many other departments).

Composite materials are an industrial gold mine, and the University of Delaware has an incomparable record on composites research. A composite is a combination of materials that together create a substance superior to any of its components. Composites are used in everything from tennis rackets to jet fighters. The school's nationally acclaimed Center for Composite Materials was established in 1974, making it a pioneer in the field. ICI, Hercules, and Du Pont are among the companies that have invested in composites research and manufacture. These companies are also involved in the race to maintain U.S. superiority in composites research and manufacturing. Through the Research Partnership Program, the Center for Composite Materials has been active in achieving this goal.

Uncle Sam's participation in the existing consortium of academia, state, and industry was being sought as early as 1987 by Delaware's U.S. Senator William V. Roth, who proposed the "Composites Technology Development Act of 1987." The act called for $45 million of funding over a five-year period.

As of 1989 state officials were pushing for federal funds for a proposed Composites Technology Park in Delaware. As put by the Du Pont Co., the Composites Technology Park "is envisioned as a multifaceted complex aimed at focusing and nurturing efforts to develop a major composites industry within the state. It would include incubator space for start-up companies, along with an array of facilities and resources for composites design, materials characterization, applied research and testing, technology demonstration, and small-batch manufacturing."

The continued success of the university's Center for Composite Materials and the realization of Delaware's dream of a Composites Technology Park could radically affect the state. Composites are expected to be a $12-billion market by the year 2000. By securing a share of that market, Delaware will add to an already impressive annual production output.

Per capita, Delaware outdid all other states in value of goods and services produced in 1988—$13.2 billion. "Made in Delaware" is stamped on everything from prescription drugs and prefabricated homes to automobiles and Vlasic pickles.

Manufacturing employed 69,700 Delawareans in 1988, which represented 21.1 percent of the work force, slightly higher than the national average. The mainstays of northern Delaware's manufacturing sectors are chemicals and auto-

mobiles. To out-of-staters, one of the most visible of New Castle County's industries is probably the chemical industry, as represented by Star Enterprise, a petroleum refinery that lies along U.S. Route 13, the primary feed route to southern Delaware's beaches. At night, the stories-high smokestacks and bristling steel structures are lit up like Christmas trees. Day or night, the huge refinery is hard to miss.

Star Enterprise is a partnership of Texaco Refining & Marketing (East) Inc. and Saudi Refining Inc. The facility itself, located in Delaware City, dates to 1956 and has a throughput rated at 140,000 barrels of crude oil per day. Two products of the refinery are aviation fuel and motor fuels for markets throughout the Northeast. Other products are liquified natural gas and numerous petrochemical feedstocks such as elemental sulphur. Petroleum feedstocks are raw materials used by the chemical industry. Another product of the refining process is petroleum coke, a fuel used by utilities.

The smokestacks that rise from the refinery are becoming an oddity in Delaware. Smokestack industries account for only a small part of the state's economic output. Less hazardous to the environment, but quite profitable, are operations such as the state's two automobile assembly plants, General Motors in Wilmington and Chrysler in Newark. Between them, they provide about 6,000 high-salary jobs. To the people that man the assembly lines of America's automobile industry, the ups and downs of the American economy usually translate to layoffs and plant closings. Delaware's plants are less susceptible to these economic fluctuations. General Motors' Boxwood Assembly Plant (as of early 1989) was the most state-of-the-art automobile assembly facility in the world, thanks to a $311- million renovation. Chevrolet Ber-

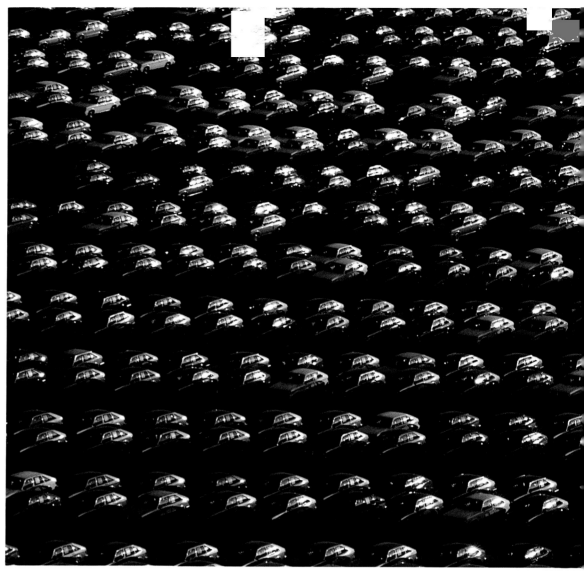

The automotive industry in Delaware means big business, not just at New Castle County's General Motors and Chrysler plants, but throughout a host of related industries supplying their needs. Photo by Kevin Fleming

ettas and Corsicas built there are hot items, and the demand often outpaces the supply. In 1988 alone, the plant produced 294,444 of the L-cars.

Chrysler followed the lead of GM's Wilmington plant, sinking $205 million into a modernization program. Modernization in the auto industry means robotics. Between the two plants, hundreds of workers lost their jobs to machines. The remaining workers, however, gained a bit of security. Huge cash expenditures make these plants globally competitive and less expendable.

An outgrowth of the state's auto industry is just-in-time manufacturing. In 1988 the Boxwood Assembly Plant was using an average of $6.5 million in parts per day, and 55 percent of parts used were supplied just-in-time. Just-in-time means the parts are brought in as needed, sometimes within minutes of when they're used on the assembly line. To do this, sup-

pliers establish facilities in strategic locations, often within a day or two's drive of several customers. Shipping costs are reduced, and the manufacturers devote much less space to storage. Among GM's in-state, just-in-time suppliers are a glass division of PPG, Delaware Seat, and Metallon Paint Corp. Chrysler, too, depends on just-in-time manufacturing to streamline and make its operation more cost effective.

Just-in-time manufacturing is applicable to a variety of industries. For instance, Sandusky Plastics of Delaware, Inc., an Ohio-based company, established a plant in Clayton, Delaware, from which it supplies Scott Paper Co. in Dover with plastic containers for paper wipes. Delaware's location and business climate, as well as the availability of raw and finished goods, make the state an ideal site for just-in-time suppliers and manufacturers. The Delaware

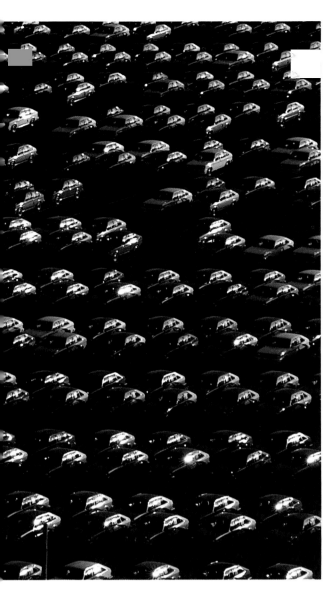

Development Office is taking advantage of these factors and working to draw more operations of this nature.

The years have managed to bring a small but important part of Delaware's manufacturing facilities to the state's pleasantly sleepy south. Southern Delaware, which comprises 80 percent of the state's land mass, contains only 11 of the state's 30 industrial parks. Major manufacturers include Scott Paper, PPG, Riechold, Playtex, Cargill, Barcroft, and Nanticoke Homes, Inc. The latter builds prefabricated homes and is growing in quantum leaps. Seaford, in western Sussex County, claims the world's first nylon manufacturing plant, built in 1938 by Du Pont. Currently, 2,300 employees at the Seaford site produce 500 million pounds of nylon a year.

Southern Delaware's dearth of manufacturing doesn't indicate a lack of high-tech savvy. ILC Dover, Inc., located in Frederica, manufactures protective equipment, including space suits used by shuttle astronauts. ILC has been NASA's sole designer and developer of space suits since the Apollo program. One of the fibers used in making the suits is produced by W.L. Gore and Associates, a Delaware-based company with 4,000 employees in the United States and abroad. Gore produces some very high-tech chemical- and plastic-based products.

Another flourishing southern Delaware industry is food processing. Among the food processors that call the area home are General Foods in Dover, Draper King Cole in Milton, and Vlasic Foods, Inc. in Millsboro. (Vlasic's Sussex location is the largest pickle processing and packaging plant in the United States.) A more ideal location for these industries would be hard to find. Delaware's farmers provide the raw goods, and the Northeast Corridor provides a tremendous and easy-to-reach market. Even the labor in the state's agrarian south is cheaper than what's available upstate.

Delaware is a small state, about 2,000 square miles. With this in mind, it is easy to believe that Delaware is among the six most urbanized states in the nation. Conversely, Delaware ranks among the top eight states in percentage of land area devoted to agriculture. This is possible because two-thirds of Delaware's population lives and works in the state's industrialized, northernmost county, New Castle.

The rolling hills of the piedmont country in the north give way in the south to a rich coastal plain where agriculture holds sway. Combine all the agrarian pursuits of this three-county state, and it's clear that agriculture is the state's number one industry. The linchpin of this agricultural economy is the chicken. In 1988 the Governor's Select Panel on the Future of Delaware Agriculture announced that "the poultry sector in Delaware agriculture, combined with the grain farming that supports it, will continue to account for 80 to 90 percent of Delaware's total agricultural output for the foreseeable future." The "grain farming" cited revolves around corn and soybeans—crops that are used almost exclusively to support the state's broiler industry, a multimillion-dollar enterprise with humble beginnings.

In 1923 Cecile A. Steele of southeastern Sussex County had an idea that would impact the entire state. Her idea was to raise a flock of 500 chickens to sell as broilers. Previously, chickens raised in Sussex were used as layers to provide eggs for nearby urban markets. However, Steele's idea worked so well that her husband, Wilmer, quit his job to raise poultry. By 1927 the Steele farm had a 25,000-bird capacity, and Steele's idea was spreading.

Sussex County now produces more broilers than any other county in the nation. (The second-place county produces only half as many.) In 1985 Sussex broilers accounted for $354 million in sales and employed 5,600 Sussex Countians. Overall, the broiler industry employs more than 20,000 Delawareans. Broiler operations on the Delmarva Peninsula, which include operations in Maryland and Virginia, ship out approximately 2 million dressed birds every weekday. Delaware's proximity to Northeast markets and the fact that it is the northernmost location of major broiler production undoubtedly give players in the industry an edge. Five prominent poultry producers take advantage of Delaware's location.

Chickens and high-tech may sound like disparate partners, but they're not. The University of Delaware works with the industry to maximize production efficiency, which, in essence, means reducing mortality rates. When thousands of chickens occupy a small area, the poten-

tial for the spread of avian diseases multiplies. The university works closely with the Delmarva Poultry Industry, Inc., to develop vaccines and study the use of growth hormones. Currently, the Delmarva Peninsula generates about 25 percent of the poultry vaccines produced for chickens in this country.

The following is an excerpt from a report issued in December 1987 by the Governor's High Technology Task Force. The task force advised the creation of "a board consisting of representatives from state government, academia, and the poultry industry to recommend agrobiotechnology programs and, in particular, develop an agenda designed to ensure that the poultry industry remains a vital and expanding force in Delaware."

Laying chickens provide another profitable rural enterprise. Delaware's layers produced 144 million eggs for market in 1987. Other products of southern Delaware's farm-based economy in 1987 included 138 million pounds of milk, 8 million pounds of beef, and more than 26 million pounds of pork.

With the huge demand of Delaware's poultry and livestock industry for feed crops, it's not surprising that much of the state's acreage is devoted to growing corn and soybeans. The dry summers and low rainfall of the late 1980s took a heavy toll on Delaware crops. In 1987 Delaware farmers raising corn as a feed crop produced 10.8 million bushels, down 23 percent from 1986. Soybean growers suffered, too, with a yield in 1987 of 4.23 million bushels, 27 percent below the yield for 1986. The poultry industry provides a built-in market for these crops. In fact, every year poultry growers tap out the Delaware market and then buy out-of-state grains to satisfy their needs.

Other important crops are rye, wheat, barley, hay, apples, peaches, potatoes, lima beans, green peas, sweet corn, watermelon, cantaloupe, cabbage, cucumbers, and mushrooms. Among these fruits and vegetables, in terms of cash, potatoes are king. In 1987 Delaware farmers harvested potatoes valued at $8 million. Delaware spuds are marketed throughout the Northeast and Canada and are also shipped to markets in the South—once Dixie's annual potato crop is depleted. Delaware once was second to only one state in raising lima beans, and while the lima bean harvest is still substantial, it is nowhere near what it was. Mushrooms, though, have grown into a $5 million a year industry.

Nearly half of the fruit and vegetable crops grown in the state are used by in-state food processors such as Vlasic Foods, ConAgra, and Draper King Cole. A variety of fresh and canned vegetables are shipped to countries in the Caribbean, the Middle East, Europe, and Canada. Grocery stores in Delaware are another pipeline for the bounty. In addition, produce is available throughout the growing season at countless roadside stands. These self-styled greengrocers don't get rich, but they do supplement their regular incomes and provide fellow First Staters with a fresh alternative to the produce aisles of local grocery stores.

A well-kept secret in Delaware is the success of the greenhouse and nursery industry. Flora for landscaping and indoor use are raised to the music of cash registers tallying up approximately $30 million in annual sales. Other agriculturally based enterprises, such as farming fish (crawfish and bass) for profit, are under consideration or in the trial stage.

With its industrial north and agricultural south, and the diverse riches produced by both, Delaware appears to be a successful experiment in the melding of America's urban and rural character.

Small business is big business in the state known as the Small Wonder. Get-

ting a business off the ground isn't easy, though, so the Delaware Development Office has a Small Business Advocate whose job it is to tell the little guy how to sidestep red tape and where to find resources that can mean the difference between success and failure.

"Small business is the basis of our free enterprise system and a vital part of Delaware's economy," said Gary Smith, who in 1989 was Delaware's Small Business Advocate. "It provides a diverse economic base that can help the state through economic swings. It also is an excellent training ground for employees. It's also a sector where new technologies develop rapidly. A lot of new ideas and technologies come from small companies—they have the flexibility to pursue something new and the guts to take the risk."

Although small business in Delaware in 1988 was responsible for only about 40 percent of jobs and 32 percent of wages, it accounted for 95 percent of the Delaware State Chamber of Commerce's membership and 98 percent of all businesses in the state. (Delaware's definition of small business differs from Uncle Sam's. The government calls any business with 500 or fewer employees "small." In Delaware, any company with fewer than 100 employees is a small business.) In 1988 there were 17,204 small businesses in Delaware, up from 14,953 in 1983. At the same time, companies such as Du Pont and Hercules streamlined and offered early retirement plans. Many well-trained and educated workers chose early retirement and used their business savvy in private enterprise.

AstroPower Inc. is a prime example of the entrepreneurial spirit and technological know-how that abounds in Delaware. AstroPower is one of only a handful of companies in the world making photovoltaic cells to harness the

Almost half of the fruit and vegetable crops grown in the state are used by in-state food processors such as Vlasic Foods, ConAgra, and Draper King Cole. In addition, produce is available throughout the growing season at count-less roadside stands. Top left photo by Kevin Fleming. Top right and bottom photos by Robert J. Bennett.

energy of the sun. Allen M. Barnett, a University of Delaware electrical engineering professor, began the company in 1983 in what once was the shop building of a junior high school in Newark. By 1988 AstroPower had $2.4 million in revenue and 55 employees, and the company was shipping state-of-the-art cells as far away as Sri Lanka and Zimbabwe.

AstroPower is a subsidiary of Astrosystems Inc., the Long Island, New York, company that holds the patent on the process for producing low-cost high-performance solar cells that Barnett developed while at the University of Delaware. Astrosystems provided the venture capital for Barnett's brainchild.

Data gathered in 1988 by the federal government indicated a shortage of small business in Delaware. It turns out that between 1980 and 1986, 79 percent of new businesses in the state were big businesses. Nationally, only 24.5 percent of the new businesses for the same period were "big." These figures are real, but they misrepresent the importance of small business to Delaware. The dispro-

Businesses of all sizes find willing markets for their goods in today's Delaware. Photo by Kevin Fleming

portionate growth in big business resulted from a huge growth in the white-collar world of banks and other financial operations—growth spurred by the Financial Center Development Act. Ironically, the FCDA is one of the reasons small business in Delaware is booming. The expanding financial sector relies on service industries for everything from janitorial services to computer maintenance, and as the corporations multiply and expand, the service industry follows suit.

"In many cases, the service economy in Delaware is the servicing of the needs of big business," Gary Smith said. "But it goes beyond this to the needs of the people. Much of Delaware's fast-growing service economy is consumer oriented.

"We're entering the age of the service economy—the age of the brain, and it's a real race. The foundation of a service economy is education, and Delaware's educational system is good, good enough to support the continuing rise of its service sector."

Between Dover and the wetlands that creep inland from the Delaware River and Delaware Bay is the Dover Air Force Base. Giant cargo planes come and go from the base continually, casting huge shadows across the land. The shadow cast by the base, though, reaches farther and touches more lives. The base employs 8,055 civilians and military personnel. Only the state and the Du Pont Company employ more Delawareans. A tally of the base's economic impact on people and businesses within a 50-mile radius annually reaches some $324 million.

"Big" is the word most commonly used when referring to the base and its operations. It is the biggest and busiest aerial port facility on the East Coast, representing a big piece (25 percent) of the nation's strategic airlift capability. There are 37 of the free world's biggest cargo planes, C-5 Galaxies, operating out of

the air base. Galaxies are almost as long as a football field and have tails that rise six stories into the air. The 12 fuel tanks of a single C-5 hold enough fuel to fill a five-bedroom house.

Dover-based Galaxies circle the globe, providing a wide range of airlift support on a daily basis. In 1989 Dover's C-5s flew equipment to Alaska in response to America's largest oil spill. Dover also sent C-5s laden with supplies to earthquake-shattered Soviet Armenia in 1988.

The average tour of duty of servicemen stationed in Dover is 5 to 10 years, and many of these men and women and their spouses and children work full- and part-time civilian jobs. The Delaware Development Office and the Air Base Family Support Center have joined forces in a project called "Base One Work Force," a venture that helps the community tap a potential work force of more than 5,000 military personnel.

Galaxies coming in and out of the air base are a real attraction. People headed to and from the beaches often stop to look. But huge cargo planes aren't the only thing in Delaware that people come to see. According to the U.S. Travel Data Center in Washington, D.C., the year 2000 will see tourism become the leading employer in revenue-generating business in the nation. The center now lists tourism as Delaware's fourth-largest employer in revenue-generating business. In 1986 tourism put $708.6 million in the state's economy. From 1977 to 1986, the economic impact of tourism on the state increased 125 percent, and the figure rises every year.

Although southern Delaware has the pastoral setting and Atlantic beaches, it's industrialized New Castle County to the north that pockets most of the cash spent by tourists. A rough breakdown of where the money goes indicates that New Castle County gets approximately

60 percent of the flow. Sussex County's beaches and inland camping sites account for about 30 percent; Dover and Kent County draw what's left. New Castle County's huge share stems from Delaware's official definition of "tourist." Anyone using northern Delaware's eateries, hotels, and motels is part of the official tally.

The Delaware Tourism Office is in the business of developing the industry and marketing the state. Staff members work with the business people behind the travel industry in Delaware to enhance the state's appeal through, for example, hospitality training.

"Managing the growth of the industry is one of our primary objectives," says Kate Wheeler, who in 1989 was director of the tourism office. "We want growth, but we want growth with direction and quality."

With so many people nearby, the state has an excellent opportunity to draw ever larger crowds. However, contrary to the typical image of tourists as outsiders, statistics show that a number of the state's tourists are Delawareans. Another sizeable slice of the tourist trade comes from out-of-staters visiting friends in Delaware. This has prompted in-state marketing efforts by the tourism office.

Regardless of who's spending the tourist dollars, Delawareans have benefited and will continue to benefit from an industry that can create revenues without destroying environmentally valuable wetlands—it's a trade that doesn't call for smokestacks to rise from the rustic beauty of southern Delaware. Northern Delaware, too, will benefit financially and, in a sense, spiritually. The historic sites of New Castle County—more than 350 years' worth—have become profitable, and in doing so have virtually ensured their survival.

Tourism also assures the survival of the entrepreneurial spirit that has put Delaware on the fast track. Tourism offers the small businessman huge opportunities for profit. The restauranteurs, the owners of small shops, motel owners, the children selling lemonade to sunburned strangers: these people all walk away with cash in their pockets. Equally important is the money taken in by state parks, revenue that can be used to upgrade and preserve the land and water that draw the crowds.

People from all walks of life are the resource upon which Delaware's economy hinges. With this in mind, the Delaware State Chamber of Commerce has nine key items on its agenda for the 1990s: expansion of economic development in Kent and Sussex counties, the importance of an adequate water supply, the effect of shifting demographics on the state's work force, the need for education and training, affordable children's day care, a balanced approach to land use, concern for the rising cost of health care, and affordable housing.

William C. Wyer, past president of the State Chamber, addressed this agenda in a message he delivered in the chamber's annual report for 1988:

During the past year, the State Chamber focused on an agenda of new ideas for the '90s—a new agenda designed to help our state retain its 'livability' standards without discouraging the prosperity that has created so much opportunity.

The State Chamber [and Delaware] is successful because it is progressive. Our strong sense of response to our state's needs are meshed with the common interests of the business community. By serving in a leadership role, bringing public and private interests together in a meaningful public policy, we fulfill the mission stated in our annual report: 'To promote a business environment in Delaware that benefits all its citizens.'

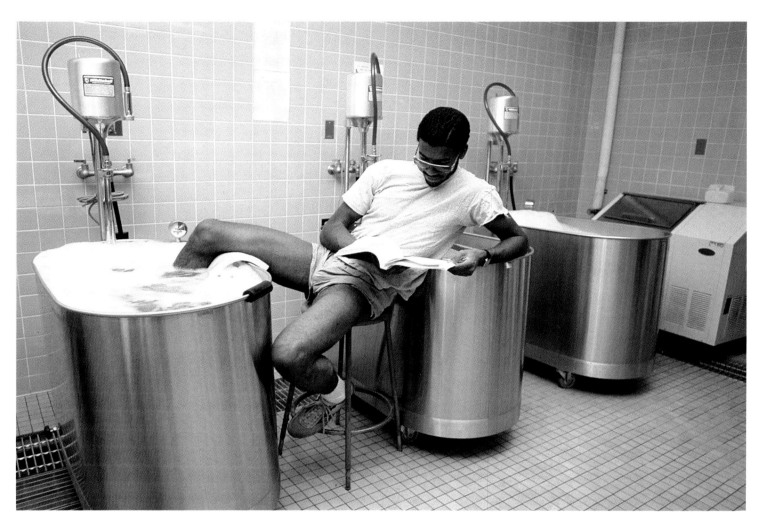

A University of Delaware athlete studies while undergoing on-campus therapy for a sports injury.
Photo by Eric Crossan

eautiful beaches and landscape and a business environment that's second to none are a big part of the good life to which most Delawareans are accustomed. However, there are less obvious but equally important benefits to life in the First State. Two excellent examples of this hidden value are top-notch educational and health care systems. Granted, a businessman spending the night in Wilmington or a family spending a weekend at a Delaware beach would have little or no reason to explore the state's educational advantages. Medical attention, though, is another story. Fortunately, hospitals such as the Medical Center of Delaware are out there and ready to fill the needs of visitors and residents.

By 1988 Delawareans were within easy reach of 9 hospitals, 49 nursing homes, and 10 mental health facilities (5 of the latter were located in short-term acute care general hospitals). A more impressive set of numbers concerns the people who administer care: In 1987 Delaware could claim 253 physicians, 50 dentists, 46 physical therapists, 1,245 registered nurses, 273 licensed practical nurses, 35 speech pathologists, and 117 pharmacists. Impressive numbers, but not as impressive as the standard of care offered First Staters.

"Health care in Delaware is equal to that anywhere in the country. We have, generally, a full range of health care offered by first class institutions that provide some of the most up-to-date technology available," said Dr. Lyman J. Olsen, director of the Delaware Division of Public Health.

Alfred I. duPont Institute

Men and women in medicine often effect cures considered miraculous by laymen. Nowhere are the miracles of medicine more evident than at Wilmington's Alfred I. duPont Institute, a multispecialty hospital for children. Since opening in 1940, the institute has served more than 100,000 children from around the world—that's almost one-sixth the state's current population.

Among institute specialties are neurology, orthopedics, genetics, intensive care, and rheumatology. Families unable to pay for services often rely on the philanthropy of the Nemours Foundation, which oversees and funds the institute. The last will and testament of the facility's benefactor, Alfred I. duPont, decreed that the Nemours Foundation work to benefit children and the elderly. DuPont not only created the Nemours Foundation and assigned it a mission, he left millions of dollars in trust for operational expenses. He also

Body and Mind

set aside half of his 300-acre Wilmington estate as a site for a hospital.

The institute has a great track record. It was the first children's hospital in the region to establish a myoelectric prosthetic program. Children missing one or both arms can turn to the program for a battery-powered prosthesis equipped with a microchip to translate message from the wearer to movement in the prosthetic limb. Another exciting institute project gives handicapped children mobility. Specialists in the rehabilitation-engineering department work with children to design control systems for wheelchairs. Beginning with knowledge of a child's physical capabilities, these engineers can design a chair that can be operated by the blink of an eye or the movement of a single finger. Study also is underway to adapt robotics as aids for the disabled—turning machineage marvels into the servants of the handicapped. The institute was also the first children's hospital in the nation to acquire digital low dose computerized radiography. Radiography is vital to treating diseases such as scoliosis (curvature of the spine). While radiography exposes patients to radiation, low-dose equipment reduces risk by reducing the patient's exposure, allowing specialists to use the equipment more freely.

Much of what goes on at the institute is on the cutting edge of medical technology and procedure. For more than a decade the orthopedic department of the institute has been able to lengthen limbs. The complex operation, entailing surgery and a long period of controlled knitting of bone, can correct a congenital defect such as disparate leg length by lengthening the bones of the affected limb. A more common but equally spectacular bit of orthopedic surgery is spinal fusion, which has been done more than 3,000 times at the institute. Spinal fusion can work when scoliosis is too severe for correction through bracing or therapy. A bone is grafted, usually from the hip, and used in concert with metal pins and a rod to literally straighten the spine.

Originally the institute focused its energies on helping orthopedically handicapped children. Now plans call for expansion into the entire gamut of pediatric surgical services. The institute's affiliation with the prestigious Thomas Jefferson University Medical College in Philadelphia and with the Medical Center of Delaware is part of the plan. Working together, these facilities can make greater steps in research while simultaneously working to train needed specialists and physicians.

As of 1989 a move involving the region's medical community was underway to create a regional pediatric medical center and to expand available services and consolidate them within the institute. Avoiding duplication of services and thereby making better use of available resources is key to anticipated growth.

Medical Center of Delaware

Tiny Delaware is also home to the Medical Center of Delaware, a giant with a fast-growing reputation for quality care. In fact, with its 1,090 beds, 970-member medical/dental staff, and 5,000 nurses, technicians, and support staff, the center ranks among the largest facilities in the nation. The center is also the principal trauma and referral center for all of Delaware and nearby areas of New Jersey, Maryland, and Pennsylvania. In its role as a major teaching hospital, it is the largest affiliate of Thomas Jefferson University Medical College. Every year more than 150 doctors undergo residency training at the center in family practice, medicine, surgery, pediatrics, obstetrics and gynecology, radiology, emergency medicine, and dentistry.

Comprising the center are three

hospitals: Christiana Hospital, just south of Wilmington; Wilmington Hospital; and Eugene du Pont Memorial Hospital (Pelleport), also in Wilmington.

Christiana Hospital, which houses the region's much touted trauma unit, is the newest, shiniest jewel in the center's crown. Every year more than 32,000 patients are admitted to the hospital, and more than 6,000 babies are born in Christiana's maternity ward. An excellent pediatric staff provides a program of comprehensive care, including trauma, neonatal and pediatric intensive care, cardiovascular surgery, general surgery, and adolescent medicine. Also, Christiana is the only hospital in Delaware to offer on-site Magnetic Resonance Imaging (MRI). In 1989 MRI was the most recent and exciting advance in computerized diagnostic imaging.

Wilmington Hospital, another branch of the center, has been serving Delawareans since before the turn of the century. Among key programs and services offered by the hospital are an ambulatory surgery center; a state-of-the-art, same-day surgery and outpatient center; and a Family Practice Office staffed by physicians who offer continuing medical care for infants, children, and adults. (Patients may be cared for in the home, in the Family Practice Office, in the hospital's inpatient unit, or in nursing homes.) Wilmington Hospital also has a department of psychiatry that offers adults and adolescents a broad range of programs, including the Herman Rosenblum Adolescent Center, Delaware's only psychiatric day-treatment for teens with psychological, behavioral, or developmental problems. Also within the hospital is the Wilmington Eye Center, which offers excellent ophthalmologic care—from routine exams to intricate eye surgery.

The center's third branch, Eugene Du Pont Memorial Hospital (Pelleport),

is a place where patients with severe or permanent impairments can relearn ordinary tasks of daily life. Pelleport uses the most advanced methods of physical medicine and rehabilitation. Conditions dealt with at Pelleport include amputation, arthritis, acute and chronic back pain, chronic pulmonary disease, stroke, head injury, multiple sclerosis, Parkinson's disease, joint replacement, and spinal cord injury. A specialized team of health care professionals provides services that include physical and occupational speech therapy, clinical nutrition counseling, psychiatry, rehabilitation medicine and nursing, social services, and pastoral care. Vocational rehabilitation and prosthetic/orthotic services also are available. Special programs include a stroke support group and an amputee support group.

Nanticoke Memorial Hospital

The Dupont Institute and the Medical Center are stellar examples of state-of-the-art facilities, but they aren't the only option available. A network of health care providers exists that stretches north, south, east, and west. This infrastructure provides residents of every town, no matter how small or secluded, with up-to-date and easily accessible medical treatment.

Nanticoke Memorial Hospital, in Sussex County, is a fine example of the medical treatment available in southern Delaware. This general acute-care facility has 80 doctors on staff and provides everything from 24-hour emergency service to skin care and ostomy specialty nursing. A vital service of the hospital is its continuous recruitment of physicians to various Sussex County locations. By mid-year 1989 the hospital had recruited more than 50 doctors. In the same year, to further fill the ranks and meet future needs, the hospital set a recruitment figure of 40 to 50 more doctors.

Among other goals set by the hospital during the late 1980s was the opening in 1991 of a psychiatric and substance-abuse center—Sussex County's first substance-abuse center. Nanticoke administrators also planned to consolidate rehabilitation services within a single center.

Another first for Nanticoke, and for the First State, is the hospital's mobile lithotripsy unit. A lithotripter is a machine used to shatter kidney stones by targeting and then bombarding them with ultrasound waves, allowing patients to pass the shattered fragments without having to undergo surgery. Treatment takes about three hours and is technically known as extracorporeal shock wave lithotripsy. Nanticoke is the only hospital in Delaware serviced by the mobile unit, which also services hospitals in Pennsylvania, West Virginia, and New Jersey. Nanticoke Memorial Hospital is a strong link in a health care chain that stretches throughout Sussex, Kent, and New Castle counties. Other links in the Sussex "chain" are Beebe Medical Center in Lewes and, in northern Sussex, Milford Memorial Hospital, a 141-bed nonprofit community hospital. Kent Countians can either head to facilities in New Castle and Sussex counties or have their needs attended at Kent General Hospital. In New Castle County, where the bulk of the state's population lives and works, residents can choose between Alfred I. duPont Institute, the Medical Center of Delaware, St. Francis Hospital, or Riverside Hospital. The latter two are in Wilmington, which is also home to the Veterans Administration Medical Center.

Aside from these hospitals, myriad specialty centers exist throughout the

state: the Birth Center of Delaware in Wilmington; the Curative Workshop in Wilmington, an outpatient facility specializing in physical, occupational, and speech therapies for adults and children; the Central Delaware Oncology Center in Dover, the only such facility in Delaware south of Wilmington; the Newark Emergency Center, a 24-hour outpatient and emergency care unit; Fenwick Medical Center in Fenwick Island, Delaware, a walk-in emergency care

Left: Not surprisingly, Delaware's renowned high-tech community includes many researchers specializing in medical issues. Areas of excellence are numerous, and range from genetics to computerized diagnostics. Photo by Eric Crossan

Facing page: The man behind the Alfred E. duPont Institute has his final resting place beneath the Carillon Tower on its grounds. At his death in 1935, duPont left the lion's share of his massive fortune to create the institute, the Nemours Health Programs for senior citizens, and other philanthropic programs. Photo by Kevin Fleming

unit; and the Millsboro Family Health Center. And this is only a partial list of what's available.

For those choosing to go outside the state for health care, a list of hospitals within easy driving range reads like a roll call of the care providers hall of fame. These include Bethesda Naval Hospital in Bethesda, Maryland; Johns Hopkins Hospital in Baltimore, Maryland; Hahnemann University Hospital in Philadelphia; Georgetown University Hospital and George Washington University Hospital, both in Washington, D.C.; Children's Heart Hospital in Philadelphia; and Childrens Hospital of Philadelphia.

The Governor's Committee On Health Care Cost Management

The state itself shoulders a yeoman's share of responsibility for health care. The Delaware Department of Health & Social Services states its mission thus: "To improve the quality of life for Delaware citizens by promoting health and well-being, fostering self-sufficiency, and protecting vulnerable populations." Annually some $250 million in state and federal funds goes for health care services in Delaware. This figure includes Medicaid expenditures, funding for community health programs, and expenses accrued by three state-run nursing homes, a mental hospital (Delaware State Hospital), and the Stockley Center for the Mentally Retarded.

In the mid-1980s concern over rising health care costs prompted Governor Michael N. Castle to appoint a commission to study the problem. In 1987 the Governor's Committee on

Health Care Cost Management released its findings. The commission made recommendations that fall under four general headings.

First, better planning for future health care needs should be a priority. Two recommendations toward achieving this goal were the creation of a committee to advise the secretary of the Department of Health & Social Services, and improvement of the health data service, already one of the best in the nation. (Improvements have been and continue to be made to the system. Accurate statistics make it easier to target those in need and thereby use resources more efficiently.)

Second, there should be a focus on health promotion and wellness education. The commission recommended that a move be made to reduce negative risk factors. Almost 50 percent of deaths in Delaware are due to negative risk factors, such as the failure of motorcyclists to wear helmets, drug and alcohol abuse, and the use of tobacco. The commission recommended that the state attack these negative risk factors through a campaign of public education, begin-

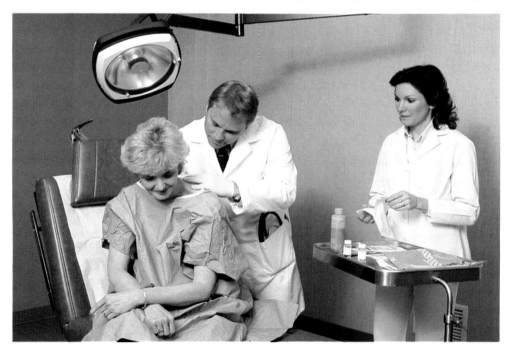

Delaware holds a remarkable position in the health care field. Patients from other states and countries travel to its facilities for specialized treatment, while its own residents benefit from the best in modern health care. Photo by Eric Crossan

ning with health education in the schools.

Third, to develop alternative financing and delivery strategies and long-term cost management strategies. In line with this, the commission advised that the nursing shortage be addressed. The commission went on to suggest that Delaware enhance community-based services. The report suggests that costs could be reduced and service improved if, for instance, more of the load were to be shifted to private organizations that help people function in the home. (An example of such community-based organizations is the Visiting Nurse Association of Delaware, a company that provides complete in-home health service.)

Fourth, that uncompensated care/ medical indigency should be dealt with. Recommendations pertaining to this came under two headings, public sector and private sector. Under public sector, the commission advised that Medicaid be extended to women—especially pregnant women—who can neither afford insurance nor qualify for state or federal funds. The commission also recommended that Medicaid be extended to aged, blind, and disabled people who don't qualify for Supplemental Security Income and are below the federal poverty level. (In 1989 a committee created by Governor Castle was looking for ways in which the public and private sector could join forces in extending insurance coverage to more low-income people.) Based on data available at the time of its study, the commission estimated that 80,000 to 90,000 working Delawareans do not have adequate health insurance coverage. So, under the heading of private sector, the commission suggested that a minimum health care benefit package be established for full-time employees. And, to the extent feasible, that coverage include dependents. The commission also advised that further study

be done and recommendations be made on creating incentives for companies to provide coverage. For instance, tax cuts could be given employers who provide coverage, and taxes could be levied against those who don't.

The commission's report set the tone of the state's response to health care needs for years to come. As early as 1989 progress had been made toward initiating certain recommendations. Delaware now has a health resources management council, and a health data center has been established within the Department of Vital Statistics. The data center allows officials to collect and track health-related data, information that can help identify and deal with future trends.

In keeping with the maxim that an ounce of prevention is worth a pound of cure, the Center for Wellness was established. The center serves as a source of advice and information for employers who want to initiate a wellness plan. Another preventative measure was the establishment of the Division of Aging's RX Check. Statistics indicate that the average elderly person takes some 14 different medications. Elderly Delawareans now can turn to RX Check to make sure their prescriptions don't pose a threat when taken together.

For the young, school districts are establishing comprehensive health education starting in kindergarten and continuing through the twelfth grade. The program's emphasis is on personal health and fitness and prevention of the big three: tobacco, alcohol, and drug abuse.

Under financing and delivery of services, case management is being provided to medium- and low-income pregnant women. Also, within the Medical Center of Delaware, there now is a program called "Child Watch." This program targets newborns thought to be at risk— for example, low birth-weight babies.

Another result of the commission report is a new nursing-home reimbursement methodology. This new approach takes a case-by-case look at a patient's needs and reimburses nursing homes accordingly. Prior to this, funds for nursing home patients were tied to a one-size-fits-all school of thought. It was a method that didn't allow for variances in patients' needs.

Some of the concepts that sprang from commission recommendations are startlingly innovative. One new program has the Department of Health & Social Services using state money to buy up to a year's worth of HMO coverage for women leaving the state welfare roll. The idea is to provide health insurance for women who can't afford coverage and whose employers do not provide insurance. When losing welfare means losing insurance coverage, the incentive to work is greatly reduced.

Another innovative idea—based on preventive medicine—is the state's network of school-based clinics. By 1989 there were two of these clinics and two more were being established. The clinics aren't geared toward sex education or abortion counseling, but toward general health care. Children sign up, with their parents' consent, and the clinics provide for their basic health needs. Physicals, annual as well as check-ups required for sports, are one of the services offered. A real benefit of these clinics has been a reduction of absenteeism.

Another service-related response to the commission's findings is a growing network of Women's Health Centers. These centers offer accessible and comprehensive health care for women of all ages. Children are also accommodated. The primary concern of the centers is reproductive health care, as better prenatal care is a significant means of reducing infant mortality. One of the services offered is genetic screening and counseling for families with a history of genetic problems. As of 1989 there was at least one center in each of the state's three counties.

Changing the means and mode by which health care is provided is nothing new. Medicine is a volatile field. Even the term "modern medicine" implies change. Compare outdated medical practices with what's current and it becomes obvious just how drastic that change has been. For instance, Delaware's Nanticoke Indians once subscribed to a cure for chicken pox that called for placing the patient in the open doorway of a chicken house. Supposedly, a cure would be initiated when chickens flew over the person to get outdoors. These days the belief in the curative power of flying chickens is an amusing bit of medical history. Laughing at this old-fashioned cure is easy when, as in Delaware, patients and doctors have easy access to state of the art facilities, equipment, and practices—and when the state itself is willing to keep pace with the medical needs of its residents.

* * *

According to Benjamin Franklin, "Early to bed and early to rise, makes a man healthy, wealthy, and wise." Delaware's health care network goes a long way toward putting a rosy glow in the cheeks of residents, and business ventures often are greeted with success and wealth. That leaves wisdom, and education is the only sure way to cultivate wisdom.

University Of Delaware

A wealth of options presents itself to those seeking higher education in the First State. The University of Delaware, the largest and one of the most prestigious schools in Delaware, lists more than 200 degree programs at undergradu-

The University of Delaware works hand in hand with the business community to train students in very marketable skills, like poultry farming. The results benefit all: industry builds the skilled workforce it needs, students develop solid career skills, and unemployment is kept to a minimum. Photo by Eric Crossan

ate, graduate, and postgraduate levels.

Established in 1833, UD is a land-grant institution with an enrollment of about 19,000. Although the main campus is in Newark, many students attend classes at auxiliary sites, one of which is the College of Marine Studies in Sussex County. Located on the Atlantic coast near the mouth of the Delaware Bay, the College of Marine Studies has master's and doctoral programs in oceanography, marine biology and biochemistry, applied ocean science, and marine policy. A high tech research vessel belonging to the college cruises the Atlantic—a prime classroom for the study of the waters and creatures surrounding the Delmarva Peninsula.

Because UD works to align the needs of the real world with the desires of students, it has become a bulwark of business and industry. A fine example of this is its College of Agricultural Sciences, which has a national reputation in research in poultry health and nutrition—a response to Delaware's booming broiler industry. The university's College of Business and College of Engineering are also renowned for their programs. Together these and other UD colleges and departments strive to meet the staffing needs of Delaware's agrarian, corporate, and industrial sectors.

Widener University

With the abundance of corporate headquarters in Wilmington, it should come as no surprise that well over 1,000 lawyers operate out of the city. Many of these lawyers are homegrown and locally educated—thanks to Widener University School of Law in Wilmington. Widener is known nationally for its specialization in corporate law. It is a specialty reflected in the university's law review, a publication with a bona fide reputation for intelligently covering pertinent issues.

Delaware's elementary and secondary students consistently score above national norms on standard achievement tests. Low pupil/teacher ratios, good funding, and highly educated faculty are some of the reasons for their success. Photo by Kevin Fleming

Widener's Delaware campus originally was the Delaware Law School, which was founded in 1971 and merged with Widener in 1975. The school works to serve the needs of Delaware, but addresses international needs, too. With an eye for the ever increasing reality of Earth as a global village, the university began two international studies programs, one in conjunction with the University of Padua in Italy and a second with the University of Nairobi in Africa. These programs broaden students' cultural experience and expose them to a global perspective on legal issues.

Another campus of Widener University's law school opened in Harrisburg, Pennsylvania, in 1989. If projected enrollment is realized, Widener will be one of the largest law schools in the nation, second only to Georgetown University.

Of course, a degree from Widener doesn't always add "esquire" to a name. Widener University's Brandywine College, also in New Castle County, offers two-year programs in accounting, fashion merchandising, management, parale-

gal studies, and criminal justice. Its Office Technology Department offers executive and legal secretary programs and a computer applications specialist program.

In addition to the state's two universities, Delaware is home to five colleges: Wilmington College, which offers career-oriented programs at each of its five Delaware campuses; Wesley College in Dover, which offers two- and four-year degrees in a variety of fields, including computer science, environmental science, medical technology, nursing, and physical education; Goldey-Beacom College, a

renowned, multilevel business college, which has three Delaware campuses, two in New Castle County and another in Kent County; Delaware State College in Dover, founded in 1891, which offers bachelor's and associate's degrees "to students seeking marketable skills" ; and Delaware Technical & Community College, which has campuses statewide that offer associate's degrees, diplomas, and certificate programs in semi-professional and occupational areas.

All of the aforementioned colleges and universities cater to working adults. According to the Delaware Development

Office, "More than 2,000 courses are scheduled throughout the state each year at convenient times and locations. These provide opportunities to pursue undergraduate and graduate degree programs, fulfill business and professional objectives, sharpen existing skills, or develop new ones."

Wilmington College is a good example of a school that can meet the educational needs of working adults. In 1989 nearly 200 of Delaware's working teachers turned to Wilmington College for master's degrees. For the 1988-1989 school year, 80 percent of Wilmington College's student population was composed of working adults, many of whom were active in entry-level and middle-management jobs in the business world—

often in banking and finance. To meet the scheduling needs of students such as these, Wilmington College offers flexible scheduling within a framework of traditional and accelerated class formats.

Systems addressing adult and continuing education in Delaware don't limit themselves to master's or Ph.D. programs. Sometimes services offered are lifelines cast to those who otherwise would fall through the cracks of the educational system. The James H. Groves Adult High School, which has six centers, is a statewide school system for adults and out-of-school youths seeking high school diplomas. It is the only statewide adult high school system in the nation. Some 500 Groves diplomas are issued every year, annually accounting

University of Delaware president E.A. Trabant stands proudly before the largest school in the state—and one of the best. Chartered in 1769 as the Academy of Newark, the institution has grown through its two centuries into a community of world-renowned faculty and some 19,000 students, with degree programs in more than 100 subjects. Photo by Eric Crossan

for 1 out of 32 Delaware high school diplomas. The Groves program, which is free to Delaware residents, is accredited by the Middle States Association of Colleges and Schools. This puts a Groves diploma a cut above a General Education Development diploma, or GED, the government's equivalent of a high school diploma. While many postsecondary institutions acknowledge GEDs, the state itself doesn't. There are, however, seven GED testing centers throughout the state, and a GED can be used to buy credits toward a Groves diploma. All Groves

Left: Acutely aware that the young are its future, Delaware spends almost half its budget on education. Photo by Kevin Fleming

Facing page: The marching band entertains sports fans at a University of Delaware event. Photo by Kevin Fleming

centers run GED preparatory classes.

Education is serious business—ask any high school dropout. However, to members of Delaware's Academy of Lifelong Learning, education is almost a recreational pursuit. The academy's stated goal is to "provide opportunities for intellectual and cultural exploration and development for men and women of retirement age." Classes, held during the day from September through mid-May, are academically oriented, covering the arts, finance, politics, humanities, languages, and more.

A University of Delaware player emerges from heavy guarding to score a fast two points. Photo by Eric Crossan

The academy, which comes under the aegis of the University of Delaware, has more than 1,000 members—some of them in their 90s—who support the program through annual dues of $160. Throughout the 1980s, most of the academy's activity was in northern Delaware. Now the program has been expanded to include southern Delaware.

Apprenticeships as Benjamin Franklin knew them are a thing of the past. Times change, needs change, and schools change with them. These days, the three R's often give way to the big T, training needed to enter specific blue-collar professions. Delaware provides

adult vocational-technical education through schools in New Castle, Kent, and Sussex counties. Among skills taught at these centers are machine trades, construction trades, welding, plumbing, automotive, instrumentation, air conditioning, refrigeration, and aircraft maintenance.

Delaware's twentieth century version of apprenticeship is administered by the state Department of Labor. To join, an individual must be at least 16 years old and out of high school. In 1989 some 1,050 Delawareans were in the program. For hands-on training, participants are paired with union and non-union employers in more than 600 trade areas. State vocational-technical schools handle the classroom training. Organizations in the private sector also afford an arena for vocational-technical training. A list of approved professional, business, and trade schools has been compiled by the state. It includes the Beebe Hospital School of Nursing, a three-year program that graduates registered nurses; Dawn Aeronautics, a full-time school offering private and commercial airplane pilot licenses; USA Training Academy, which offers training for aspiring tractor-trailer drivers and secretaries; and Professional Staffing Associates, a school that prepares individuals for entry-level positions in the banking industry. Numerous other training and apprenticeship programs are out there for the choosing, including those provided by the Private Industry Council and the State Department of Labor's Division of Employment and Training.

Delawareans needn't wait until they've graduated from high school before beginning a vocational-technical education. In fact, nearly two-thirds of Delaware's high school students choose some form of vocational-technical training. Delaware is one of only a few states with a vocational school district in each county. Through these schools, the state has moved to fill the needs of business and industry. In fact, leaders of business and industry help direct these programs through positions on local and state boards of education and vocational advisory councils. These councils review school programs and recommend ways to keep instruction close to the realities of the shop and marketplace.

"Within the vocational-technical educational centers, we go well beyond blue-collar and into technical career areas," said Dr. Thomas M. Welch, state director of vocational education. High school vocational-technical centers offer train-

ing in areas such as chemical technology, electronics, marketing, and business. Welch cited the system's pre-tech, or Two Plus Two program. Two Plus Two stands for two years of vocational-technical training at the secondary level followed by two years of related postsecondary schooling.

"The key here is that it is an articulated program in which high schools and postsecondary institutions work together to assure that training received at the postsecondary level is a continuation, avoiding redundancy within the programs," Welch said.

Sometimes workers need additional training to help deal with specific business situations. According to the Delaware DataBook, a publication of the Delaware Development Office, employers with training needs can contact the development office and access more than 60 recognized educational facilities, many of which "provide skill training designed to company specifications."

Many of Delaware's postsecondary institutions work with business and industry to deliver programs tailored to specific training needs. In 1988 the University of Delaware designed training programs for about 50 Delaware companies. Upon request, the university designed and instituted training programs in management and organizational behavior, law, law enforcement, security, accounting, and finance—to name only a few. One university client was the Du Pont Company, which requested help in team building: uniting managers and their staff in a joint effort to target and meet company objectives. In many cases, state and federal funding for such programs is available to new and expanding companies. The amount and type of funding hinges on a company's size and its potential to impact the Delaware economy.

First Staters have a fondness for private schools. In fact, the percentage of young Delawareans attending nonpublic schools in 1988 was the highest in the nation. In New Castle County alone, 21,600 (about 20 percent) of students attended nonpublic primary and secondary schools. For the same year, the State Department of Public Instruction listed 123 Delaware nonpublic schools in its annual educational directory.

"This preference for independent schools doesn't signal an exodus from the state's public schools," said Ronald R. Russo, principal of St. Mark's High School in Wilmington and president of the Delaware Association of Independent Schools. He explains this predilection for stepping outside the public school system as a matter of allegiance: past graduates of nonpublic schools are sending their children to their alma maters. Russo believes that a strong system of nonpublic schools is good for the whole system. Competition for enrollment encourages all schools to put together good programs and hire good teachers.

In spite of the popularity of nonpublic schools, it is the public school system that invariably affects the lives and minds of most Delawareans. In 1987 Delaware's 169 public schools, including 22 special schools, took on the job of educating 94,410 youths—a staggering but well-placed responsibility. Delaware earmarks almost 50 percent of its budget for education. In fact, public schools receive more than 67 percent of their financial support from the state. What's more, the pupil/teacher ratio in Delaware schools in 1988 was 16.1:1, compared with a national average of 17.6:1. In addition, more than 36 percent of public school teachers in the state hold advanced degrees.

Average levels of achievement by Delaware students, for all grades in all content areas, are consistently above national norms as measured by the Comprehensive Test of Basic Skills. Elementary test scores were 22 percent higher than the national average in 1988, and Delaware's eleventh graders scored 17 percent above the national average. To make sure students aren't pushed through the system, graduating seniors face a final hurdle that must be cleared. Before they receive diplomas, seniors must demonstrate minimum competency levels.

"Delaware's public schools are probably far better than those in most other states, but they're still not good enough—given the challenges that we face today," said the governor's education advisor, Helen K. Foss. "Because of our size and the resources available to us today and the talent here, we ought to be the best in the nation."

"We're always learning more about how children learn, and we have to put that to work," Foss said.

We need to work to replace instructional strategies that have been around since the '60s in order to meet the needs of today's students— to prepare students for the technological advancements that have taken place. We must shift our focus from institution or program centered to student centered, from a focus on input to a focus on output. The concept of education as the business of the educator must change to that of a community partnership.

Toward making Delaware's school system the nation's best, concepts are being considered that on the surface appear to have nothing to do with education. Students' physical and emotional condition has become a real consideration. The reasoning behind this social worker's approach to education is simple. A student who is physically and emotionally unprepared to learn can't really take advantage of a school system, regardless of how good the school is.

Delaware, therefore, is attacking these problems long before students reach school age. An umbrella program is in place that focuses on the first 60 months of a child's development, beginning with prenatal care. The gist of the program is to connect children in need with the proper agencies. By the time a child begins school, should he or she still have problems that interfere with learning, then the schools will have to be ready to play an uncharacteristic role. "Although social services are not part of the educational community's responsibility, schools can act as brokers, identifying children with needs and connecting them with the proper agency," said Foss.

Several innovative programs aimed at improving Delaware's public school system were either being considered or just getting off the ground in 1989. Delaware is one of five states involved in a program known as "Re:Learning, From Schoolhouse to State House." This program puts the onus on faculties and principals—with the support of their school district and board—to rethink and revamp the structure and delivery of the teaching process. A big part of this is to allow teachers more of a say in how they do their jobs. Central to this program is the concept of teaching students how to think, steering them away from a diet of force-fed facts, turning them on to a process of thought that leads to learning. Four Delaware schools were involved in the program during the 1988-1989 school year, and another five took part in 1990.

"The idea is to ask students essential questions; in a sense, to tease them into participating, helping them use their minds well, focusing on essential concepts that trigger the mind." Foss explained. "In the end, they understand more; they actually learn."

Some students, however, just don't fit into today's system. Rather than trying to hammer these square pegs into round holes, an effort is underway to square the "round holes." In 1989 the governor was seeking funds for the Alternative Secondary Education Initiative, a program designed to target and assist students on the verge of dropping out. Faculty members are relied on to designate students as at risk. These students are offered an alternative: a flexible schedule that can include day classes at the home school and afternoon and evening classes at a Groves school. Classes are offered year-round at the Groves school, and students can schedule schooling around their daily lives. Once the necessary credits are accumulated, students receive diplomas from their home school. Career counseling, planning, and placement are major components of the Alternative Secondary Education Initiative.

"We have an agenda for education," said Dr. William B. Keene, state superintendent of public instruction. He continued:

In addition to strengthening the regular programs, we have fully implemented an evaluation system for teachers and specialists. We are developing a similar program for principals. We are making gains in teachers salaries. The state board's goal is to bring the average salary up to that of the four-state area. We are working more closely with other state agencies in evaluating and developing education programs. We are developing partnerships with business and industry . . . We meet frequently with our advisory committees on career and vocational education, desegregation, recruitment, youth organizations, and get input from local boards of education.

Delaware youth continue to profit from the cooperative environment that exists with the State Board of Education, the Department of Public Instruction, and education oriented organizations.

*Leisure time in Delaware can quickly fill up with museum outings, symphony or jazz concerts at
the Grand Opera House, dinner theater, rowdy dance parties, and gala soirees.*
Photo by Sarah Hood

5

*A*sk a few Delaware grade school students. They'll tell you there are a multitude of museums in the state—enough for a month of class trips, and then some. But Delaware's historic houses and museums appeal to far more than the field-trip set. These first-rate tourist attractions draw visitors from across the country and across the globe. One can journey back in time, amid superb collections of decorative objects in a grand manor house. Or get a close-up look at the remains of an early black-powder mill along the banks of the Brandywine. Or peek into the tiny ticket booth of one of the country's earliest railroads. And then there are Victorian villas, 300-year-old churches, art galleries lined with Wyeth paintings . . .

The best spot to begin touring museums and historic houses is in northern New Castle County, on and around Route 52. This tree-lined drive takes one past gently undulating hills, open fields, and sprawling country estates. One such property—the former chateau of Henry Francis du Pont—is now home to one of the greatest collections of decorative arts ever assembled.

Opened to the public in 1951, the renowned Winterthur Museum and Gardens annually attracts nearly 300,000 visitors. The seven-story, 196-room mansion houses more than 89,000 decorative objects, including furniture, ceramics, textiles, paintings, and prints. Representing the design periods from 1640 to 1840, the collection includes such treasures as a set of silver tankards by Paul Revere, pewter by Philadelphian William Will, a cake plate made for Martha Washington, and Chippendale furniture made by Newport cabinetmakers John Townsend and John Goddard.

Winterthur's 45-minute general admission tour, the Two Centuries Tour, follows the chronological development of American craftsmanship in six style periods: the seventeenth century, William and Mary, Queen Anne, Chippendale, Federal, and Empire. Winterthur offers a variety of other tours, including the very popular "Yuletide at Winterthur," showcasing selected rooms decorated for traditional American holiday celebrations.

The Finer Things

Winterthur's 980 acres contain more than 200 acres of native and exotic plants in English-style gardens. In spring the gardens bloom with dogwood, Korean forsythia, daffodils, rhododendrons, magnolias, azaleas, and tree peonies. Summer brings such field and meadow flowers as black-eyed Susans and blue lobelia. Autumn and winter have their own pleasures, from the riotous colors of October leaves to the stark drama of branches etched against a snowy silhouette in midwinter.

Children especially enjoy the tramcar ride through the gardens, which is offered mid-April through October. Children under 12 get to ride the tram for free. On the other end of the spectrum, serious academics also find much to love at Winterthur. The museum is a valuable resource for scholars, with a highly rated 72,000-volume library. And its graduate programs—offered in conjunction with the University of Delaware—are well recognized in the field. Master's degrees are offered in art conservation and early American culture, and a doctorate is available in the history of American civilization. In addition, scholarly conferences are held on a periodic basis, with topics ranging from "Beyond Necessity: Art in the Folk Tradition," to "Robert Mills: The Years of Growth."

Appealing to a broader base is the range of conferences and lectures available to Winterthur Guild members, who currently number about 13,000. The guild also sponsors a variety of other activities, such as concert series, travel programs, and theater trips.

In addition to influencing the serious student of design, the guild member, and the casual visitor, Winterthur has also come into the lives of thousands more who have never set foot on the Montmorenci staircase or gazed at the Chinese parlor. Some even go to sleep with Winterthur every night. That's if they own bed linens from Wamsutta Mills' Winterthur collection. The collection features a variety of patterns, including "Peony Garden," a design of birds, flowers, and butterflies based on the wallpaper in the museum's Philadelphia bedroom; and "Portsmouth," a flame-stitch pattern taken from an antique needlework chair.

In all, Winterthur had about 30 licensees in 1988, representing 1,200 products adapted from the museum's collection. Besides Wamsutta's sheets, these reproductions include furniture, ceramics, glass, silver, pewter, brass, textiles, wallcoverings, carpets, miniatures, garden furniture, and decorative accessories. Licensees include Hallmark Cards, Reed and Barton, Hamilton Clock Company, and Kindel Furniture.

The museum continues to grow—its latest project is a new exhibition build-

ing, scheduled to open in 1992. The building will add 35,000 square feet of space for permanent and traveling exhibits.

Just across from Winterthur on Route 52 is the Delaware Museum of Natural History. Within this museum are more than one-and-a-half-million shells—one of the largest collections in this hemisphere. Popular with school groups—particularly for its child-oriented Discovery Room—the museum is also frequented by naturalists, nature lovers, and those who just want to get a look at the largest bird egg in the world.

Continuing the northern Wilmington museum tour, Hagley Museum and Library is located just off Route 52, at routes 141 and 100. It was here, on the banks of the Brandywine, that E. I. du Pont built his first black powder works in 1802. Almost two centuries later the Du Pont Company still thrives, long abandoning its black-powder for such chemical creations as nylon, Lycra, and Stainmaster.

Fortunately, Hagley is far from being a mere company museum or a monument to the success story of a French expatriate. Rather, this National Historic Landmark can be seen as a fascinating exploration of the Industrial Revolution, with numerous exhibits tracing America's expansion from small, water-powered mills to giant steam- and electric-powered industries. Hagley features a working waterwheel, a water turbine, a steam engine, and a working machine shop. Of particular note is the restored workers' community. Its artifacts of home, work, worship, and play create a picture of life as it was led by the Irish immigrants who manned the mills.

The 230 acres of Hagley are lovely for strolling; or one can hop aboard an open-air jitney that travels the grounds. A restored French garden and an early twentieth century Italianate garden are

Facing page top: The seven-story, 196-room mansion of Winterthur Museum is set among 980 acres of English-style garden, showcasing a huge variety of familiar and exotic specimens. Photo by Kevin Fleming

Facing page bottom: The Hagley Museum and Library and its 230 lush acres include exhibits on the Industrial Revolution such as this millwright shop, E.I. du Pont's Georgian-style first home, and French and Italian gardens. Photo by Brad Crooks

Granogue, another du Pont home, is a well-known New Castle County landmark on its rolling 515-acre site.
Photo by Kevin Fleming

Located in what was then a busy port town, Odessa's Corbit-Sharp House did double duty in the nineteenth century as a stop on the Underground Railroad.
Photo by Kevin Fleming

popular outdoor attractions. Also on the museum grounds is E.I. du Pont's first home, Eleutherian Mills. This Georgian-style residence is furnished to reflect the taste of the five generations of du Ponts who lived there.

Completing the museum loop of northern New Castle County is Nemours Mansion, about five minutes east of Route 52. Extravagant is the operative word for this 300-acre site and 100-room mansion. Nemours was the home of the late Alfred I. duPont, who was something of the family renegade. Shards of colored glass jut from the top of the nine-foot stone wall surrounding the property; it is said this was done to keep out intruders (especially those named "du Pont," as some raconteurs tell it). Some also say that Alfred chose to estrange himself from the rest of the family by spelling his name "duPont," rather than "du Pont." Visitors to duPont's lavish mansion can view more than 30 rooms, includ-

ing his billiard lounge, exercise room, bowling lanes, and darkroom.

From Nemours, it's about a 10-minute drive into the heart of Wilmington, which boasts an abundance of historic sites and buildings. Old Swedes Church—built on the banks of the Christina River in 1698—is the oldest church in America still in use. Nearby Christina Park is home to "The Rocks," the site where the Swedes landed in Wilmington in 1638. Also notable in the city of Wilmington is Old Town Hall, built between 1798 and 1800. Old Town Hall houses antique furniture, silverware, paintings, books, and manuscripts. Children enjoy gazing at the eighteenth and nineteenth century toys, games, and dollhouse, and peeking down into the basement's old city jail cells.

Delaware's capital city of Dover is also rich in history. In fact, it was William Penn who directed the laying of the Dover Green in 1683. Directly on

A band of costumed "soldiers" stand ready outside Fort Delaware on Pea Patch Island. Photo by Kevin Fleming

the Green is the Old State House—built in the 1780s—and the second-earliest state house still in use. The nearby Hall of Records houses the public archives of the state of Delaware, including such historic documents as the state's original land grant by King Charles II; William Penn's title to the "three lower counties on the Delaware"; and an original copy of the 1787 U.S. Constitution. And five miles southeast of Dover, off Kitts Hummock Road, is the impressive old John Dickinson Plantation. Dickinson, known as the "penman of the Revolution" helped draft the Articles of Confederation.

About halfway between Dover and Wilmington is the once thriving port town of Odessa, which boasts an exceptional cluster of historic houses, many maintained by Winterthur Museum. The 217-year-old Corbit-Sharp House is particularly noteworthy, with its ingeniously concealed crawl space designed to hide runaway slaves. And the Brick Hotel Gallery, also owned by Winterthur Museum, features a stunning collection of Rococo-Revival furniture crafted by mid-nineteenth century cabinetmaker John Henry Belter.

The gem, though, of all historic communities in Delaware is Old New Castle. Old New Castle—"Old" to distinguish it from the larger suburban sprawl of New Castle—is a picturesque community of well-maintained historic homes on brick and cobblestone streets. An amalgamation of Georgian, Federal, Greek Revival, Italianate, and early Victorian architecture, much of New Castle is designated as a National Historic Landmark.

The Dutch, Swedes, and English all made settlements here, on the banks of the Delaware River. And William Penn first set foot on New World soil in the town of New Castle, as he stepped off the *Welcome*'s deck in 1682.

Major attractions include the Georgian-style Old Courthouse, built in 1732. The Declaration of Independence was read to assembled crowds from the balcony of the courthouse in 1776. A popular spot for picnicking and strolling in New Castle is Battery Park, which once had fortifications to protect the city from naval attacks. Battery Park is home to the tiny ticket office of the New Castle and Frenchtown Railroad, one of America's earliest railroads. Another prime pick for ambling is The Strand, a cobblestone street of substantial brick homes along the Delaware River. Particularly striking is the George Read II House, considered one of the finest examples of Georgian architecture in America. It's replete with gilded fanlights, carved wood, and relief plasterwork.

Architecture and design are not the only cultural gems of Delaware. In fact, few geographic regions have played such an integral role in the evolution of American art as Delaware's lush Brandywine Valley. The valley, situated on the state's northern edges and extending into southeastern Pennsylvania, has nurtured the "Brandywine School" of artists, which includes such talents as Howard Pyle and N.C. Wyeth.

The legacy began with artist-illustrator-author Pyle, who was born in Wilmington in 1853. Considered by many to be the "father of American illustration," Pyle's first accepted illustration was for *Harper's Weekly*. That drawing was followed by a legion of illustrations and books, including *The Merry Adventures of Robin Hood*. At the turn of the century, Pyle began an art school in Wilmington, taking his pupils on frequent excursions to the Brandywine. Successful pupils included N.C. Wyeth and Frank Schoonover.

The Brandywine River Museum, just over the Pennsylvania line in Chadds Ford, is recognized for its outstanding collection of works by artists of the Brandywine School. Opened in 1971 and housed in a converted Civil War-era grist mill, the museum is also acknowledged for its major collection of regional landscapes of the nineteenth and twentieth centuries. Representative artists include Jasper Cropsey, Thomas Doughty, William Langston Lathrop, Edward Moran, William Trost Richards, James Brade Sword, and Henry Lea Tatnall.

The museum also houses a comprehensive collection of American still-life paintings, including a selection of late nineteenth century trompe l'oeil works. Some of the artists who appear in this collection are Soren-Emil Carlsen, George Cope, DeScott Evans, and John Haberle.

As notable as these collections may be, there is a reason why people like to call the Brandywine River Museum the "Wyeth Museum." From the very beginning, the museum has been closely associated with the work of the Wyeth family—its riverside neighbors and probably America's best-known family of artists. The museum's permanent collection includes major paintings by N.C. Wyeth, his children Andrew, Carolyn, and Henriette, and his grandson Jamie. In fact, the Brandywine River Museum has the largest collection of paintings by Andrew Wyeth on display in the world.

From the outside, the museum is austere red brick, and inside it remains unpretentious in design, with rough plaster walls and wide-plank pine floors. Although young, the museum has already attracted more than 2 million visitors from every state and 80 foreign countries. With the addition of a $3.6-million wing in 1984, the museum now contains 60,000 square feet of space, with four galleries and a research library.

Art from the Brandywine tradition is also well represented at the Delaware Art Museum. Located on Wilmington's handsome Kentmere Parkway, the Delaware Art Museum boasts a sizable collection of works by Howard Pyle and his students, including Frank Schoonover, N.C. Wyeth, Stanley Arthurs, Elizabeth Shippen Green, and Maxfield Parrish. The recently renovated museum is particularly noted for its superb collection of English pre-Raphaelite paintings, one of the largest such collections in the world. The pre-Raphaelites, acquired in 1933, include paintings by Dante Gabriel Rossetti, Edward Burne-Jones, John Everett Millais, and William Holman Hunt. The collection, with its related archival material, has become a significant resource for scholars from around the world.

The Delaware Art Museum has its roots in the Wilmington Society of Fine Arts, which was founded in 1912. The first acquisition for this small group of arts supporters was a collection of 48 paintings by Howard Pyle. Pyle's work is the basis of a collection that focuses on American fine art from 1840 to the present. Included are works by Homer, Church, Henri, and Hopper. Important works by contemporary artists are also showcased, including works by Al Held, Paul Wiesenfeld, Jack Beal, and Jerome Witkin.

The museum now boasts more than 8,000 works in all. But the Delaware Art Museum is much more than a repository of fine paintings. It is a dynamic cultural institution, sponsoring monthly trips to New York for gallery viewing, shopping, and theater; hosting film and lecture series; and offering studio art classes for children and adults. Kids enjoy their very own Children's Gallery, a hands-on area for play, experimentation, and discovery.

For the scholar, the museum library houses more than 35,000 volumes of art reference and research materials, including exhibition catalogs and art periodicals. The pre-Raphaelite, Pyle, Sloan, Schoonover, and Shinn archives are of particular interest.

For corporate clients, or for those who just want to splurge on a grand work of art for the living room wall, there is the Delaware Art Museum Sales and Rental Gallery. Sales and Rental features a changing selection of contemporary original art from leading galleries in Philadelphia, Baltimore, Wilmington, and Washington, D.C., as well as selected work by regional artists.

For modern art, the Delaware Center for the Contemporary Arts (DCCA) fits the bill. The two galleries of the DCCA host temporary exhibits in a variety of media, from watercolor to pottery.

A group of volunteers founded the DCCA in 1979 to encourage the growth of contemporary artists in the Delaware Valley and to provide a resource for artists and the community. The center is in Wilmington's old city Water Department Building, a neoclassical structure that is a National Historic Site. In 1987 its public exhibition areas were renovated and expanded into a main gallery, an artist-members gallery, and a sales and rental gallery.

In its short history, DCCA has displayed the works of more than 500 artists. The center holds about 10 shows a year, including an annual all-member juried show. It also sponsors artist critiques, workshops, gallery talks, and artist-in-residence programs. Working studio space above the gallery gives artists a chance not only to create, but also to interact with each other and exchange ideas.

The Christina Cultural Arts Center also showcases contemporary artwork, much of it by minority or women artists. Christina, a community center and educational resource for Wilmington residents, periodically holds fine art exhibitions. It also sponsors theater, music, dance, painting, pottery, and yoga classes, along with a wide variety of other programs for children and adults. Such programs have included a musical salute to Dr. Martin Luther King, an annual kite-flying day at Rockford Park, archeological exhibits, gospel recitals, and poetry readings.

In downstate Delaware, the premier art facility is the Rehoboth Art League, located on 3½ acres in Rehoboth's upscale residential enclave of Henlopen Acres. The 1,000-member group, founded in 1938, sponsors member and nonmember exhibitions, lectures, classes, demonstrations, poetry readings, trips to New York and Washington, D.C., galleries, and even theater productions. The League is a bustling place, filled with everyone from regulars attending Sketch Group to the crowds of nonmembers who show up for special events, such as the Edible Art competition, held late each summer.

The Rehoboth Art League is housed in four buildings; the main structure is one of the oldest in Rehoboth. Named the Homestead, this cypress-shingled house was built in 1743 and is listed on the National Register of Historic Places.

It's not uncommon to find many of Delaware's leading cultural institutions housed in grand old historic buildings such as the Homestead. It's so common, in fact, that sometimes Delawareans take their historic treasures for granted. They're just a part of everyday life; the commuter motors by a 300-year-old church on the way to work, eats lunch in a 150-year-old mansion, then has a drink after work at a tavern once frequented by Edgar Allen Poe.

But the Delaware Children's Theatre building, on Wilmington's Delaware Avenue, is such a stunning historic property that even the jaded sneak an appreciative glance as they drive by. The theater is a big hit with the kids and equally as popular with grown "kids"; half of the season subscribers are adults. Recent offerings have included such time-tested favorites as *Heidi, Charlotte's Web*, and *Alice in Wonderland*.

Delaware has an active, healthy theatrical community, ranging from amateur thespians giving their all at a local dinner theater to seasoned professionals trying out an experimental one-act at the Delaware Theatre Company. A young but robust organization, the Delaware Theatre Company presents a mix of the classics and innovative material, all performed by Equity actors. Located on the banks of the Christina River in Wilmington, the theater is directed by Cleveland Morris, one of its founders.

The Delaware Theatre Company has become something of a new tradition for the state's theatergoers. But getting dressed up for a night at Three

Little Bakers Dinner Theatre is a ritual that has lived on for many, many years. Located in Pike Creek Valley, southwest of Wilmington, Three Little Bakers is known for its glitzy, plush auditorium and lavish buffet dining. Three Little Bakers is big on musicals and is a fashionable place for a night out, especially for families and seniors.

Another popular dinner theater is the Candlelight Music Dinner Theatre in the town of Arden, north of Wilmington. The rousing musicals performed at this rustic wood-framed theater attract large crowds, who often linger afterward for a stroll in the bohemian enclave of Arden, which has long been a haven for actors, artists, writers, and artisans.

Community theater groups in the Wilmington area include the Wilmington

A student pores through a reference work in the University of Delaware's renowned library. Non-students are also welcome and can obtain a library card for a small fee. Photo by Kevin Fleming

The Christina Cultural Arts Center (Christina Community Center) provides an outlet for the creativity and concerns of Wilmington's people, and particularly the black community. Programs range from gospel music to archeology. Photo by Brad Crooks

Drama League and the Brandywiners. The Wilmington Drama League, which dates back to 1933, is considered one of the best community theaters in the state. The organization, with more than 1,000 members, often performs old Broadway hits. Large-chorus musicals and tried-and-true chestnuts are what the Brandywiners typically choose for its annual production at Longwood Gardens Open Air Theatre. The outdoor stage—with its colored fountains serving as a curtain—is set in a pleasant grassy knoll bordered by Kentucky coffee trees and hemlocks.

The Brandywiners was started in 1932 by Wilmingtonians Frances Tatnall Ball and W.W. "Chick" Laird, who persuaded his uncle, Pierre S. du Pont, to lend his stage at Longwood Gardens. Today there are about 250 members in the Brandywiners, which attracts large audiences to its productions.

In southern Delaware, there are several community theater groups, including the Kent County Theater Guild and the Possum Point Players. The Kent County Theater Guild presents four productions a year in its Patchwork Playhouse on Roosevelt Avenue in Dover. The Possum Point Players performs for a Sussex County crowd, presenting its shows in Georgetown.

In the town of Newark, south of Wilmington, there is a strong community theater tradition in the Chapel Street Players, which has been entertaining audiences for more than 50 years. Newark is also home to the newly revamped theater department of the University of Delaware. After 12 years at the University of Wisconsin, the faculty that created the nationally recognized Professional Theatre Training Program has relocated to the University of Delaware. Once every three years a select group of new students is admitted into this rigorous program. Training is provided through

tutorials, classes, and public productions, most from the classic repertoire. Students pursue training in one of five areas: acting, costume production, directing, stage management, and technical production. The costume production program is one of the few degree-granting programs of its kind in the nation.

A discussion of theater in Delaware isn't complete without mentioning the Playhouse, an elegant, 76-year-old facility owned by the Du Pont Company and housed in the Hotel du Pont in downtown Wilmington. The 1,250-seat theater has hosted a cast of notables throughout the years, including Sarah Bernhardt (who appeared on Christmas night in 1916), Al Jolson, Mary Martin, Betty Grable, Imogene Coca, Jane Fonda, Marlo Thomas, Gilda Radner, and many, many others. The Playhouse was once well known as a pre-Broadway tryout stop; it was the site of the world premiers of *The Odd Couple* with Walter Matthau, *On Golden Pond* with Henry Fonda, and *Auntie Mame* with Rosalind Russell.

The Playhouse subscription season runs from September to May, typically with six shows, most of them musicals. Recent offerings have included *Pippin, 42nd Street,* and *Singing in the Rain.* In addition to the subscription season, the theater is utilized for stockholder meetings, assorted company functions, and for an annual performance of the *Nutcracker* by Wilmington's Academy of the Dance.

In contrast to the Playhouse's fairly light schedule of performances, the Grand Opera House hosts a concert, lecture, or travelogue just about every week of the year. The Grand has become Wilmington's cultural gathering place, presenting an eclectic blend of top-notch entertainment, such as the Preservation Hall Jazz Band, the Joffrey Ballet, Kris Kristofferson, Marcel Marceau, Bill

Cosby, Chuck Mangione, the San Francisco Symphony, and Itzhak Perlman.

The Grand is a beauty—its ivory facade rises proudly above Wilmington's pedestrian-only Market Street Mall. It is a National Historic Landmark and a founding member of the League of Historic American Theatres. But just two decades ago the structure was in disrepair, until a dedicated band of volunteers stepped in to save it from ruin.

Considered one of the finest examples of cast-iron architecture in America, the Grand was built by the Masons of Delaware and opened in 1871. Influenced by the Second Empire period of nineteenth century Paris, the Grand is a classical revival with free-standing columns and a mansard roof. In its symbolism, Freemasonry relies heavily on odd numbers, particularly the numbers three, five, and seven. These numbers were used as a recurrent theme in the design of the Grand's facade. On the second and third floors, each of the five sections includes three arches and three keystones. On the mansard roof, the windows are set in groups of three, two, two, three so that there are seven windows when counted from left or right to center.

In its early days the Grand hosted such big-name entertainers as Edwin Booth, Ethel Barrymore, George M. Cohan, and Buffalo Bill Cody. The best comedy, drama, and minstrel troupes performed at the Grand on their national tours. Ironically, the opera house was host to relatively few opera performances. Around 1910 moving pictures replaced the live performances. During the 1910s and 1920s admittance to the theater was five cents for the entire day. *The Perils of Pauline, Marni,* and *Dr. Jekyll and Mr. Hyde* were some of the popular attractions. The Grand declined considerably by the 1960s, when it became a movie house for horror films.

But by 1973 the nonprofit Grand Opera House Inc. had been established, paving the way for the current mélange of high-quality entertainment.

Each season more than 100,000 people attend performances at the 1,100-seat theater, which is noted for its outstanding acoustics. When conductor Eugene Ormandy appeared at the reopening of the Grand in 1976, he was one of many who have praised the acoustics, noting the "bright, clean sound" that was projected to the audience.

When one thinks of the Grand Opera House, an invariable association is the Delaware Symphony Orchestra. Delaware's only professional orchestra plays most of its performances in the old-fashioned splendor of the Grand. Since 1979 the group has been led by charismatic music director and conductor Stephen Gunzenhauser. During Gunzenhauser's tenure, the Delaware Symphony has grown from a modest-sized community orchestra to an acclaimed regional orchestra with 80 professional musicians.

The symphony gives more than 50 performances a year, including children's concerts and special programs. The needs of southern Delaware are recognized, with four classical and pops concerts held at downstate locations each season. Subscription programs include classical, pops, and chamber series. The popular chamber concerts, held in the Gold Ballroom of the Hotel du Pont, feature champagne and elegant desserts at intermission, plus opportunities to talk with the musicians.

The Delaware Symphony traces its origins back to Alfred I. duPont's Tankopanicum Orchestra, a Wilmington musical organization popular at the turn of the century. In 1929 the Wilmington Symphony Club and the Wilmington Music School merged, forming the Wilmington Symphony. In 1971 the Wilmington

Symphony became the Delaware Symphony Orchestra.

OPERADelaware also makes use of the splendid Grand Opera House stage to present its two major productions each year. The company has presented fully staged professional opera for more than 40 years and is the fourteenth-oldest opera company in America, as listed by Opera America, the association of professional opera companies. Past OPERADelaware performances have included *Madame Butterfly, MacBeth, Die Fledermaus, Cosi Fan Tutte,* and *The Magic Flute.* The organization has produced several world premieres, including works by Gian Carlo Mennotti and Alva Henderson, and has featured artists who have gone on to perform with the Metropolitan Opera, the New York City Opera, and other major companies.

OPERADelaware strives to make opera accessible. It presents most of its operas in English and distributes special programs and study guides to introduce young audiences to opera. The company also produces touring productions in area schools and a family production each season, with students in the cast, chorus, orchestra, and technical crews.

Groundbreaking for a new OPERADelaware building was held in February 1987. OPERAStudios, at Poplar Street in the Christina Gateway section of Wilmington, will have rehearsal space, shops for sets and costume construction, storage facilities, and administrative offices. Performances will continue to be held in the Grand Opera House.

Vocal musicians can join a host of community choral groups in Delaware, from Dover's Community Singers to Wilmington's Chorale Delaware. For good old-fashioned barbershop singing there is the Wilmington chapter of the Society for the Preservation and Encouragement of Barbershop Quartet Singing in America. Mercifully, the group also goes by

the shorthand name of the Chorus of the Brandywine. The 60-member group of men has been performing annual shows in the Wilmington area for more than 50 years.

Theater, music, opera, dance, art, and architecture—Delaware boasts a rich heritage and a promising future in all of these cultural arenas. But Delaware is also blessed with an abundance of other cultural opportunities—perhaps one of the most significant is its first-rate libraries. There are numerous local lending libraries in Delaware, the foremost being the Central Branch of the Wilmington Library. Housed in an architecturally acclaimed building on Wilmington's Rodney Square, the library had its start in 1850, when it was incorporated as a private institution. It was opened to the public in 1883, and the present build-

Above: In addition to its relaxed quality of life, Delaware's endless possibilities for cultural enrichment make it a wonderful state to move into—or to grow up in. Photo by Kevin Fleming

Facing page top: The Delaware Art Museum infuses a little bit of fantasy into local life with such events as the annual Beaux Arts Ball. Photo by Kevin Fleming

Facing page bottom: A troop of patriots commemorate Separation Day at a New Castle County event. Photo by David Greenfield

ing opened in 1923. In addition to its superb collection of books, periodicals, films, videocassettes and tapes, the library owns N.C. Wyeth's "Robinson Crusoe" series, which is displayed on the building's third floor.

But the consummate library in Delaware is surely the University of Delaware's, consisting of the Hugh M. Morris Library and branch libraries for agriculture, chemistry, marine studies, and physics.

The Morris Library was expanded and renovated in the mid-1980s, at a cost of $15 million. Originally opened in 1963, the refurbished building now seats about 3,000 and is about twice as large as the original structure. In sheer numbers, the Morris Library is a book lover's utopia. As of the 1987-1988 school year the library had some 1.8 million books and periodicals, 1.6 million microforms, 450,000 government publications, 100,000 maps, 1,500 films, and 500 videocassettes. The university library is a depository for U.S. government publications, a patent depository for U.S. patents, and a repository for State of Delaware publications.

More than one million people used the library in the 1987-1988 school year, checking out 400,000 items and getting the answers to more than 150,000 reference questions. The library's computerized card catalog—dubbed DELCAT—makes tedious hours of research a bit less wearisome. The system can access more than 650,000 library holdings, with bibliographic descriptions of the items, call numbers, location in the library, and even circulation status. DELCAT is available by computer access from anywhere in Delaware, free of charge.

The library is also recognized for its Special Collections section, which includes books, manuscripts, prints, broadsides, and periodicals from the fifteenth to the twentieth centuries. Special Collec-

tions features a pleasant glass-walled gallery for special public exhibitions. Recent exhibits have included a show of manuscripts, notes, and drafts of works by Tennessee Williams, and publications printed by the Hogarth Press, which was founded by Virginia and Leonard Woolf. Other highlights of Special Collections include a comprehensive collection of the work of Rudyard Kipling; numerous letters of George Bernard Shaw; first or early editions of works by Einstein, Newton, Galileo Galilei, and John Dalton; and the works of William Faulkner, Ernest Hemingway, Henry David Thoreau, Theodore Dreiser, Herman Melville, Howard Pyle, and Carl Sandburg.

The university library is an asset not only to the students on campus but also to the community at large. Borrowing privileges are available for a small fee, and community members can join the University of Delaware Library Associates and participate in dinner lectures, exhibition openings, and fundraising. It's all quite a development from the library's beginnings as a modest college library with a handwritten card catalog of 35 titles.

If you delve into today's card catalog, you'll come up with a few shining stars in literature who were born or lived in Delaware. One of the most notable is Pulitzer Prize winner John Q. Marquand, who was born in Wilmington in 1893. Marquand was a prolific novelist who won his Pulitzer for *The Late George Apley*, which was later made into a Broadway play in collaboration with George S. Kaufman. Other Marquand novels include *H.M. Pulham, Esquire, So Little Time, B.F.'s Daughter*, and *Point of No Return*.

In addition to Marquand, Wilmington was also home to novelist Anne Parrish, who penned her novels in her grandmother's house on Philadelphia Pike, south of Claymont. It was here that she wrote *The Perennial Bachelor,* which won a Harper prize.

Another Delawarean recognized in the world of literature is Henry Seidel Canby, who was born in Wilmington in 1878. From 1924 to 1936 he was editor of the *Saturday Review of Literature.* He wrote numerous books, including *The Brandywine,* which was illustrated by Andrew Wyeth.

Delaware can even rightfully claim to be the home—albeit a temporary one—of F. Scott Fitzgerald. Fitzgerald, his wife Zelda, and daughter Scottie spent two years at Ellerslie mansion, north of Wilmington, in the late 1920s. While at Ellerslie, Fitzgerald entertained such literary luminaries as Ernest Hemingway and John Dos Passos.

Fitzgerald, known to frequent several raucous speakeasies in and around Wilmington, was very fond of the whirlwind of lavish social activities that characterized the 1920s. He probably would have enjoyed the glittering social scene of modern Wilmington just as much. Surely, there has been no time in the city's history proffering such a wealth of balls, soirees, parties, cotillions, and bashes as there is today. The majority of cultural institutions throw at least one big black-tie affair each year, and some organizations plan two or three.

The Delaware Art Museum is the sponsor of the wildly popular Beaux Arts Ball, an annual costume party that's a "must do" on innumerable social calendars. One year the theme may be "Circus Under Glass"; the next time around the ball may focus on a fairy tale motif.

Other can't-be-missed events include the Delaware Symphony's Rhapsody in Bloom; the Wilmington Music School's Beggars' Ball; and Holidazzle, sponsored by the Delaware Foundation for Retarded Children. Held in November at Longwood Gardens, Holidazzle is a splashy fashion show featuring modeling by local celebrities and personalities.

The Grand Opera House is also known for throwing a good party—namely the black-tie Grand Gala and its youthful offshoot, the Baby Grand. The Gala fundraiser, held late each January, is always a fanciful soiree, complete with an extravagant new theme each year. And the Baby Grand—designed for Wilmington's younger patrons of the arts—is a looser, rowdier version of its older sibling. The premiere Baby Grand in 1987 featured the antics of Buster Poindexter—aka David Johansen—and his Banshees of Blues. "Creative black-tie" is requested at the Baby Grand, so patrons good-naturedly add a sequined cummerbund, a glow-in-the-dark bow tie, or a pair of beach shorts to their ensembles.

Sundresses, shorts, and even bikinis are the apropos garb for Delaware Theatre Company's Barefoot Ball, an island party with West Indian steel bands, plenty of rum punch, and an instant beach—created by heaping two tons of sand in the parking lot of the riverfront theater company. Another party for the young is the Symphony Sizzler, a dance thrown by the Delaware Symphony.

The young and young-at-heart also have the Halloween Loop, an annual excuse to get costumed and get crazy. The bars in downtown Wilmington aren't known to thrive at night, with most folks sticking close to home at suburban watering holes. But on the weekend closest to Halloween those downtown streets don't roll up at 5 P.M. That's when ghosts, goblins, and a cast of thousands of other costumed creatures descend on the Market Street Mall and the bars in and around that pedestrians-only street. The Halloween Loop is always an exuberant good time, a chance to let loose on Wilmington's biggest party night of the year.

Many of Delaware's beaches are known for a particular atmosphere; Dewey Beach, for example, is a favorite hangout of the young and high-spirited. Photo by Kevin Fleming

6

*T*he casual visitor to Delaware—someone on a business trip to Wilmington, or buzzing by on I-95 en route to New York or Washington, D.C.—may be surprised to learn that the state boasts a plethora of natural wonders.

At first glance, the traveler may notice only the massive corporate towers zigzagging the Wilmington skyline, or the light manufacturing at industrial parks on the city's edge.

But Delaware is essentially an agrarian state. Even well-populated, well-developed New Castle County has its open spaces, particularly in the hilly northwestern edges. And below the Chesapeake and Delaware Canal, New Castle County becomes downright bucolic, with acre after acre of farmland, fresh- and saltwater marshes, and peaceful hamlets like Port Penn and Taylor's Bridge. The meadows, marshlands, and tilled fields continue through Kent and Sussex counties, right down to the bare sand dunes of coastal Sussex.

Much of Delaware's scenic lands are well preserved through a fine system of state parks, extending from Bellevue and Brandywine Creek in northern New Castle County to Holts Landing and Trap Pond in the southern regions of Sussex.

There isn't much in the way of outdoor recreation that you can't do at one of Delaware's 11 state parks. Feel like boating or camping? How about fishing or swimming? And there's always horseback riding, hiking, and picnicking available for the outdoors-minded.

Delaware's state parks reflect the amazing diversity of leisure options found in a state that's only 96 miles long and 35 miles across at its widest point. Park settings run the gamut—grassy fields, rolling meadows, millponds, shady patches of woods, marshlands, and ocean and bay beaches.

The Great Outdoors

Even the most discriminating of beachgoers tend to get impassioned when talking up the coastal state parks. In a world of overdeveloped beaches lined with condominiums and amusement piers, Delaware's state parks are one last bastion of an old-fashioned seashore experience. Bathhouses, a discreet refreshment stand or two, and a park office are about the only visual clutter between you, the sand, and the surf.

For a day devoted to swimming and sunning, Fenwick Island State Park—right below South Bethany—is an excellent choice. Sunbathers also swear by Delaware Seashore State Park, as do surf fishers and windsurfing aficionados. Delaware Seashore has broad swaths of unsullied sand on both the ocean and bay sides, extending from Dewey Beach to Bethany Beach and encompassing the Indian River Inlet.

There's even a bit of treasure at Delaware Seashore State Park, at a section aptly known as Coin Beach, north of the Indian River Inlet. The *Faithful Steward* sank there in 1798, breaking up only 100 yards from land, and copper Irish coins from the cargo have been known to wash ashore. One never knows . . . and the odds are probably better than they are a few miles up the coast, in Atlantic City's casinos.

For those who get restless just sunning on the beach, Cape Henlopen State Park, near Lewes, offers plenty of alternatives. There's more than 2,000 acres for strolling and exploring at this sandy hook, with ocean and bay views on three sides. Cape Henlopen is windswept dunes, cranberry and blueberry bogs, petrified forest, quiet stretches of beach, and nature trails that twist through the pines and brush.

The park is the site of the decommissioned Fort Miles, which protected the coastline during World War II. That explains the tall, curious-looking concrete towers throughout the park—and, in fact, all the way down the Delaware coastline. During World War II the towers served as lookout stations, guarding against enemy submarines and ships. One tower in the park is now open to the public, providing spectacular views of the Atlantic.

Inland from the ocean, but still water oriented, is Holts Landing State Park, eight miles northwest of Bethany Beach. Holts, on the Indian River Bay, is popular for swimming, fishing, boating, crabbing, and clamming.

Farther west in Sussex County is Trap Pond State Park, near the community of Laurel. There are fishing and swimming in the pond and a large number of hiking trails and campsites. Canoeists can venture out to investigate the gnarled bald cypress trees that have their knees sticking out of the water. To see even larger numbers of bald cypress, one should venture to nearby Trussum Pond and Big Cypress Swamp.

The swamp, also called the Great Pocomoke Swamp and the "Great Delaware Everglades," is 10,000 acres of eerie fog, black water, cypress, and murk . . . but it is more pleasant than it sounds. At one time the swamp boasted thousands of acres of bald cypress. Now, however, only scattered clumps remain of what are the northernmost stands of bald cypress in the United States.

Big Cypress has hidden its share of outlaws, moonshine stills, and, some say, even spirits of a more ethereal nature. Ghost stories are a staple of the local old-timers' collection of swamp yarns.

Kent County's sole state park is Killens Pond, south of Frederica. The 580-acre park offers harried Dover professionals and hard-working local farmers the chance to swim, fish, boat, hike, picnic, and just leave behind workaday worries.

New Castle County is home to five

What would a vacation paradise be without sailing, sunshine, and great seafood at the end of the day? Delaware Bay has all the requirements. Photo by Kevin Fleming

These "tubers" have made a major expedition of it, with fancy colored tubes and the whole gang in attendance. Once under way, though, it's just "go with the flow" down the Brandywine. Photos by Brad Crooks

Above: A deer studies a photographer who has wandered into the Brandywine Valley area, a natural habitat for both species. Photo by Brad Crooks

Left: Cape Henlopen State Park is a wonderful place for young explorers, with 2,000 acres of varied natural terrain, an old fort, and a number of towers once used as lookout posts. Photo by Sarah Hood

Facing page: A lone fisherman tries his luck year day's end at Indian River Inlet. Photo by Kevin Fleming

state parks. Bellevue State Park, in north Wilmington, is particularly noted for its equestrian facilities. Bellevue had its auspicious beginnings as the estate of William du Pont, Sr. Du Pont's family were avid riders, so they built stables, an indoor exercise ring, and an outdoor mile-and-an-eighth dirt track. Joggers are the ones lapping the track these days, but trails through the woods and fields are well frequented by the horses from Bellevue's privately operated stables.

North Wilmington is the quintessential suburb. The houses are substantial Colonials and the lawns are generally large and well tended. But the Colonial-filled subdivisions don't leave much room for wide open spaces.

But no, that's not exactly right. For one can't overlook the pastoral appeal of Brandywine Creek State Park. The car odometer will show that Brandywine Creek is just a few short miles from the strip shopping centers of Concord Pike. But odometers have been known to lie; one look at the fields and wooded trails and it's clear that Brandywine Creek is worlds away from suburbia.

Brandywine Creek's 400 acres, in the verdant Beaver Valley, are particularly noted for hiking trails, superb bird-watching vistas, and some 300 species of wildflowers. Even so, it seems that on the average sunny Saturday most park visitors are simply there for picnicking or playing catch. For those who do want a short introduction to the park's nature life, the Tulip Trail provides a one-third-mile-long, half-hour hike. The 15 stations on the Tulip Trail help the nature neophyte to identify trees, plants, and wildlife.

At the opposite end of the county from Brandywine Creek sits Fort Delaware State Park. Fort Delaware—on Pea Patch Island in the Delaware River—isn't the kind of parkland that's replete with swing sets and fitness trails. In-

stead, Fort Delaware is the site of imposing gray stone walls; grim, dank dungeons; and faint remnants of prison graffiti—that's because the massive, five-sided fortress served as a detention center during the Civil War. More than 30,000 Confederate soldiers were imprisoned on this boggy island, and a larger percentage of the prison population died—about 2,500 in all—than in the Confederacy's infamous prison at Andersonville, South Carolina.

The island's origins and name came from a crop of sprouted peas that were incredibly good growers, so say the local raconteurs. A long-ago ship loaded with peas wrecked on a shoal where the island now stands. The peas were said to have sprouted, flourished, and collected floating debris until the little island was born. Ferry boats bound for Fort Delaware leave from the historic town of Delaware City. It's a short, relaxing jaunt across the Delaware.

In addition to state-preserved parklands, Delaware is also home to national wildlife refuges. Bombay Hook National Wildlife Refuge is one of the state's most important environmental resources and an essential link in the chain of refuges that extend from the Gulf of Mexico to Canada. Bombay Hook is more than 16,000 acres of brackish marsh, swamp, freshwater pools, croplands, and woods, located on Route 9, east of Smyrna.

Established in 1937, the refuge's cord-grass marshes are a haven for more than 250 species of birds, including the bald eagle, which nests at the refuge from early December to about mid-May. Situated on the Atlantic flyway, Bombay Hook is most spectacular in mid-October through November, when more than 100,000 migratory birds, including snow and Canada geese, make the refuge their temporary home. Bombay Hook also supports white-tailed deer, foxes, otters, opossums, woodchucks, and a large population of muskrats.

As valuable as Bombay Hook is now recognized to be, in the year 1679 it was casually sold by the Indians for a couple of coats, a gun, black powder, liquor, and a kettle.

Ornithologists make Bombay Hook first on their list of places to bring the binoculars. But there are a number of other notable birding spots in Delaware, including Prime Hook National Wildlife Refuge, Woodland Beach, Assawoman Wildlife Area, the Nanticoke Wildlife Area, and Big Cypress Swamp. Egrets, herons, waders, shorebirds, and waterfowl abound in the coastal wetlands and marshy regions.

Although some can stand for hours equipped with field glasses and guidebooks and still not be able to distinguish a snowy egret from a great white heron, any novice can become an expert by afternoon's end with a journey to the Brandywine Zoo. The zoo, in Wilmington's Brandywine Park, is small and child-oriented. It's home to a menagerie of South American monkeys, North American otters, pythons, birds, and tigers. It's nothing like a bustling, large-city zoo, but Brandywine has its following. Young families in particular find the zoo an attractive spot for a Sunday outing, followed by a romp on the jungle gym just up the hill.

Below the zoo, down a twisting cobblestone drive, is what may well be the prettiest plot of land in the entire city. Josephine Gardens, on the banks of the Brandywine, is an intimate, grassy oasis from the city's hustle and bustle. It's perfect for dog-walking, jogging, or solitary strolls. In spring it's worth a daily trip just to be sure to catch the peak moments when more than 100 Japanese cherry trees burst into bloom.

The second weekend in September is another can't-be-missed time in the gardens. That's the weekend of the annual Brandywine Arts Festival. The festival was first held in the 1960s and has become a high-quality, juried show attracting more than 350 artists and artisans. Browsers can find oils, watercolors, pen-and-ink drawings, photography, custom jewelry, fine earthenware, leather goods, and more.

While Brandywine Park is marvelous for jogging, strolling, or picnicking, Rockford Park, with its wide open spaces, is just right for touch football, kite-flying, Frisbee-tossing, and wintertime sledding. There are four tennis courts and a baseball diamond, which is regularly used by local softball and baseball teams. Rockford is also big with cross-country runners and weekend joggers.

Need directions to get to Rockford Park? Just look for the landmark stone water tower jutting out of a canopy of trees off Pennsylvania Avenue (Route 52). The open field in front of the tower is utilized for many special events throughout the year, including a rousing tribute to Independence Day by the Delaware Symphony, followed by fireworks.

But ask a longtime Wilmingtonian to talk about Rockford Park and the words "Flower Market" will come up sooner or later. The name of the event, held the second weekend of May, is a little misleading. Sure, plenty of flowers and plants are peddled, just as they were when the fair was first organized by a group of society matrons in 1921. But most fair-goers aren't there to pick out a pot of geraniums or a flat of impatiens. They come to hop on a Ferris wheel with the kids, splurge on a sketch by a local artist, grab a bag of popcorn or an ice cream cone, get the youngest one's face painted, and wander past the crafts and clothing displayed on tables under candy-striped tents.

It's a good bet Rockford Park, with its full schedule of activities, is the best-

The translation "room enough" does indeed fit Rehoboth Beach. There's room for endless flocks of sunners, swimmers, shoppers, drivers, and spectators where Rehoboth Avenue meets the sand. Photo by Kevin Fleming

known park around town. It's equally likely that Valley Garden Park is the best-kept secret. This city-owned property isn't even within the city limits, but tucked between palatial Centreville and Greenville five miles northwest of downtown. The rolling hills in these environs are dubbed Chateau Country. That's because the high stone walls and the curtains of greenery hide 100- and 200-room mansions—many built by various members of the du Pont family—and acres of woodland and formal and country gardens.

Roam through Valley Garden's 100 acres and it's easy to fantasize that

you're surveying your own country garden. In the spring Valley Garden is truly spectacular, with hundreds of flowering trees and shrubs and thousands of daffodils carpeting the woods and fields.

A few miles past Valley Gardens is Longwood Gardens. There's only one word to sum up these internationally recognized gardens: incomparable. Longwood, just over the Pennsylvania line in the town of Kennett Square, is pure utopia for the serious gardener. It's 350 acres of magnolias, daffodils, tulips, wisteria, roses, peonies, chrysanthemums, and countless other blooms, amid statuary, reflecting pools, waterfalls, a bell tower, and an Italian water garden. Inside the stately conservatory are an additional 3½ acres of garden, accenting everything from poinsettias to palms. In all, there are 11,500 different types of plantings at Longwood.

Some of these plantings date back to the 1700s, when the land was used as an ornamental tree park. But it wasn't until Pierre Samuel du Pont purchased the property in 1906 that the formal gardens of Longwood were created and nurtured. Du Pont, former president of the Du Pont Company, opened his gardens to the public and created the Longwood Foundation before his death in 1954.

Longwood is spectacular year-round, from November's Chrysanthemum Festival to 350 Acres of Spring, held in April and May. But for many, their favorite season at Longwood is summer, with the dazzling Festival of Fountains. Blankets and lawn chairs are staked out for prime viewing spots near the Main Fountain Garden, as adults relax and children catch fireflies while they wait for the sun to set. With nightfall comes a whooshing sound as the fountains switch on, propelling tons of water through 300 jets, up as high as 130 feet in the air. Highlighted by colored lights, the fountains are accompanied by the resonant sounds of one of the world's largest privately owned pipe organs. On special nights there are fireworks along with the fountains.

Longwood's fountain displays are more popular with many Delawareans in midweek, rather than on the weekends. Likewise, those who wander into most Wilmington nightclubs on a Saturday night in July or August are likely to get the VIP treatment. That's because they'll probably be the only customers in the place.

The city clears out on summer weekends, with young singles, families, and retirees alike making the two-hour trek southward for a sandy (and hopefully sunny) weekend at the beach.

It's only about 25 miles from Lewes—Delaware's northernmost ocean resort—to Fenwick Island, a narrow strip of a town by the Maryland border. But you can't lump the coastal communities together— Rehoboth is as different in attitude and atmosphere from Lewes as Dewey is from Bethany.

Lewes is a picturesque fishing port with a fine collection of historic cypress-shingled homes that are increasingly being purchased by out-of-towners. Despite the new infusion of tourist capital, Lewes manages to retain its low-key, small-town ways.

Lewes is the oldest town in Delaware—it was first settled by the Dutch in 1631. Established as a whaling colony, the commu-

nity was named Zwaanendael. But Zwaanendael didn't last long, for in less than a year the settlers were massacred by Indians.

Today, Lewes' Dutch roots are remembered through displays and artifacts at the Zwaanendael Museum. This ornate, brightly painted building was designed after the Town Hall of Hoorn, Holland. Lewes also has a maritime museum at Front Street's Cannonball House, so named because of the cannonball lodged in its foundation, a remnant of the British bombardment of the town in the War of 1812.

Lewes is famous for its shipwrecks— stories abound of the caches of gold bullion and coin lying on the ocean floor. It's reputed that the shipwrecks got there in the first place because unsavory looters would light lamps to lure ships toward rocky shores. One of the most talked-about wrecks is the *De Braak,* a British sloop that foundered during a storm in 1798, sending a million-dollar cargo

The urbane young visitors to the Nation's Summer Capital take the bench—or are they chairing the boardwalk? A famous journalist or politician could walk by at any moment. Photo by Robert J. Bennet

of copper and gold down to Poseidon. Amid much publicity, the *De Braak* was raised in 1986. The sloop was laden with artifacts valuable to historians, but, alas, not a single gold nugget could be found.

Lewes is also known as the home of the Delaware dock for the Cape May-Lewes ferry, which runs hourly in the summer. The ferry offers a scenic 70-minute cruise for those on foot, on bike, or arriving by car, to the restored Victorian town of Cape May, New Jersey.

A few miles south of Lewes is Rehoboth, probably the best-known and most popular of the Delaware resorts. "Rehoboth," which began life as a Methodist camp ground, means "room enough," and it seems the town does manage to make room enough for the enormous number of visitors that flock to its shores.

Rehoboth is a *de rigueur* element of summer for diplomats, legislators, and assorted political figures from Washington, D.C., which is a two-and-a-half hour drive south. Political correspondent Roger Mudd owns a condominium in the Henlopen Hotel, and Chuck and Lynda Robb and Jack Anderson are

among the many others who are regulars.

Directly south of Rehoboth is Dewey Beach, an offshoot of Rehoboth that's now an incorporated town of its own. Dewey has something of a reputation for boisterous partying and good-natured rowdiness. Dewey also has a reputation for getting under your skin and leaving you just a bit obsessed about the place. Maybe it's because of the chummy ambience of a Sunday morning at Theo's diner, munching eggs and reading the *Washington Post*. Maybe it's for the fun of a cheap, quick meal at an outdoor chicken pit by the side of the highway. Or the high-spirited excitement of a afternoon-into-evening marathon of music—better known as a jam session—at the Bottle & Cork Pub. Or maybe it's for the beach itself—clean, white sand peopled with a young, noisy, happy crowd. Whatever the reasons for the love affair, it's certainly a public one; dozens of cars all over the state bear bumper stickers that proudly proclaim, "Dewey Beach—A Way of Life."

Next stop south on the Delaware coastline is Bethany Beach and South Bethany. Like Rehoboth, Bethany was

Facing page: The comings and goings of surf fishermen are evident from the tracks on this beach near the Indian River. Photo by Kevin Fleming

Left: The local boys of Leipsic, a small town in Kent County, line up for a sand-lot ball game. Photo by Kevin Fleming

founded as a camp meeting place, hence its Biblical name. The Mission Society of the Christian Church set up its camp in 1901 and quickly built a boardwalk, a post office, a pavilion for camp meetings, and a set of cabins.

The early missionaries wouldn't recognize Bethany now, with its half-dozen or so immense oceanfront towers and its hundreds of contemporary cottages. But Bethany remains true to its origins in that it's the most family-oriented of the beach resorts. Billed as one of the "quiet resorts," Bethany is where middle manager types from Wilmington spend their two weeks' vacation. On Bethany's modest boardwalk, the emphasis is on the saltwater taffy, caramel corn, ice cream and pizza stands, beach sundries, and clothing shops. Ardent arcade aficionados would be well advised to hot-foot it up to Rehoboth.

In addition to attracting middle-class families, Bethany is also a holiday destination for older, well-heeled professionals, who own the contemporary beach

houses that line Route 1 to the north and south of town. Actress Lynda Carter and her husband, Washington attorney Robert Altman, are one of the many capitol couples who like to spend a few weeks in Bethany.

Fenwick Island—which isn't really an island, technically speaking—concludes the expedition down Delaware's coast. Like its neighbors to the north, Fenwick began life as a camp meeting ground. That early abstemious spirit is still much in evidence, especially when comparing restful, low-key Fenwick to the glitz, crowds, and neon-lit boardwalk of Ocean City, Maryland, directly south. In contrast, Fenwick has no boardwalk—a small sports center with miniature golf, bumper boats, and video games just about does it in the entertainment department. There are a dozen or so good restaurants in town and an equal number of nice, cozy motels.

An excursion to the beaches isn't really complete without a side trip to Leipsic, on Route 9, north of Dover. Some Wilmingtonians make Leipsic their lunch stop to or from the beach. The big appeal in this fishing village (population 228) is Sambo's tavern, which many say have the best steamed crabs on the face of the earth. Sambo's is nothing fancy, just a slightly ramshackle building on the banks of the Leipsic River. Sambo's serves up bushels and bushels of steamed, spiced blue crab, at tables covered in newspapers and bearing rolls of paper towels. Plain-talking locals, trendy types from Wilmington, politicos—anybody and everybody—indulge in the fat, succulent, just-caught crab at Sambo's.

Devouring crab at Sambo's could almost be called a ritual for the true-blue Delawarean. And there's a host of other rites—ceremonies, fairs, festivals, and celebrations that separates the outlanders from the longtime residents. Sure, a newcomer may stumble upon one of these

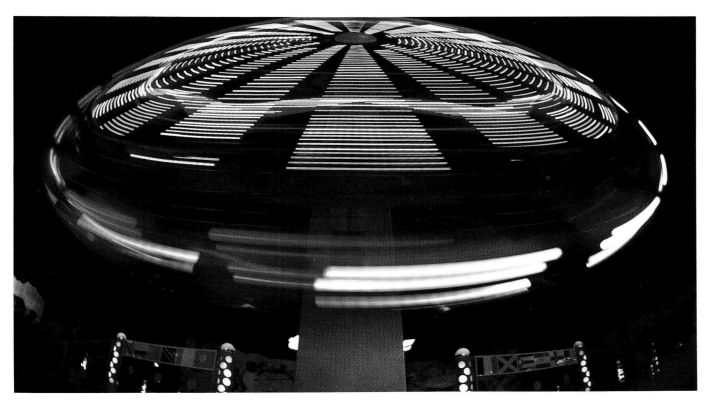

events, but the native Delawarean will be there year after
year.

Some of Delaware's fairs
and festivals are a bit on the unusual side. Like the "piping-out"
of summer in Rehoboth each Labor Day, a ragtag, anything-
goes, costumed parade thrown
by the locals, thrilled to see the
passing of summer, with its
crowds and headaches. Or like
a similarly rowdy New Year's
march in Middletown called the
Hummers' Parade, a campy send-
off of Philadelphia's Mummers' Parade.

There are a few events of a more conventional nature that shouldn't be
missed, either. Like Old Dover Days,
held in the state capital. For more than
50 years, Dover has turned back the
clock for one weekend in May, with may-
pole and colonial dancing, tours of
homes and gardens, and a parade complete with fife and drum corps.

Following on the heels of Old

Dover Day, June brings a duo of ethnic
festivals: Greek and Italian. The Greek
Festival, sponsored by Wilmington's
Greek Orthodox Church is a four-day
orgy of dancing, drinking, and good
eating—of moussaka, souvlakia, gyros,
baklava, and more.

The granddaddy of all Delaware
carnivals is the Italian Festival held at
St. Anthony of Padua Church, in the
heart of Wilmington's Little Italy.

*Above: Carnival rides are another fea-
ture of the state fair, along with athletic contests, famous country music
acts, and more. Photo by Robert J.
Bennet*

*Left: A couple dancing in traditional
garb at the Country Fair "smacks" of
authenticity. Photo by Kevin Fleming*

During festival week, the neighborhood's tidy red-brick rowhouses are festooned to the hilt with red, white, and green streamers. And the church's athletic fields are transformed into a huge midway, complete with funhouse, Ferris wheel, and merry-go-round. Lining the edges of the midway are duck ponds, basketball throws, and booth after booth of Italian and all-American cuisine—pizzelles and cream-filled horns at the Italian bakery, Sicilian-style pizza from a red-white-and-green hut, and cotton candy and candy apples at the brightly lit concessionaire van. Up by the school

such favorites as country and Western singers, demolition derbies, professional wrestling, and draft-horse pulling contests. The fair is held in the town of Harrington in late July.

In September there is an authentic Indian powwow, with plenty of ceremonial dancing, storytelling, traditional food, and crafts. The powwow is held near Millsboro by Delaware's Nanticoke tribe, which now numbers about 500.

Perhaps the one event that most uniquely says "Delaware" is November's Return Day, a post-election occasion for politicians to bury the hatchet—literally.

A horse and his jockey warm up for the evening's harness event at Brandywine Raceway. Photo by Kevin Fleming

there's always a death-defying feat, maybe a human cannonball shot into midair, or a trapeze artist inching up a high wire to the top of the church steeple. More than 250,000 people show up for the eight-day event to eat, drink, and socialize at the biggest block party in town.

What the Italian Festival is to upstate residents, the Delaware State Fair is to their counterparts in Kent and Sussex counties. The fair is down-home style fun, served up in equal portions of blue-ribbon livestock, fresh-baked pies, midway rides, and award-winning crops. Evening entertainment centers around

Winners and losers ride side-by-side in antique carriages through the streets of Georgetown, then they bury the hatchet in a few inches of sand before feasting on traditional roasted ox. The ceremony dates back to the 1830s, when Sussex Countians gathered in Georgetown to hear election results.

Sports
Delaware doesn't have a pro sports team to call its own. But the Eagles football, Flyers hockey, and 76ers basketball teams in nearby Philadelphia serve as surrogate hometown teams. In the summer,

it's off to the ballparks of the Philadelphia Phillies or Baltimore Orioles, depending on whether the fan lives in upstate or downstate Delaware (or sometimes depending on how well each team is doing.)

Fan fever has its own local outlet in autumn, when the University of Delaware's Blue Hens try to trample a few feathers at Delaware Stadium in Newark. The Yankee Conference football team has a reputation for being as tough as the state bird for which it's named.

Tough team or not, there's a certain set at the football games who probably couldn't tell you the colors of the players' uniforms (they're blue and gold, for the record.) These are not sports fans but fans of the tailgates—those dawn-to-dusk parties thrown in the parking lot outside the stadium gates.

Tailgating doesn't actually start at dawn, but the serious tailgaters do show up at 9 or 10 P.M. for prime parking. Kickoff's at 1:30 P.M., giving ample opportunity for eating, drinking, and socializing. Some tailgaters treat the whole affair nonchalantly—dressed in jeans and sweats, they're content to sprawl on the back of station wagon bumpers and munch fried chicken and hoagies. But others dress to impress, resplendent in silk dresses or suits and ties, nibbling paté from linen-covered tables topped with candelabra.

The most lavish tailgates around aren't at the football games, though, but at the annual Point-to-Point races on the grounds of Winterthur Museum, northwest of Wilmington. Elaborate luncheons are artfully arranged on the bumpers of Rolls Royces and Jaguars—no sandwiches and compact cars for these tailgaters.

In addition to Point-to-Point's five feature races—most over post-and-rail fences—there are junior pony races and a parade of horse-drawn antique carriages. A new addition to the day's schedule is a juried tailgate competition. Noted epicureans judge the merits of a host of creative feasts, including, at one recent Point-to-Point, a whimsical beach tailgate—complete with windsurfer, sand, and all the other accouterments for a day at the shore.

Equestrian activities are abundant in Delaware, from Point-to-Point to the harness racing at Brandywine Raceway. Delaware racetracks include Brandywine, in north Wilmington; Delaware Park, in Stanton; and Harrington and Dover Downs in Kent County.

Delaware Park, a well-landscaped, 52-year-old facility, offers the only thoroughbred racing in Delaware. At one time, the park drew large crowds from the entire Eastern Seaboard—daily attendance figures hit 35,000 in the 1950s. Today Delaware Park no longer draws the giant crowds, yet its old-fashioned ambience and grassy picnic grove are still appealing.

Those who'd rather ride the ponies than wager have a ample selection of stables, trails, and lessons from which to choose in New Castle, Kent, and Sussex counties. And polo enthusiasts can travel to nearby Toughkenamon, Pennsylvania, to watch or participate in the fast-paced action of the Brandywine Polo Club.

Of course, there's much more to the sporting life in Delaware than just horses and football. Options include the genteel pleasures of lawnbowling at the Du Pont Country Club—followed by a light repast in the club's Wedgewood Room—or the rough-and-tumble allure of rugby, played by a tough bunch of jocks called the Killer Worms, also known as the Wilmington Rugby Club.

In the way of team sports, there are all manner of formal and informal teams and leagues sponsored by companies, counties, towns, and neighborhoods. Softball is the big game in

Delaware, with more than 700 adult teams and 80 youth teams. In New Castle County there's even an annual Icicle Softball Tournament, held in January for the most die-hard of softball fanatics.

There's one crowd, though, that scoffs at softball; it's strictly hard ball for the 100 or so players on the eight teams of the Delaware Semi-Pro Baseball League, which was started more than 40 years ago. These baseball lovers—many of them ex-minor league or ex-college stars—play three or four games a week from May through the end of summer.

Golf is a popular pastime with Delawareans, especially those corporate employees who can tee off at their own company country clubs. Those clubs include Hercules Country Club, off Lancaster Pike in Pike Creek Valley, and Du Pont Country Club, with three golf courses at its Wilmington site and another course at its Newark facility. Outstanding private and public links include Wilmington, Brandywine, Cavaliers, Newark, Delcastle, and Rock Manor country clubs in New Castle County; Garrison's Lake and Maple Dale country clubs in Kent County; and Rehoboth Beach, Seaford, and Cripple Creek country clubs in Sussex County. The biggest spectator event on the local golf calendar is the McDonald's Championship tournament, an LPGA event held at the Du Pont Country Club each summer.

Tennis players can work at their backhands at a variety of public and private courts throughout the state. In New Castle County the public courts at Rockford Park and Delcastle Recreation Center are particularly popular, as are the private facilities at Bellevue State Park.

Runners can pound the pavement in 5K, 10K, or half-marathon runs just about every weekend. The Caesar Rodney Half-Marathon is the event for runners who take their sport seriously;

it's a challenging course winding in and around Wilmington. In a lighter vein, the Harriers' Harvest Run at Halloween attracts all sorts of running clowns, jogging rag dolls, and race-walking creatures of the night.

New Castle County bicyclists can get into gear with the White Clay Bicycle Club, which sponsors a variety of weekday evening and weekend rides. The club also holds special events, such as the Delaware Doublecross, a 28-mile ride across state, and the Twin Century, a two-day, 200-mile ride from Wilmington to the beach and back. Serious racers can join the racing arm of the White Clay Club, called the First State Velo Club. Downstate bikers can pedal with the Diamond State Bicycle Club, which starts most of its rides in the Dover area.

Almost every sport imaginable can be enjoyed in Delaware or nearby states. The 600-member Wilmington Trail Club sponsors 5-mile weekday hikes and 18- to 20-mile weekend treks. Croquet enthusiasts can join the mallet-whackers of the Delaware Croquet Club and the Vicmead Mallet Club. Whitewater rafters can plummet down the Lehigh River, located two hours from Wilmington in Pennsylvania's Pocono Mountains.

Of course, the Poconos also mean skiing, at more than a dozen ski areas and resorts. Doe Mountain is one of the closest ski areas to Wilmington, offering beginning- and intermediate-level skiing. More advanced skiers travel on to Blue Mountain, Big Boulder, Jack Frost, Camelback, Shawnee, or Alpine, all located in the heart of the Poconos. At the first sign of snow (or the first days cold enough for artificial snowmaking) Delaware skiers eagerly strap their skis on the car and make the trek north, either on their own or on group trips sponsored by the Wilmington Ski Club. This organization plans ski trips and just about everything else—from overnight camping to skiwear fashion shows—for its more than 1,000 members.

Water sports abound in Delaware, for obvious reasons. One reason is called the Brandywine, another the Indian River Inlet, then there's the C&D canal, Lums Pond, Killens Pond, Rehoboth Bay, the Atlantic Ocean . . . the list goes on and on. And in nearby Maryland, the upper Chesapeake Bay beckons, promising Saturdays of crabbing, fishing, swimming, water-skiing, and boating.

In New Castle County, most recreational water activity takes place on the Brandywine—called a river by many, but actually a creek. Whatever you call it, this body of water flows past handsome, unspoiled countryside. It has been the inspiration for works by three generations of the Wyeth family, who make their home by the creek's banks upstream in Chadds Ford, Pennsylvania.

Canoeing is a popular pastime on the Brandywine, and at least one north Wilmington outfitter arranges daily excursions. To some, the mellow pleasures of tubing are even more appealing. No need to exert a single muscle—"tubers" just pop into an inner tube and laze downstream. Sociable types like to tie a few tubes together and float *en masse*. Over on the Christina, on the west side of Wilmington, the scullers set out at dawn to polish their skills. The Wilmington Rowing Club is a young organization that is growing in popularity with urbanites.

Delaware's coastal region is also host to every water sport under the sun. Enthusiasts can parasail, water-ski, fish, sail, surf, jet-ski, windsurf, go skimboarding, powerboating or paddleboating, and even dive for buried pirate treasure.

In the frothing surf, skimboarders do their double flips—and some even do triple flips—on equipment that looks

a bit like pint-sized surfboards. Dewey is the site of the annual East Coast Skimboarding Championships. And over on the bayside in Dewey, the graceful forms of windsurfers slide by in the sun, past the diners on the decks of the Rusty Rudder restaurant.

Sailors head to the Rehoboth Bay Sailing Association for its full schedule of activities, including the Governor's Cup regatta held in June. And the surf fishermen swear by the Indian River Inlet, above Bethany.

But that's only one of the prime picks. Fishermen have a wealth of wonderful decisions to make. Do they want to drop line in bay or ocean? Millpond or stream? Are they fishing for large-mouth bass and pickerel or maybe weakfish and bluefish?

Charter fishing boats ply the ocean and bays all through the summer, and as late into the autumn as November. The ocean and bays yield trout, sea bass, tautog, bluefish, weakfish, tuna, and flounder.

Stream fishermen usually cast out their lines in New Castle County's waters for panfish, chain pickerel, bass, and brook trout. Rainbow, brown, and brook trout are stocked each spring in the Red Clay, White Clay, Christina, Pike, and Mill creeks, and Wilson's and Beaver runs.

And freshwater angling can be had at most of the 60 ponds throughout the state. The small ponds dotting Bombay Hook National Wildlife Refuge are hot spots, so say those in the know. Or are they just telling us a fish story?

Delaware, the state, and the quality of life it yields draw rave reviews, no matter who you talk to. A prime location, scenic surroundings, pleasant climate, public awareness, prosperous living, good neighbors, and time to enjoy it all. This is the legacy Delaware provides. Who could ask for anything more?

Incoming Volkswagon imports await shipment at the Port of Wilmington. Photo by Kevin Fleming

Part
2

Delaware's Enterprises

EXIT 6

4

Wilmington Blvd.
Maryland Ave.
3/4 MILE

Photo by Kevin Fleming

7

Diamond State Telephone
Company, 132

Keen Compressed Gas
Company, 134

Delmarva Power, 136

Artesian Resources
Corporation, 137

WILM NEWSRADIO, 138

Chesapeake Utilities Corporation, 140

Networks

*Delaware's energy and communication providers keep
resources, power, and information circulating
throughout the state.*

Diamond State Telephone Company

From the first telephone in Delaware in 1878 to the hundreds of thousands of subscribers today, from the simple telephone service of a century ago to the sophisticated information-management network of today, the history of the telecommunications industry in the Diamond State has been marked by rapid growth and technological milestones.

The Diamond State Telephone Company has been a vital part of that history since its incorporation in 1891. A member of the Bell Atlantic family of companies since 1984,

the firm has made a commitment to ensure that progress and outstanding customer service go hand in hand. From its headquarters office at 911 Tatnall Street in downtown Wilmington, Diamond State Telephone directs a network that extends throughout Delaware and employs slightly less than 1,100 people.

Compared with the six other Bell Atlantic companies, Diamond State is small in size. However, it has been a pioneer of sorts, an innovator responsible for a number of firsts.

In the 1950s Diamond State became the first telephone company in the nation to offer direct-distance dialing. Diamond State was the first telephone company to computer control all of its switching centers. It became the first telephone company in the nation to offer statewide 911

service, in 1984. And it was the first company to offer all of its customers access to their long-distance carriers.

The Diamond State Telephone network is valued at more than $360 million. The company completed 1988 announcing the third consecutive year of record growth. Diamond State supports 389,000 access lines providing residential, coin telephone, and business service. Of this number, 128,000 are business lines.

Diamond State has been especially responsive to the needs of both existing businesses and the new enterprises moving into the state. It is committed to offering the most sophisticated types of service to its customers, and tailoring its "product" to meet the individual needs of the business.

One pair of fiber-optic cables (at left, splayed, and right, bound) provide the same message-carrying capability as traditional 1800 copper cable (shown at center) and is eight to 13 times more efficient.

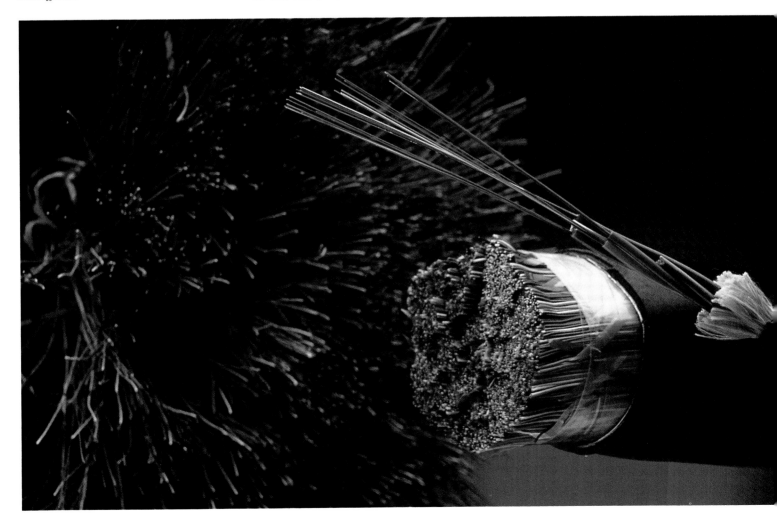

A call taker at one of Delaware's six 911 Enhanced Centers is ready to take emergency reports from callers, determining the appropriate dispatch.

The firm has been a pacesetter at installing fiber-optic cable in both its public network and in private networks for major customers such as The Du Pont Company. In a fiber-optic system, tiny lasers convert voice and data communications into pulses of light that are carried on pure glass fibers thinner than human hair.

Computer-controlled switching machines allow Diamond State to offer sophisticated services that meet the complex information-management needs of businesses as well as the growing needs of residential customers for services that help them streamline their lives. These include Bell Atlantic I.Q. Services, a family of features that includes now-familiar services such as call forwarding, call waiting, and three-way calling. I.Q. Services also include newer features that give customers unprecedented control over their telephone service. These features, for example, allow customers to block calls from certain numbers or to identify important callers with a distinctive ring. The latter service, called Identa Ring, is especially geared for residential and small business customers. It is much less expensive than running

separate lines for one household or business.

In the near future, among several brand-new features will be a residential telephone answering service that will eventually replace answering machines; a voice mailbox that will categorize messages as urgent, private, or normal; and call delivery, which will record and deliver a message at a designated time.

Diamond State also works with other organizations and institutions within Delaware to upgrade their information retrieval systems. The company recently formed a new computer link with the University of Delaware for a public data network. Any Delaware residence—home or business—with a personal computer and modem can access the university library on-line catalog, DELCAT. If the desired book is in the university library, the individual can request that it be sent to the local public library for checking out at no cost to the user. The University of Delaware Library has a broadly based comprehensive collection, including business, science, and the arts.

The Diamond State Telephone Company network's greatest strength is clearly that it is designed to grow as customers' needs change and expand. The network's latest technology, along with the skill and vision of the company's employees, enable Diamond State to work in

partnership with its customers to design custom solutions to new and evolving information-management needs.

The foundation of Diamond State's relationship with its customers is not based on technology alone, however. It is built upon a long tradition of outstanding service. This spirit of service has been nurtured by generations of employees, and they display it both on and off the job. Through volunteer activities with a wide range of organizations, employees demonstrate their commitment to the communities in which they live. These outside involvements vary from volunteering to work with handicapped children to Junior Achievement programs to programs that benefit senior citizens.

Diamond State is deeply committed to Delaware. Its high-tech network has helped make the state an attractive place for businesses to locate, and the spirit of service of its employees has helped make Delaware an outstanding place to live.

Diamond State Telephone president Joe Hulihan (left) presents the Award of Excellence to central office technicians John Watts (center) and Robert Moore (right) for their outstanding contribution to service. Watts and Moore were instrumental in developing a synchronized data clock, necessary for efficient data transmission.

Keen Compressed Gas Company

The willingness to adapt to changing times and a fluctuating economy—plus the know-how and competence to enter new markets with new products—are the hallmarks that characterize the Keen Compressed Gas Company.

As the area's leading supplier of compressed gas, the Keen family has served Delaware for more than 70 years. Businesses and consumers alike have relied on Keen to provide industrial gases, welding gases, and related items. The firm's customers range from sophisticated research and development laboratories to large, bustling refineries and include small businesses and consumers. But the family-owned and -operated company has developed a product line that extends beyond gas. This includes welding equipment, consumer appliances, medical and laboratory supplies, safety products, and heating/air conditioning equipment. The company also specializes in services such as piping de-

sign, sizing, and layout; equipment safety inspections; and gas-mode analysis and evaluations.

Indeed, the corporate philosophy of "Keen Service Counts" is more than just another slogan—it aptly describes the way Keen does business on a day-to-day basis.

Keen Compressed Gas Company was established in 1919 by Stanley H. Keen, a native Delawarean. The firm's first offices were at 34th and Market streets in Wilmington. During the company's first 30 years, welding was its mainstay. This was especially true during World War II,

when a shortage of new products created a greater demand for welding in the repair and maintenance of existing products. During the years that followed the war, Keen saw an opportunity in the propane-gas field, and it was not long before the company was heavily involved in this area.

The year 1969 proved to be a turning point for Keen, which at the time was operating as a successful but small company with 15 employees. That year Keen acquired Anchor Welding of Wilmington, a distributor of Airco products. Airco

Right: J. Merrill Keen, president (left), and Willard Keen, sales manager, carry on the family tradition begun in 1919 by Stanley H. Keen.

Below: Delaware's premier supplier of compressed gas and related products is headquartered at 101 Rogers Road in Wilmington.

is among the top three suppliers of gases in the country. Today Keen is one of 200 Airco distributors in the United States.

Other acquisitions of small welding companies followed during the 1970s and 1980s, resulting in greater expansion: a Dover company in 1975; a Millville, New Jersey, company in 1977; a Concordville, Pennsylvania, firm in 1982; an Elkton, Maryland, business in 1985; and a Wilmington branch of a larger company in 1988. The latest Keen acquisition occurred in March 1989, when it purchased a West Chester, Pennsylvania, welding supply company.

But Keen's spiral of growth has not been without its obstacles. A major loss took place during 1982 and 1983 with the closing of a large regional steel company, a heavy user of Keen products and services. This was followed by a slowdown in other large industries that were traditional users of welding gases and supplies. With its customer base dwindling, Keen was faced with the need to refocus its business. Keen bounced back: It shifted its emphasis from industrial gases to gases for the home and medical/laboratory field. The move has proven to be profitable. During the past decade the company's business has quadrupled.

Today Keen is considered small by national standards, but it is the largest business of its kind in Delaware. The company consists of three distinct divisions: welding/industrial gases and supplies, medical/laboratory gases and equipment, and propane gas service.

In the medical/laboratory gases area, Keen serves as both a wholesaler and a retailer. Its customers include research laboratories, environmental companies, home-care companies, hospitals, nursing homes, and private physicians and dentists.

Welding and industrial gases and suppliers still constitute the basis of Keen's business. However, over the years, this aspect of the business has been reduced considerably.

The propane gas service arm of the company, which accounts for about 38 percent of Keen's volume, is geared to both businesses and consumers. It includes the sale of related propane appliances and serves about 4,000 customers.

Keen Compressed Gas now serves its customers from eight locations in four states: Wilmington, New Castle, and Dover in Delaware; Millville, New Jersey; Concordville and West Chester, Pennsylvania; and Elkton and Edgewood, Maryland. All eight sites include self-service showrooms—an area in which Keen has served as a pioneer. The showrooms range from welding supplies in Wilmington and all branches to consumer appliances in New Castle.

The company's inventory includes one million dollars in equipment and supplies plus 40,000 cylinders of gas that can be delivered generally within 24 hours to customers via a fleet of more than 50

Right: Gas is stored in giant tanks at Keen's Wilmington facility.

Below: Everything for the welder can be found at Keen's showroom in Wilmington.

company-owned trucks and trailers.

There are now more than 100 employees—many of whom have worked for Keen for more than 10 years. Most of the employees work in one of the Delaware sites.

Although Stanley H. Keen died in 1965, his work has carried on through his family. Today his youngest son, J. Merrill Keen, serves as president and general manager of Keen Compressed Gas Company, and a daughter, Ruth Keen Lloyd, is secretary. Some of the founder's grandchildren—Willard Keen, Richard Keen, Jon M. Keen, Kim Keen, and Bryan Keen—are also involved in one aspect of the business or another.

Delmarva Power

Delmarva Power serves more than 340,000 electric customers throughout the Delmarva Peninsula and 79,000 natural gas customers in northern Delaware.

The utility was incorporated in Delaware in 1909 and today employs more than 2,600 people. Major generating facilities are in Edge Moor, Delaware City, and Indian River in Delaware and in Vienna, Maryland.

Over the years Delmarva Power has earned an outstanding reputation for meeting the needs of its residential and industrial customers. The utility's customer-approval rating has consistently ranked highly, with its reliability rate exceeding 99 percent. In fact, reliable electric power was the reason given by one New York bank for locating a subsidiary in Delaware. Customers also benefit from Delmarva Power's stable utility rates. Its industrial electric rates in particular are among the lowest in the Northeast.

Delmarva Power works closely with industrial customers to help them identify and meet their energy needs. It provides regular communication with its corporate customers through newsletters.

The major challenge facing Delmarva Power in recent years has been growth: how to provide energy for the future at the lowest reasonable cost in an environment where electrical-load growth is coming much more rapidly than expected. Between 1985 and 1989 the demand for electricity on the Delmarva Peninsula has grown 38.9 percent—compared with 12.6 percent for the entire decade between 1975 and 1984. In short, the utility now has more customers using more electricity than ever before, and this growth is expected to continue.

To meet future energy needs, Delmarva Power has developed Challenge 2000—a blend of alternatives that will provide flexibility so the utility can respond quickly to changing demands for energy, emerging technologies, and fluctuating fuel costs. This differs from the traditional approach that relies mainly on a single source for supplying energy needs and simply builds more power plants.

On the demand side, Challenge 2000 consists of programs aimed at reducing electric use during peak periods. This includes residential load management and commercial/industrial interruptible and peak management rates.

Delmarva Power recently completed two 100-megawatt combustion turbines to meet the growing energy needs of its customers.

On the supply side, Challenge 2000 focuses on new ways to generate electricity by building smaller power plants, acquiring alternative power sources that use the most advanced technologies available, and installing power sources that add smaller increments of energy. To this end, Delmarva Power has completed two 100-megawatt combustion turbines. The utility is also talking with cogeneration developers about new projects that might provide base-load generation in the 1990s. Delmarva Power also plans to purchase electricity from other companies, as well as upgrade its existing plants.

The major challenge facing Delmarva Power in recent years has been the rapid growth on the burgeoning Delmarva Peninsula.

Artesian Resources Corporation

Artesian Resources Corporation is the umbrella organization consisting of a major water utility and diversified businesses involved in environmental testing, data processing, and real estate. The water utility has experienced record-breaking growth each year, and the other units are also thriving.

The original enterprise is Artesian Water Company, an investor-owned utility established in 1905 that serves more than 46,000 primarily residential customers. Artesian's

challenge is constructing additional storage facilities and developing new sources of supply to meet the demands of its customers.

In 1984 Artesian was reorganized into a holding company system with Artesian Resources as the umbrella, employing 125 people. Artesian Water became a subsidiary, and new businesses were created to handle environmental testing (Artesian Laboratories), data processing (Artesian Computer Services), and real estate development

customers in Delaware, New Jersey, Pennsylvania, and Maryland. Government certified for drinking water in Delaware, Pennsylvania, and Maryland, it is one of the more prominent environmental-testing facilities in the Mid-Atlantic region.

Another part of the Artesian group is a new data-processing business that serves both the water utility and commercial customers by providing consulting services, medical billing, and the development of software packages.

The laboratory and data-processing subsidiaries recently moved into modern facilities at the new County Commerce Office Park, built by Artesian Development Corporation. The 15-acre office park, which overlooks I-95 from Churchmans Road, is adjacent to Artesian's corporate headquarters. It is perhaps the most visible symbol of the organization's growth. Now completed, it spans 200,000

distribution system spans 600 miles of water main over a 125-square-mile area from the Pennsylvania and Maryland state lines to the Chesapeake and Delaware Canal. Artesian Water has 42 pumping stations and an average daily pumpage of 15 million gallons. Eighty percent of its water comes from its own wells. The rest is purchased from other water utilities.

The water company's operations remain a solid, consistent source of growth, both in its customer base and its service territory. Its greatest

A mirrorlike facade greets visitors at the Artesian Resources Corporation headquarters in County Commerce Office Park.

(Artesian Development).

Artesian Laboratories is the first full-service laboratory in Delaware doing commercial environmental testing. Current services include conducting about 25,000 tests annually of drinking water, solid waste, and soil for more than 200 industrial, commercial, governmental, and residential

square feet and includes other commercial tenants.

Artesian Resources Corp.'s ongoing commitment to serve Delaware is very much in evidence. As an example, in 1987 it agreed to lease to the state part of the company's property on the Christina River for use as a public boat ramp. The company is justifiably proud of its many employees who actively participate in community services—for example, fire fighting or fund raising for charitable organizations.

WILM NEWSRADIO

WILM NEWSRADIO (1450 on the AM dial) broadcasts news and information 24 hours per day, seven days per week from its headquarters at 1215 French Street in Wilmington. Although its primary market is New Castle County, the station has a broadcasting pattern that extends 35 miles from Wilmington.

The station has helped area residents understand their communities and their environment and has responded to the needs of its listeners for years. Although it is a local radio station, its vision matches that of a much larger medium. The station has been a pioneer in a number of areas and has never hesitated to take risks in its programming.

WILM is the only all-news radio station between Philadelphia and Washington, D.C. In fact, Wilmington is one of the smallest markets in the country with an all-news station. WILM is considered one of the forerunners of news and information radio in the region.

WILM has 41 employees, and more than half of them are professional journalists. It not only has the largest broadcast staff in Delaware, but the size of its staff is considered above average for any AM radio station in a market its size. During the past 13 years WILM has more than doubled its program staff.

WILM was the first radio station in its market to have a regular professional weather forecasting service and was the first to carry daily Dow Jones and Company stock reports on the Wall Street Journal radio network. It also pioneered traffic reports via helicopter, and it is still the only Delaware station with daily helicopter traffic reports.

WILM had one of the first two-way talk shows in the country. In 1976 the station won a major victory for taped-delay broadcasts of political debates in 1976. That year WILM won an appeal to the Federal Communications Commission that gave all radio stations more

flexibility in scheduling public-interest programs. The victory made it possible to tape segments and then broadcast them later for the convenience of listeners.

It is the only affiliate of the CBS Radio Network between Philadelphia and Baltimore, and WILM

carries weekend news programming from the major international broadcasters.

The state's second-oldest continuously licensed broadcast station, WILM was licensed by the FCC in 1923. It was acquired by the Delaware Broadcasting Company in 1929 and operated independently for the next 10 years. In 1939 WILM became affiliated with Intercity Network through a sister station, WDEL. A year later WILM changed its affiliation to the Mutual Broadcasting System. In 1949 a group headed by Ewing B. Hawkins acquired the Delaware Broadcasting Company, and Hawkins became WILM's president and general manager. By 1959 Sally V. Hawkins had joined her husband's firm as treasurer, and since 1972 she has served as station president.

The station began broadcasting on a 24-hour basis in 1952. In 1976, to serve the needs of an increasingly information-oriented society, it converted from its middle-of-the-road contemporary-music format to an all-news and information format.

The family-owned and -operated station has become a fixture in the

Left: Delaware Governor Michael N. Castle is interviewed by WILM NEWSRADIO reporter Debbi Pernick.

Wilmington community. The staff itself is involved in numerous civic and charitable organizations, and the station has earned countless awards for its community service programming and its up-to-the-minute news coverage. The emphasis at WILM has always been on live coverage and quick response to current events.

The station traditionally sponsors more debates than any other station during election years. During the most recent national primary campaign, it was the only local radio station to send journalists to New Hampshire to cover the progress of presidential hopeful and former Delaware governor Pete du Pont. WILM is the only radio station in Delaware that has a full-time legislative correspondent in the state capital. It provided the only continuous radio or TV news on primary-election night. WILM also has a bureau in Washington, D.C.

The station also excels in the business and economics realm. Since 1981 it has had a full-time business editor—the only broadcast

medium in Wilmington to hold that distinction. Business news encompasses corporate relocations, Chancery Court proceedings, plant openings and closings, financial news, and stock reports. WILM carries live hourly newscasts from the Wall Street Journal Radio Network throughout the day supplemented with local business and market reports.

Eighty percent of WILM's programming is locally originated. With the exception of one network-originated talk show, all of the talk shows are local. Topics range from science to family matters and from political analyses to popular culture.

WILM NEWSRADIO is the number-one radio station in New Castle County for news, traffic reports, and talk radio. It reaches 45 percent of all radio listeners age 18 and over in the county, and its listeners are loyal—86 percent listen daily.

Below: Chopper 1450 provides Delaware's only aerial traffic and news report.

Chesapeake Utilities Corporation

Chesapeake Utilities Corporation has been serving the Delmarva Peninsula for more than 130 years. The company's roots date back to 1859 in Dover, when early gas industry pioneers provided the basic service of street lighting. Chesapeake's Delaware Division still provides gas for those streetlights today.

Chesapeake Utilities Corporation and its subsidiaries have evolved into a multiple energy supplier primarily engaged in natural gas distribution in Delaware from Delaware City to southern Sussex County and extending into the eastern shore of Maryland and the central Florida area; natural gas transmission in Delaware and the eastern shore of Maryland; and propane distribution in Delaware, Maryland, Virginia, and Florida. In 1988 Chesapeake Utilities acquired certain propane and oil distribution assets of Kellam Delivery, a subsidiary of Kellam Energy, Inc., as part of its diversification process. As a result of this acquisition, Chesapeake's propane distribution subsidiary, Sharpgas, Inc., tripled its distribution operations. Sharpoil, Inc., its oil products distribution subsidiary, acquired the oil products distribution assets of Kellam, Inc., representing a new line of business for the company. Other acquisitions in 1988 were Capital Data Systems (CDS), a computer facilities management service, and Currin and Associates, a utility, financial, and rate consulting firm, both based in North Carolina.

During its expansion and diversification, Chesapeake Utilities has always maintained its strong ties with the First State. The company's executive headquar-

Chesapeake Utilities supplies the natural gas used for industrial and commercial applications in Delaware City.

ters is located in Dover. Its largest natural gas distribution division as well as its transmission pipeline company (Eastern Shore Natural Gas) and propane distribution operation (Sharpgas, Inc.) have offices and major operational facilities in Delaware.

Among Chesapeake's community-related projects is the ongoing sponsorship of SHARING, a heat share fund that helps to pay winter heating bills for the elderly, handicapped, and low-income households.

Delaware City industrial consumers receive their natural gas via a 12-inch pipe on a pipeline suspension bridge that traverses the C&D Canal.

In its commitment to meet Delaware's future needs, the company has been systematically expanding its service territory to offer natural gas services to Delaware's growing communities. Intricate computerized compressor stations have been strategically added to increase the distribution capabilities. The company works closely with area builders and developers to meet the needs of new residential and commercial/industrial users.

With the changing nature of the natural gas industry, the firm has positioned itself to effectively offer innovative rate structures and aggressive marketing programs without sacrificing the quality of service.

Propane and oil products distribution are also flourishing in Delaware. The demand for competitively priced energy products, coupled with excellent service, has made Sharpgas and Sharpoil a viable part of the Chesapeake energy services package. With the addition of service industries, Chesapeake can now also offer data-processing (CDS) and consulting services (Currin and Associates) to Delawareans.

Chesapeake Utilities Corporation will continue to provide energy and energy-related services with the same commitment, enthusiasm, and tradition of the nineteenth-century entrepreneurs that first brought gaslights to the City of Dover 130 years ago.

Photo by Eric Crossan

Photo by Kevin Fleming

8

FMC Corporation, 144   General Chemical   Chrysler Motors Corpora-   ICI Americas Inc., 150   Wilmington Finishing
                Corporation, 146   tion, 148   Company, 154

General Foods USA, 155   NOR-AM Chemical Com-   Kaumagraph Corporation,   CIBA-GEIGY Corporation,   The Du Pont Company, 162
                pany, 156   158   160

Townsends, Inc., 166   Atlantic Aviation Corpora-   The Aqualon Group, 170   General Motors Corpora-   Slocomb Industries, Inc., 174
                tion, 168   tion, 172

Industrial Strength

*A rich industrial tradition combines with the
technology of tomorrow to spell success
for many Delaware firms.*

FMC Corporation

"Without the Newark plant and its team of people dedicated to producing products of the highest quality, we would not be in business."

That comment, from top management at the Chicago-based FMC Corporation, underscores the Newark plant's key role in the multinational's Food and Pharmaceutical Products Division. The plant, situated on a 27-acre tract on Ogletown Road, produces and markets pharmaceutical excipients and food additives. Excipients include binders, disintegrants and coatings for tablets and capsules that help the active ingredient perform.

The high-tech Newark plant is the original, largest, most advanced, and best equipped in FMC's Food and Pharmaceutical Products Division. The operation is headquartered in Philadelphia and is the recognized leader in the worldwide pharmaceutical excipient industry. Every product manufactured and sold by the division worldwide originates in Newark.

This includes the division's star product—Avicel®, a microcrystalline cellulose, an additive marketed to leading food and pharmaceutical companies in more than 80 countries. Avicel, a light, tasteless powder, is derived from a specially purified alpha cellulose, the same kind found in many fruits and vegetables. It binds, thickens, stabilizes, and can replace fat and absorb moisture in food products such as frozen desserts, salad dressings, nonfat yogurt, and pie fillings.

Eighty percent of Avicel sales, however, are to pharmaceutical firms. In fact, virtually every major pharmaceutical company in the

world uses Avicel for at least one of its products. Its primary uses are as a binding agent for tablets and capsules and as an aid to rapid disintegration of active drugs in the stomach. Avicel is found in medications that treat cardiovascular disease, hypertension, diabetes, and ulcers, and in over-the-counter pain relievers, cough/cold remedies, and vitamins.

Avicel was discovered in the late 1950s in the laboratories of the old American Viscose Corporation in nearby Marcus Hook, Pennsylvania, where manufacture of the product began in 1961. The following year a new plant start-up began at Newark, Delaware. The company introduced

Above and right: FMC's Newark plant, the major source of the pharmaceutical and food additive Avicel®, is the largest and most modern plant in FMC's Food and Pharmaceutical Products Division.

Avicel as a low-calorie food ingredient, but the product characteristics were found to have potential as a binder and filler for pharmaceutical tablets. In 1963 FMC purchased the American Viscose operations. The effort to find multiple uses for the product has paid off handsomely with an expanded product line and market share. There are now 15 variations of Avicel, and FMC is the world's leading supplier of microcrystalline cellulose.

FMC Newark plant management staff is (standing, from left): G.K. Riley, employee relations manager; W.W. Heckcrote, controller; D.A. VonBehren, quality-control manager; and S.P. Sabatino, operating superintendent. Seated are (from left): E.G. Fleck, senior engineering associate; B.S. Phalen, plant manager; and S.A. Reed, purchasing manager.

major research
and development
facility in Prince-
ton, New Jersey,
which is consid-
ered the best of its
kind in the excip-
ient supplier in-
dustry. At both
Princeton and
Newark the focus
is new product
development and
applications re-
search, plus a
strong technical
customer service
program.

Longevity and
stability are hall-
marks of the
Newark site. Its
employees have
accumulated more
than 1,200 years

In 1978 the firm expanded
beyond the original Newark plant
by building a prototype facility in
Cork, Ireland. Meanwhile, the Newark plant has expanded steadily
since its start-up to accommodate a
growing product line. In the late
1970s and early 1980s a number of
new pharmaceutical excipients were
introduced, including Ac-Di-Sol®

(used to speed up the disintegration
of tablets and capsules, resulting in
faster drug action), and Aquacoat®
and Aquateric® (high-performance
latex film coatings that modify the
rate or target of delivery of active
drugs, mask bitter taste, and control
dissolution patterns, as in sustained
release).

The most recent expansions occurred in 1985 to accommodate the
production of Ac-Di-Sol and in 1987
with the opening of a new, multimillion-dollar high-tech coatings
plant to produce Aquacoat, Aqua-
teric, and a series of cellulose esters
used in novel drug delivery systems.

The computerized Newark plant
features an enclosed continuous process system where 108 employees
on three shifts work a 24-hour schedule. Also at Newark is a state-of-the-
art automated packaging center,
bright modern offices, warehousing
space, and a pilot plant facility. The
latter is supported by the division's

*Avicel® comes off the packaging line, ready for
use by food and pharmaceutical manufacturers
worldwide.*

of service. At least 16 employees
have service records ranging between 20 and 30 years, having
started with American Viscose.
Bruce Phalen, plant manager since
1978, leads a seven-person management staff with another 111 years of
experience and technical expertise.
The hourly workers are represented
by U.S. Steel Workers of America,
Local 13028, and labor-management
relations have been characterized
by a longtime record of freedom
from labor strife.

The plant scores high in safety:
Over the past three years there have
been no lost-time injuries. Plant management is also proud of its low rate
of personnel turnover, which aver-
ages less than 2 percent per year.

FMC Corporation is one of
the world's leading producers of
machinery and chemicals for industry, government, and agriculture. A
Fortune 200 company, it employs
25,000 people and has 112 manufacturing and mine facilities in 26
states and 15 foreign countries.
The Food and Pharmaceutical
Products Division is part of its
Chemical Products Group.

General Chemical Corporation

General Chemical Corporation traces its roots to 1899, when William H. Nichols, a pioneer in the U.S. chemicals industry, merged with 11 other small, independent heavy chemical producers. The firm's establishment was consistent with the trend of that era, in which groups of small businesses consolidated with large, financially stable operations that offered greater product diversity.

When General Chemical was formed, it produced 33 different chemicals. Today the Parsippany, New Jersey-based company's scope is international. It manufactures more than 200 high-performance specialty and industrial chemicals in 50 North American plants.

General's Delaware Valley Plant has long been a keystone plant and one of the largest in General Chemical's production network. The plant manufactures more than 110 specialty and industrial chemicals. These include sulfur dioxide-based photochemicals, fluoborates, sulfuric acid, and an array of acids, etchants, solvents, and strippers for the electronics industry. The plant is the largest producer of photo salts in the United States and the largest spent-sulfuric acid regenerator on the East Coast.

The Delaware Valley Plant employs 460 people and occupies 130 acres between the Delaware River and Philadelphia Pike. Its North Plant contains batch reactors used to make specialty and electronic chemical products. The South Plant houses the 1,000-ton-per-day sulfuric acid facility and equipment for making sulfur dioxide-based photographic chemicals.

The site's support facilities include 100,000 square feet of warehouse space, product packaging lines, and loading and unloading sections for trucks, railcars, and barges. The plant also maintains its own cogeneration unit, as well as one of the company's key research and development laboratories.

The Claymont facility plays a leading role in General Chemical's company-wide statistical quality-control program. A product testing laboratory—created in 1988—houses both basic and advanced testing equipment, such as an inductively coupled plasma device that measures impurities in the parts-per-billion range. A special software package statistically analyzes product test results and provides customers with product quality reports.

The Delaware Valley Plant's history is deeply intertwined with General Chemical's evolution into an industry leader. In 1910 the corporation purchased land for the South

Located in Claymont, General Chemical's Delaware plant is among the company's largest facilities, employing 460 people and occupying 130 acres.

Plant, choosing the site due to its access to East Coast markets. Two years later construction began on this sulfuric acid plant. Its production processes would have far-reaching effects on American industry.

The plant's operation, which began in 1913, marked the first commercial application of the contact process for sulfuric acid. This new process yielded acid that could be produced more efficiently in any desired strength and in quantities never before feasible. The contact

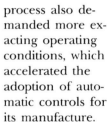

process also demanded more exacting operating conditions, which accelerated the adoption of automatic controls for its manufacture.

General Chemical's introduction of this breakthrough technology is recognized as one of the most significant achievements in American acid-making history, as sulfuric acid probably has more commercial uses than any other chemical. The sulfuric acid and sulfur dioxide made in the South Plant formed the basis for all other products manufactured there.

With its own power plant, railroad tank car repair shop, laboratory, and warehouse facilities, the Delaware Valley Plant became the forerunner of today's integrated chemical complexes. Moreover, in an era of horse-drawn vehicles, the plant was unique because it operated without horses. Instead, materials were moved via a plant-wide, elevated train track, electrically driven tram cars, and electric cranes

Left: General Chemical's Delaware Valley Works manufactures more than 110 specialty and industrial chemicals essential to the production of industrial and consumer products.

Right: The Delaware plant is the largest producer of photographic chemicals in the United States and one of the largest facilities for chemical regeneration in the country.

Below: Recognized as one of the nation's outstanding producers of consistently high-quality chemicals, the plant's Delaware Development Laboratories are a focal point for General Chemical's statistical quality-control and process-development programs.

that unloaded ore vehicles.

The plant's growth, along with the region's rapid manufacturing development, attracted many workers to the area, causing a housing shortage. To alleviate the problem for its employees, the company, in 1916, voluntarily purchased a 213-acre tract of land one mile from the plant and constructed a planned community named Overlook Colony. This $2-million development still exists today.

During World War I the Delaware Valley Plant produced chemicals needed for the war effort. The plant filled a national sulfuric acid capacity shortfall when its contact process quickly supplied high-strength acid for TNT production.

Between the two world wars more products and production facilities were added at the Delaware Valley Plant. This increased production prompted an expansion into an adjacent idle chemical site in 1940. Called the North Plant, this facility began operation in 1945.

Specialty chemicals have been a mainstay of the North Plant ever since. Among the products manufactured at this site are numerous fluorine derivatives—primarily inorganic fluorides and metallic and alkali fluoborates.

Metal fluoborates produced at the Delaware Valley Plant were first used commercially as electroplating chemicals. They were used extensively to plate airplane and truck bearings and other automotive and aircraft parts. General Chemical was the first company to make these commercially in concentrated solution form, and it spearheaded their development, leading to widespread electroplating applications.

Use of alkali fluoborates is now standard practice in the metals industry because they offer higher efficiency, cost savings, and improved quality.

Production of chemicals for the flourishing electronics industry was added at the North Plant in the 1970s.

The Delaware Valley Plant figures prominently in General Chemi-

cal's future, as the company strives to enhance its position as a high-quality, low-cost chemical producer in today's highly competitive market. Through cooperation, innovation, and diligence, the focal points of its past, General Chemical Corporation and the Delaware Valley Plant will continue to thrive through the addition of new product lines and new chemical processes.

Chrysler Motors Corporation

The Chrysler Motors Newark Assembly Plant is one of the most highly automated facilities of its kind in the United States. The plant, which spans 2 million square feet and occupies 246 acres, employs approximately 4,200 hourly and salaried workers. It is the only Chrysler plant in the country that produces the new Dodge Spirit, Plymouth Acclaim, and Chrysler LeBaron four-door family sedans. Chrysler is one of Delaware's major employers, with an annual payroll of $160 million. Chrysler pays more than $10 million each year in state and local taxes.

The Newark plant recently completed a $205-million modernization project that included a dramatic conversion to a state-of-the-art, high-technology manufacturing operation. The modernization took place to prepare for the introduction of Chrysler's new 1989 models: the Dodge Spirit and Plymouth Acclaim. These cars replaced the Dodge Aries and Plymouth Reliant. Prior to the plant modernization, the Newark site also produced the Town and Country station wagons and the Le Baron four-door sedan.

Employees gather for a team meeting to discuss plant concerns as part of Chrysler's Modern Operating Agreement.

Of the plant's $205-million expenditure on the modernization, about $110 million was spent on a 230,000-square-foot body-shop expansion and associated machinery and conveyors. The plant has nine miles of conveyors, and the body shop and assembly areas have a total of 4.5 miles of high-technology power and free conveyors installed, including two-way tilting conveyor line for improved operator ergonomics during the installation of underbody components. Newark is the first Chrysler assembly plant in the nation to make use of these unique tilting carriers

The Newark Assembly Plant, as seen from the front administration office (above) and from an aerial view (facing page).

in the production process. They allow workers to perform required job assignments more easily, with less stress, resulting in an overall enhancement of quality levels.

The modernization also resulted in an increase in the number of robots used at the Newark assembly plant from 75 to 221. The robots are used in such areas as welding, material handling, and sealing.

Other new developments at the plant include a product-quality improvement team. The team is comprised of 12 hourly workers who are known as the "blue coats" because of the distinct blue jackets worn by each member. They are charged with the responsibility of pinpointing and recommending solutions to any quality problems found throughout the plant. Another new development is the Simple Flexible Manufacturing System (SIMFLEX), a robotic application system that improves product quality, simplifies tooling systems, reduces investment costs, increases the use of flexible assembly systems, and reduces lead and changeover times. SIMFLEX was installed in the body shop. The Newark plant is

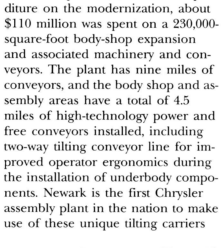

Chrysler's second assembly plant to receive the system.

The new high-technology plant makes use of an automatic-framing system wherein major body components are automatically positioned and welded. The paint department also uses the latest technology in applying protective coatings to the car. In addition, the plant has five computer-controlled front-end alignment machines.

Fifty-five computer terminals were installed to expand the integration of computers into the manufacturing process, including the Chrysler-developed Factory Information System (FIS). This sophisticated plant-wide data-gathering procedure provides instant communication between the plant's manufacturing and maintenance divisions. The addition of these computer terminals, plus existing terminals, results in a to-tal of 207 terminals monitoring more than 2,500 quality items.

To prepare for the extensive modernization and the new car launch, the Newark employees completed nearly one million hours of classroom and on-the-job training. Part of this training included sessions involving a new way of working, based on cooperation. The Newark facility was the first Chrysler assembly plant to implement a Modern Operating Agreement (M.O.A.) with an existing work force. The M.O.A. was signed in June 1987 and implemented at the start of the 1989 model launch. This flexible working agreement is designed to boost productivity and quality through a total team effort and commitment. It gives the employee a bigger say in the production process and a role in the participative style of manage-ment, as well as greater earning potential. Overall, it allows for a more efficient use of the work force and resources.

Built as a tank plant in 1951 at the height of the Korean War, the assembly plant was later converted to an auto-assembly plant in 1956. Since April 30, 1957, when the first car rolled off the assembly line, the plant has produced almost 5.4 million vehicles. Of this number 1.4 million were various models of the famous and popular compact "K" car—the Dodge Aries and Plymouth Reliant. Newark was one of only two Chrysler plants to launch the "K" car, the vehicle credited with turning around the company.

Today the plant produces the Dodge Spirit, Plymouth Acclaim, and Chrysler LeBaron four-door sedans at the rate of more than 60 cars per hour. Total daily production is 962 cars during two shifts. The Newark plant is one of 59 Chrysler manufacturing and assembly plants in the United States.

Founded in 1925, Chrysler Motors has been recognized as a world leader in the design, development, manufacture, and sale of automotive products—passenger cars, trucks, vans, mini-vans, wagons, vehicle-component systems, and replacement parts. It is the third-largest automobile company in the United States and the eighth-largest producer in the world. It ranks 11th among *Fortune* 500 companies.

ICI Americas Inc.

ICI is the world's fourth-largest chemical group, manufacturing in more than 40 countries and selling products in more than 150.

In the United States, ICI Americas Inc. is a wholly owned ICI operating subsidiary and one of the fastest-growing chemical companies. Headquartered in Wilmington, Delaware, ICI Americas Inc. has annual sales of more than $4 billion and employs more than 17,000 people at manufacturing sites, research centers, laboratories, and offices nationwide.

Today ICI Americas Inc. is organized into eight business units that serve virtually every major industry. ICI's portfolio includes a broad line of agricultural products, pharmaceuticals, Glidden paints, plastics, polyester films and resins, polyurethanes, specialty chemicals, dyes and colors, fibers, security devices, aerospace components, and advanced composite materials.

The rapidly growing ICI Pharmaceuticals Group in Wilmington, which includes Stuart Pharmaceuticals and ICI Pharma, is a business unit of ICI Americas Inc. Other U.S.-based health care units of ICI are Coe Laboratories (dental composites and supplies) of Chicago, Illinois, and Cellmark Diagnostics (DNA Fingerprinting^{SM}) of Germantown, Maryland. Together, Stuart and ICI Pharma rank 10th among U.S. pharmaceutical companies.

Founded in 1941, Stuart Pharmaceuticals became part of ICI's U.S. operation with the acquisition of Atlas Chemical Industries by ICI in 1971. Since the merger, Stuart has grown substantially, and in 1987 the company was restructured to create a second business unit, ICI Pharma. Stuart retained the hospital and consumer products, Stuart Prenatal® and Stuartnatal® 1+1 prenatal vitamins, Hibiclens® surgical scrub, and Cefotan® antibiotic. Zestril® (lisinopril), an important ACE inhibitor for hypertension launched in 1988, was also assigned to Stuart.

ICI Pharma was assigned Tenormin®, Tenoretic®, and Sorbitrate®

A surfactant/oil mixture dispersing in water is shown causing an emulsion bloom. Surfactants and related products manufactured by ICI Specialty Chemicals serve many manufacturing operations by facilitating the formulation and creation of special effects in products.

cardiovascular agents and Nolvadex® breast cancer treatment.

ICI Pharmaceuticals Group in the United States employs some 700 scientists, who, with more than 2,000 researchers in the United Kingdom, support the research effort of ICI. Research and development expenditures worldwide exceed $300 million annually.

By the early 1990s ICI Pharmaceuticals Group will introduce several new drugs to the U.S. market: a compound for treatment of diabetic complications, an intravenous anesthetic agent, a unique drug to treat mild to moderate congestive heart failure, and a treatment for advanced prostate cancer. Further in the future, agents are being researched for treatment of asthma, emphy-

sema, and mental disorders, including Alzheimer's disease.

The Glidden Company, headquartered in Cleveland, Ohio, is part of the ICI Paints worldwide business. The Glidden Company has technologically shaped the paint industry with the invention of Spred® Satin, the first waterborne latex paint, in 1948.

The Glidden and Spred brands rank among the top in retail sales. These paints and Endurance® stains are sold through a broad network of independent dealers and company-owned paint and wall covering stores.

The other part of the Glidden business is Industrial Coatings, which focuses on six markets—appliance, automotive, building products, container, general industrial, and Gel-Kote® marine.

In the container market, Glidden is the world leader in waterborne coatings that protect the contents of more than 100 billion beer and beverage cans annually. Glidden is the established leader in powder, a dry coating for major home appliances; steel, aluminum, and wood building products; parts for automobiles and trucks; fiberglass-reinforced boats; and various other consumer/industrial products, as well as plastic parts.

Glidden's Macco Adhesives Group produces a line of building and construction adhesives, caulks, and sealants. Its Liquid Nails® brand is the top-selling do-it-yourself construction adhesive in the United States.

The ICI Agricultural Products Group is helping the American farmer grow food and fiber safely and efficiently—through its agrichemicals and seeds businesses.

One of the products that literally changed some methods of farming and helped bring ICI to the forefront is Gramoxone® Super herbicide, which introduced the idea of no-till farming and offers numerous economic savings and environmental advantages to farmers. ICI is a leader in developing pyrethroid products such as Karate® and Force® insecticides that safely and effectively help farmers protect their crops from harmful insect pests.

ICI Agricultural Products has also made significant inroads in helping farmers control unwanted grasses and broadleaf weeds. Fusilade® and Reflex® herbicides were developed for use with soybean and cotton crops. Eradicane® and Sutan® selective corn herbicides and Ordram® and Arrosolo® rice herbicides give farmers a number of herbicide options from which to choose for controlling weeds. ICI has also devel-

oped a leading plant growth regulator that permits controlled growth of grasses, trees, and ornamentals.

The Professional Products section has made significant contributions to the control of other pests with Talon® rodenticide, Torpedo® termiticide, and Demon® insecticide for control of roaches.

ICI, through its Garst Seed business, is a leader in seed breeding and is active in the development of hybrid seeds through the application of advanced biotechnology. The company also markets sorghum and alfalfa seed.

ICI Films is a leader in the supply of high-performance films, resins, and film-based products and systems. The films' product range includes Melinex® polyester films, Propafilm® polypropylene films, Stabar® polyethersulphone and polyetheretherketone films, Upilex® polyimide films, as well as Melinar®

Left: Specially trained representatives from ICI Pharmaceuticals Group supply essential information about currently marketed ICI products to physicians and other health care professionals.

Below: Through innovative technology, ICI Agricultural Products is feeding "A Growing America."

polyester (PET) polymer.

ICI Films is the global leader in the development of specialized film material for use in the optical imaging markets. Applications include photographic films, X-ray films, and microfilm, as well as reprographic and drafting films and specialty printing applications.

ICI Films Melinex and Propafilm films are used in a wide range of packaging applications for food products such as snack foods, microwaveable foods, and coffee, and for nonfood uses such as medical and electrical components.

ICI Films also offers films for the electrical and electronics industries. There, the dielectric and temperature-resistant properties of polyester, polyethersulfone, polyetheretherketone, and polyimide films find applications in such markets as electric motors, communication cables, flexible printed circuits, and membrane touch switches. The thermal and chemical-resistance properties of the PES, PEEK, and polyimide films also make them ideally suited for aerospace and defense applications.

Polyester film is used in flexible disc, computer and data recording tapes/cartridges, professional and consumer video tapes and cassettes, and audio recording products.

Newest additions to the ICI Films family are ICI Imagedata and Flex Products, Inc. ICI Imagedata is a part of ICI Films, which was established to capitalize on the major business opportunities in the rapidly expanding market for color imaging and data storage. ICI Imagedata is developing new products by combining the color, films, and coating technology of ICI.

Flex Products, Inc., is a new company formed as a result of a venture with Optical Coatings Laboratory, Inc. Flex Products, Inc., combines ICI's innovation in polyester and high-performance films with OCLI's technical leadership in vacuum deposition and coating.

For more than 25 years ICI

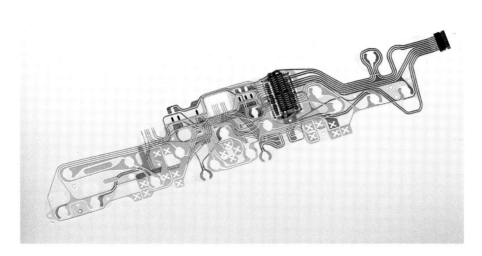

ICI Films is a leader in supplying high-performance film. Pictured here is an automotive flexible circuit made from Melinex® polyester film.

Polyurethanes has participated in all major sectors of the polyurethanes industry: rigid foams (home insulation, refrigerators, paneling, simulated wood parts, packaging for electronic products, and computer housings); flexible foams (automotive and transportation seating, cushions, carpet underlay, auto dashboards, armrests, and athletic equipment); elastomers (shoe soles, air filters, sports ball covers, industrial tubing, and housing); and coatings and adhesives (commercial/industrial finishes, heavy-duty binders, automotive/industrial sealants, circuit boards, and television parts).

ICI Polyurethanes holds the leading edge in the advancement of polyurethane technology through its development and manufacture of isocyanates, the most important raw material in polyurethanes. The group has pioneered significant applications for diphenylmethane diisocyanate (MDI) in flexible foams, shoe soling, and adhesive binders for lignocellulosic materials such as wood chips for construction use.

In the United States, ICI Polyurethanes is organized into two divisions—Chemicals and Formulated Products—as well as a spe-cialty business area for coatings, adhesives, sealants, and encapsulants. The Chemicals Division, in West Deptford, New Jersey, markets a full range of high-quality MDI and toluene diisocyanate (TDI) products under the Rubinate® brand name. The Formulated Products Division, in Sterling Heights, Michigan, develops and markets various formulated polyurethane systems such as RIMline® reaction injection molding and Rubiflex® seating systems. Product development is focused on the high-tech automotive industry, where there is a need for rapid technological innovation in both product design and materials performance. ICI Polyurethanes' North American headquarters is in West Deptford, New Jersey.

ICI Fibres sells a range of nylon textile fibers for carpeting, fashion apparel, and industrial fabrics. Tactel® fiber for apparel and Tactesse® fiber for carpeting offer luxurious natural fiber aesthetics combined with the high-performance characteristics of man-made fibers.

ICI Colors and Fine Chemicals business sells reactive, disperse acid, direct and premetallized dyes, as well as pigments used in printing inks, paints, and plastics. Nitrocellulose is sold to makers of inks and paints, and fine chemicals are supplied as intermediates to pharmaceutical and agrichemical manufacturers.

Katalco and Tracerco provide chemical catalysts, systems, and services to customer industrial plants. Katalco supplies catalysts and systems to ammonia and methanol plants, refineries, and petrochemical operations. Tracerco markets technology that "sees" inside plant equipment to provide process information so that problems can be diagnosed without suspending plant operations.

ICI Aerospace designs and manufacturers fast-acting, explosive-actuated devices for critical applications in missiles and spacecraft as well as fire protection, security, and defense weapon systems. These high-reliability devices open and close switches; cut cables tubing and wires; and pressurize, heat, initiate, release, or seal a wide range of mechanical devices in defense weapon systems. This technology has been transferred to the automotive industry, where similar devices are supplied to deploy inflatable restraint systems in cars. ICI Aerospace also markets the Security Pac® electronic protection system, incorporating the world's leading tear gas/dye pack device, which is used by banks and other financial institutions to foil robbery attempts.

The transportation, construction, graphic arts, and floor-care industries benefit from products formulated with acrylic and polyurethane polymers, vinyledene terpolymers, rubber, and precipitated calcium carbonate from ICI Resins US.

ICI is also a major importer of selected industrial chemicals into the United States. The product line is derived mainly from alkalis, chlorine, fluorine, petrochemicals, and petrochemical derivatives. A new product of particular interest is an alternative fluorocarbon, KLEA®134A, that is more friendly to the environment.

ICI Specialty Chemicals is a federation of international businesses headquartered in Wilmington, Delaware.

The product portfolio includes biocides for preventing bacterial or

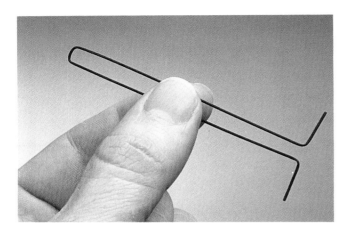

fungal growth in swimming pools, paints, papermaking, caulk, pesticides, carpet backing, and leather; mining chemicals, including organic solvent extraction reagents for recovery of purified base metals, particularly copper from aqueous solutions; and polymer additives for special effects in plastics such as antioxidants, light stabilizers, surface effect additives, nucleators, liquid dispersion, super concentrates, and additive blends.

The group's polyols products function as bulking agents and excipients in confections, pharmaceuticals, and toothpaste. Protective chemical finishes offer soil release, water and oil repellency, and stain repellency in textile and similar substrates. Surfactants and related products serve the personal care, textile, agricultural, metalworking, food, and industrial markets by facilitating the formulation and creation of special effects in products.

Flexographic and rotogravure inks from Converters Ink and Thiele-Engdahl are used to print packaging for food, beverage, and confectionary applications. High-performance lubricant systems from Tribol facilitate maintenance operations in the mining steel, pulp and paper, and auto manufacturing industries. Leather finishes from Stahl enhance the look and durability of shoes, apparel, and upholstery. Polymeric coating from Permuthane are applied to nonleather shoes and luggage, and to flexible substrates used

in automotive seat covers and interiors. Specialty building products from Thoro System Products help builders waterproof, weatherproof, restore, and maintain buildings.

ICI Advanced Materials is developing leading-edge technology in engineering plastics, advanced composites, and ceramics to meet the needs of rapidly growing high-tech industries. This ambitious business unit targets demanding applications in the aerospace, telecommunications, automotive, and defense industries for its products.

Leading the range of high-performance, space-age materials are the Fiberite® composite materials that provide extremely high strength-to-weight ratios. These materials are used in the construc-

---

Above: ICI Advanced Materials' superconductive short dipole antenna generates signals four times stronger than a comparable copper antenna.

Below: Superconductive coil produced by ICI Advanced Materials demonstrates strength of material in shape (coil), which is formed by proprietary viscous plastic processing techniques.

tion of spacecraft and aircraft, and are being investigated by the automotive industry.

ICI Advanced Materials is a world leader in engineering plastics, materials that can offer solutions to nearly every contemporary design problem. Through LNP Engineering Plastics, ICI offers a variety of resins to design engineers and processors. Among the filled and unfilled thermoplastic resins available from LNP are Maranyl® nylon, Verton® long-fiber-reinforced materials, Lubricomp® lubricated composites, and high-temperature Victrex® PES, PEEK, and PEK resins. ICI fluoropolymers, including Fluon® resins and Fluorocomp® PTFE compounds, provide materials for applications where chemical resistance, lubrication, and insulating properties are critical.

Thermoset molding compounds for a wide range of performance applications are available through the group's Fiberite Molding Materials business. These include epoxy and phenolic resins reinforced with a wide range of fillers, including glass, aramid fibers, and graphite. With the availability of both thermoplastic and thermoset resins, no other company can match the diversity and range of materials offered by ICI.

The international headquarters of ICI Advanced Materials is Wilmington, Delaware.

Wilmington Finishing Company

It's probably one of the best-kept secrets in town. On the fringe of Wilmington, in a tucked-away cul de sac straddling the Brandywine River, is a 22-acre plant encompassing two dozen nineteenth-century buildings and employing 262 workers.

This is the headquarters for Wilmington Finishing Company, a commissioned textile finisher with a national reputation, products that are exported worldwide, and a low profile locally.

The independently owned corporation has been a vital part of the city, and a pioneer in all aspects of textile finishing, for more than 150 years. Founded as a weaving mill in 1831 by Joseph Bancroft, the firm remained in his family until 1962, when a New York-based conglomerate purchased it and then began to sell off its numerous divisions. These included coating, research, licensing, and printing. Learning of plans to sell off the finishing division—and fearing a complete shutdown—a group of 12 management employees, led by Alfred Bent and John Gardiner (now board chairman), acquired the operation in 1973.

The employees then faced the task of revitalizing the ailing, cash-poor company, replacing antiquated equipment, and struggling to improve a limited product line. Once this crisis was overcome, the textile firm then weathered other economic woes: the oil shortage of the mid-1970s, which hindered the supply of raw materials.

Today it is clear that Wilmington Finishing has more than just survived. It is now a thriving enterprise, strong in a diminishing industry faced with increased foreign competition and stringent environmental regulations.

The company bleaches, finishes, and dyes 200,000 yards of solid-color fabrics per day—cotton and blends of cotton, polyester, and rayon. It is known for the durability and quality of its finishes. A process

Norman P. Hubbs, vice-president/manufacturing (left), and John O. Gardiner, board chairman, provide the leadership to keep Wilmington Finishing Company at the forefront of the industry.

called tutoring (the application of permanent patterns on fabrics) was expanded in the past seven years, and new technology has replaced old processes. Productivity has increased in all departments. The firm recently became computerized, and this has been especially useful in the dye-matching area. Two years ago Wilmington Finishing also began working with heavier fabrics used for boat cabin interiors.

End products include drapery linings, clothing, home furnishings, slipcovers, shower curtains, and sleepwear.

Wilmington Finishing Company is among the largest blue-collar employers in the city, and the major employer of semiskilled and unskilled labor. It provides comprehensive on-the-job training and this has proven effective: Many of its managers have moved up through the ranks.

Wilmington Finishing Company's benefits package is considered tops in the industry, as is its safety program. The firm expanded and formalized its safety efforts in 1986 with the hiring of a professional safety engineer.

Quality is their business: Seated from left are James Sylvester, supervisor of put-up; Charles Kane, supervisor of bleach; and Barry Sheehan, supervisor of finishing. Standing (from left) are Efrain Borges, supervisor of dye, and Phillip Smith, plant superintendent.

General Foods USA

With more than 1,200 employees, General Foods USA is one of Kent County's largest and most valued businesses.

General Foods USA's Desserts Division plant has been located in Dover since 1964. The plant—one of the company's largest—occupies 121 acres, including 26 acres under one roof.

When the Dover plant began operations, it was considered General Foods' most ambitious construction project to date. It was designed to replace four outmoded production facilities on the East Coast. In fact, the new Dover plant was to set the tone for the firm's strategy to achieve more efficient and economical operations.

Today those same principles apply: The plant revolves around the concepts of producing superior products, customer service, teamwork, joint problem solving, and the just-in-time philosophy of manufacturing and distribution.

In its early days the focal point of the Dover operation was the bulk production of chocolate and coconut for bakers and candy manufacturers. The Dover plant is the company's exclusive producer of Baker's chocolate—considered the oldest, longest-running trade name in the United States. The plant produces eight major brands comprised of more than 400 different products. These include Jell-O gelatin and pudding mixes, Dream Whip, Minute Rice, Stove Top, and other packaged products. Over the years the Dover plant has also produced Log Cabin maple syrup, Shake N Bake, and Kool-Aid mixes. Raw materials come from 55 trucks and five railcars each day. The plant recently increased production by about 20 percent when it transferred its Jell-O pudding and Stove Top stuffing operations from a plant that closed in Indiana. This most recent expansion resulted in six more production lines and approximately 120 new jobs.

Headquartered in White Plains, New York, General Foods USA traces its beginnings to 1895, when C.W. Post began selling a cereal called Postum in Battle Creek, Michigan. Many of its current brands had been established independently before 1925, when the Postum Cereal Company began a series of acquisitions resulting in an organization that in 1929 took the name of General Foods.

Since then other products associated with General Foods have included the Post cereals, Jell-O Gelatin dessert, Maxwell House coffee, Walter Baker chocolate, Log Cabin syrup, Birds Eye frozen foods, Kool-Aid soft-drink mixes, Open Pit barbecue sauce, Sanka decaffeinated coffee, Oscar-Mayer processed meats, Crystal Light powdered beverages, Entenmann's baked goods, and Ronzoni's Italian specialties. The firm was acquired in 1985 by Philip Morris Company.

Today General Foods USA is one of the largest U.S. corporations operating solely in the food and beverage business. It is considered a leading innovator in the food industry, employing 20,000 in more than 50 manufacturing and sales sites in 22 states. The company's brands have become among the world's most trusted and respected products.

The General Foods USA plant in Dover employs more than 1,200 workers and spans 26 acres under one roof.

NOR-AM Chemical Company

NOR-AM Chemical Company is one of the most diversified chemical businesses in the United States and Canada. The firm develops, manufactures, and markets a broad range of products for agriculture, professional pest control, turf and ornamentals, and other specialty areas.

The company is headquartered in Wilmington, which serves as the hub for its operations in North America. Committed to vigorous growth through a diversified product line, NOR-AM is one of Delaware's fastest-growing enterprises.

NOR-AM's parent company is Schering AG, Berlin•West Germany, a $2.5-billion manufacturer of pharmaceuticals, agricultural chemicals, industrial chemicals, and electroplating products. Schering AG is a global concern with more than 130 subsidiaries and associated companies worldwide employing approximately 24,000 people. NOR-AM represents Schering AG's commitment to the burgeoning North American agricultural/specialty chemical markets. NOR-AM employs close to 300 people, including 80 at its Wilmington facility.

The firm's existence is the result of several mergers and consolidations, including the former agrichemical business of Hercules, Inc. During the past few years its sales increased to its current level of more than $100 million. NOR-AM's growth has been impressive, and today the company is a leader in its own right.

NOR-AM's leadership position is especially evident in the agricultural chemicals industry. These products account for about two-thirds of the firm's volume. In this market, NOR-AM offers farmers and other growers a wide range of chemicals to control insects, disease, weeds,

and other problems. The business produces a diverse line of herbicides, insecticides, fungicides, plant and soil nutrients, defoliants, and fumigants. These products are found in a variety of markets, including sugar beets, cotton, tobacco, peanuts, and fruits.

NOR-AM also markets specialty chemical products for the growing turf and ornamentals market, as well as products for public health (pest control) and other specialty markets.

The firm's total product line includes about 20 compounds formulated for 15 different markets. Under development are about a dozen new compounds, giving NOR-AM an even greater opportunity for diversification and the potential to penetrate new markets. Among the products that should receive approval for launch by 1990 are an apple miticide, a promising new insecticide for cotton, and compounds for public health and turf and ornamentals markets.

This continuous introduction of new products is made possible only through a strong dedication to research and development. And it is in research that NOR-AM excels. In fact, its commitment to leadership in the markets it serves is borne out by the number of employees dedicated to developing new and improved chemical compounds. At NOR-AM, one in four employees is engaged in a research-related activity. NOR-AM draws support from Schering's large research and development laboratories in West Berlin, Germany, and in Chesterford Park, England.

These efforts are complemented by NOR-AM's research activities in the United States. The company recently acquired from ICI Americas, also headquartered in Wilmington, a 265-acre research

An aerial view of NOR-AM's Muskegon, Michigan, facility. Production of bendiocarb insecticide for worldwide distribution occurs at this site.

Left: NOR-AM markets a top-rated defoliant for cleaner, more profitable cotton. The company expects to receive approval shortly for a promising new cotton insecticide.

Right: Leading golf courses in the United States are treated and kept in excellent playing condition with a variety of NOR-AM's fertilizers, insecticides, herbicides, and fungicides.

Below: NOR-AM's newly acquired research facility in Goldsboro, North Carolina, will greatly increase the company's research and development testing capabilities in the United States.

facility in Goldsboro, North Carolina. In addition, NOR-AM operates three field stations, in Fresno, California; Pensacola, Florida; and Wonder Lake, Illinois, where new compounds are evaluated by experienced research and development teams.

NOR-AM's U.S. manufacturing activities are centered in a state-of-the-art, automated manufacturing plant in Muskegon, Michigan. This 436-acre plant is considered one of the most modern facilities of its kind in the country. It was designed with future expansion in mind. Among the products manufactured there are Bendiocarb, an insecticide, and a leading product in the public health market. NOR-AM also manufactures its products in other facilities nationwide, through contractual arrangements with other companies.

NOR-AM's sales teams focus on agricultural chemical and specialty chemical markets in key regions of the United States and Canada. Products are sold primarily through distributors, and sales offices are located in California, Missouri, Minnesota, Michigan, and Tennessee. Through these offices and its sales force, NOR-AM maintains its position as a strong, customer-oriented supplier. The firm's headquarters in Wilmington provides solid support services and important backup to its sales and marketing personnel.

One of the key elements to NOR-AM Chemical Company's success is its philosophy of stability through diversity. This, coupled with a commitment to provide quality products, emphasis on research, strong service, and professional marketing, will help ensure that the organization's future will be bright.

One in three employees at NOR-AM is engaged in research-related activities. The company draws support from Schering AG's research and development laboratories in West Germany and the United Kingdom.

Kaumagraph Corporation

Kaumagraph Corporation was founded in 1902, operating out of the east side in New York City. It was the first company in the nation to introduce and manufacture iron-on dry transfers. These product decorations enhanced such consumer goods as tennis balls, running shoes, dress patterns, children's wear, and T-shirts. Iron-on dry transfers remained the firm's sole specialty for the next 20 years. Indeed, the company's name is derived from the Greek language and means "to write with fire."

The technique for producing these transfers used Kaumagraph's proprietary hot-melt ink systems and an intaglio printing method. In the early days the company's primary markets were the knitting and weaving trades.

Kaumagraph's first diversification came in 1923, when it entered the field of lithographic printing—primarily to service a new and expanding market in printing packaging materials.

The firm became international five years later, in 1928, with the formation of Kaumagraph Canada, followed a year later by the formation of British Kaumagraph Transfers Ltd. in Manchester, England. Kaumagraph continued to add new products to its repertoire and to improve existing products during the 1930s. The company grew rapidly, and by 1939 it moved to its current headquarters in Wilmington. With that move came further diversification.

Shortly before World War II Kaumagraph was approached by the U.S. War and Navy departments and asked to develop a

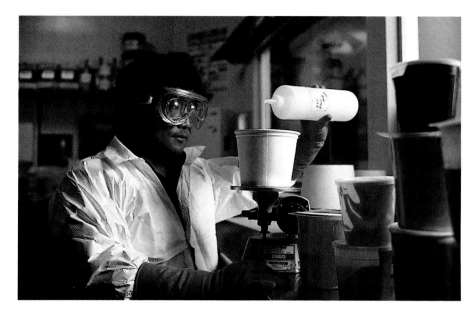

Above: Careful attention to color formulation is integral to maintaining consistency over the length of a press run.

Below: Kaumagraph performs all of its printing within a true clean room environment.

system for printing multicolor cloth survival maps that would not be adversely affected when immersed in fresh or salt water. Thanks to the development of nylon (used for the maps) by The Du Pont Company,

Kaumagraph met the challenge and won acclaim for devising a printing method to produce these complex maps. The maps were ultimately used by both American and British airmen during the war. They serve as an excellent example of innovative approach that has characterized the history of this unique company.

The years following World War II required even more changes in Kaumagraph's products and in the markets it served. In 1955 the company entered the field of wide-web (60-inch) rotogravure printing, and a year later it developed a new printing technology for the manufacture of printed overlays to decorate melamine-plastic dinnerware. The latter technique led to the firm's purchase by the Lenox Corporation, a manufacturer of dinnerware.

During the 1960s and early 1970s Kaumagraph experienced steady growth in the types of printed transfer products it manufactured and in the improvement of product identification techniques. New products included rub-on skin tattoos for the toy and novelty industries, plus a lithographic/silk-screen combination iron-on transfer (Lithofusion®) that set a worldwide standard for decorating a wide variety of T-shirts, sweatshirts, and sportswear apparel.

In August 1978 the Kaumagraph Company was sold by Lenox to Raymond G. Burke (now chairman of the board) and William H. Burke, and the name was changed to Kaumagraph Corporation. The business is now privately owned and independently operated.

Since then Kaumagraph has continued to serve as an innovator and has grown rapidly and profitably. It has branched into new markets with its expanded product expertise. For example, the company has aggressively penetrated a growing market with the development of printed automotive dashboard-instrumentation displays. In this market, the firm's clients now include General Motors,

Chrysler Corporation, and other major automotive manufacturers. In just a few short years the firm has established a reputation as a leading printer, if not *the* leading printer, of instrumentation-panel

displays in the United States.

Still other new markets for Kaumagraph have been in the medical products and consumer electronics areas. In both markets, the company is involved with developing printed panel instrumentation for membrane switches.

In the fall of 1988 Kaumagraph completed construction of its modern 45,000-square-foot manufacturing facility located on the banks of the Christina River in Wilmington. This facility has provided the firm with state-of-the-art production capabilities. The computerized plant will make use of laser printing techniques as well as a CAD (computer-assisted design) system.

Kaumagraph is now strategically positioned for broadening its product line as well as expanding the markets it serves. Also on the horizon is further expansion overseas. In January 1989 Kaumagraph Corporation (UK) Ltd. was established in England, operated by a managing director with a sales director on its staff.

Today Kaumagraph employs a total of 400 people; annual sales are in excess of $25 million. In addition to its Wilmington plant, the company opened a second plant in Millington (near Flint), Michigan, in 1985 to serve the growing automotive market.

Kaumagraph Corporation, distinguished by its commitment to finding specific market niches, is clearly prepared to enter the 1990s with a high degree of technology, innovation, optimism, and enthusiasm.

Right: Programmable die-cutting capabilities allow efficient and economical cutting of a product.

Below: Constant quality control checks assure that the printing process is always under strict control, meeting Kaumagraph's high standards.

CIBA-GEIGY Corporation

When automobile owners can see red and still be happy, it is probably the result of products made at the CIBA-GEIGY Newport Plant.

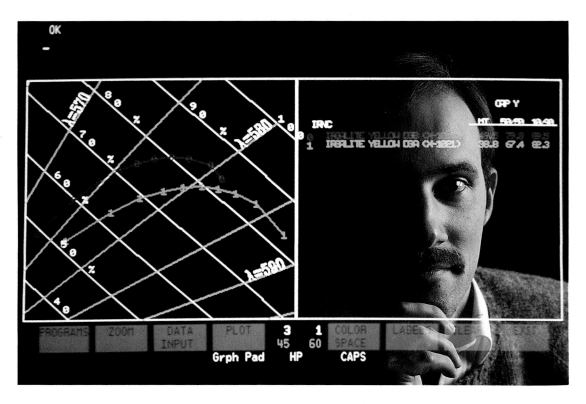

The plant, located on Water Street just off Route 141, is one of the largest producers of red quinacridone pigments in the world. Quinacridone reds and red shade pigments (commonly abbreviated as QA pigments) are most popular in the automotive industry, where they are used in both finishes and interiors.

Until the development of QA pigments in the 1950s, purchasing a red car resulted in the color of the car changing before long, unless extraordinary exterior maintenance and polishing were administered. Sunlight, along with other weather elements, tended to rapidly fade red cars. QA pigments changed all that.

The first QA pigment-coated production model was the 1958 Corvette. Since then all domestic as well as many European and Japanese automobile manufacturers have turned to lightfast QA, and more colors have been developed. In addition to the red shades, QA pigments of violet, magenta, and gold colors are also manufactured.

Efforts to develop improved QA pigments for the automotive indus-

Above: Joe Ketternacker, Colorimetry and Computer manager, evaluates chromaticity at the Newport Laboratory.

Right: Fran Dalgarn, a technician at the Newport Laboratory, works on the two roll mill.

try have continued unabated at the Newport plant for more than 30 years. In addition to production, a research and development staff at the Newport plant works continuously to develop pigments that have improved color fastness, better flow characteristics, and different hues.

Since 1984, when CIBA-GEIGY acquired the Newport facility from The Du Pont Company, growth has accelerated. Sales of QA pigments increased substantially; the work force has grown from 185 to 276; and CIBA-GEIGY has invested millions of dollars in modernization and new facilities at the site. The com-

pany is considered Newport's largest employer.

A new automotive technical development and service center has become the hub of customer service

activity for *all* CIBA-GEIGY pigments used by automobile coating manufacturers. A new pilot plant was built to manufacture small quantities of new products for customer sampling and to test various production improvements. In 1988 another major investment was completed when the new finishing facility began operation. This facility, which occupies an entire building, converts "crude" pigment into a "finished" product, ready for use by the Newport plant's customers.

The Newport plant compound, which spans 25 acres, and its employees have come a long way since the CIBA-GEIGY sign was placed at the entrance in 1984. But in many ways this is just the beginning.

Plans for still another expansion were announced in January 1989. Plant capacity is expected to grow by roughly 20 percent in early 1990. This should relieve some of the pressures that have pushed Newport employees to produce at capacity limits since CIBA-GEIGY purchased the plant.

The popularity of red and red-containing colors is now at an all-time high. Due to the advantages they offer to the plant's customers—the paint manufacturers, as well as the final consumer—demand for quinacridones is also exceptional.

The Pigments Division of CIBA-GEIGY has earned a global reputation for the production of high-quality, high-performance colors. Headquartered in Hawthorne, New York, the division is part of

Left: Technician Dave Jarrell is shown making drawdowns at the Newport Laboratory.

Below: Technician Pat Bonk, at the Newport plant, works in the blending area.

CIBA-GEIGY Corporation, a multidivisional research-based chemical company with annual sales surpassing $3 billion. The corporation, in turn, is a subsidiary of CIBA-GEIGY Limited, the Swiss-based parent with consolidated sales exceeding $12 billion. In addition to pigments, the Swiss-based conglomerate has established major interests in pharmaceuticals, agricultural products, dyes, plastics, industrial chemicals, biotechnology, contact lenses, and laser optics.

CIBA-GEIGY is also expanding its pigment operations in Europe and Asia. New facilities and/or expansions are currently under way in Korea, Scotland, Germany, and Switzerland.

Throughout the company's remarkable growth in recent years, CIBA-GEIGY's Newport employees have continued to be among the premier pigment developers and manufacturers in the world. The product they manufacture is consistent and of high quality. Over the past three years, in particular, plant employees have been recognized by several major manufacturers for the quality of the colors they produce.

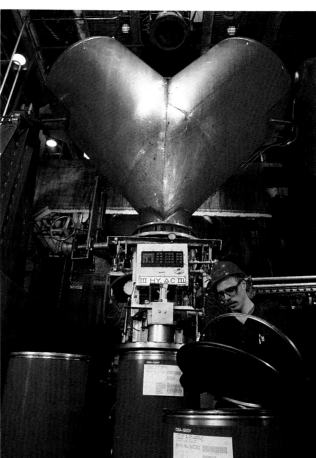

The Du Pont Company

E. I. du Pont de Nemours and Company is one of the largest and most diversified industrial corporations in the world and the largest private employer in Delaware. With more than 140,000 employees and 200 manufacturing and processing plants worldwide, the firm has annual sales in excess of $30 billion. It is involved with more than 90 major businesses, and its thousands of products and services are found in most major markets, from agriculture to transportation.

The company is globally diversified, with manufacturing or processing operations in about 40 countries on six continents. In fact, 25 percent of all Du Pont employees work outside the United States. The firm markets in more than 150 countries, and its international sales account

In 1802 E.I. du Pont de Nemours formed a company on the banks of the Brandywine River near Wilmington, Delaware, to manufacture black powder. The original Du Pont powderworks have been restored and are now part of the Hagley Museum, which depicts the industrial development of the United States.

E.I. du Pont, founder of E.I. du Pont de Nemours and Company.

for more than 40 percent of its revenue—a figure expected to increase to 50 percent by the mid-1990s.

However, when Du Pont was established in 1802 on the banks of the Brandywine River near Wilmington, its sole purpose was to manufacture black powder. Du Pont remained essentially an explosives company through its first century, although today it has largely withdrawn from this enterprise. But during its first 100 years the firm grew primarily by expanding its markets geographically—first to the American West and later overseas. Within three years of its founding, Du Pont powder was being sold in Europe, marking the beginning of the company's evolution into the global corporation it is today. By the middle of the nineteenth century, Du Pont products were being sold around the globe, and the corporation had earned a worldwide reputation for quality.

Over the years Du Pont has acquired interests in many other compa-

nies, and acquistions have become an important growth strategy. The firm made its first acquisition more than a century ago, when it purchased a powder mill in Pennsylvania. This was its first manufacturing expansion outside the Wilmington area. Beyond the explosives business, Du Pont's first important acquisition was the 1910 purchase of Fabrikoid, an artificial leather used by the then-fledgling automobile industry.

Among the more significant purchases that helped propel the company into new markets are Remington Arms in 1933, Endo Laboratories in 1969, Berg Electronics in 1972, and New England Nuclear and Conoco, both in 1981. These acquistions marked the firm's diversification into the sporting arms, pharmaceuticals, electronics, nuclear medicine, and energy businesses. Du Pont has continued to pursue an acquisitions strategy. For example, in the 1980s it has invested more than $10 billion to fund more than 50 major acquisitions and joint ventures with other companies.

Du Pont's growth has also been channeled internally through such decisions as the one to diversify by developing new products through research. On the firm's 100th anniversary in 1902, it opened its first laboratory in New Jersey. It was among the first research facilities operated by any corporation in the United States. A year later the Experimental Station opened in Wilmington on a 152-acre site overlooking the Brandywine River, near the company's original powder mills. The decision to undertake a formal research program transformed Du Pont into a science-based organization and gave birth to a tradition of discovery and innovation that it has nurtured ever since.

Du Pont's Experimental Station, located on a 152-acre site overlooking the Brandywine River, transformed the company to a science-based organization on the cutting edge of research technology.

The research effort has included the discovery of nylon, the first of many synthetic fibers to be developed by Du Pont scientists. In fact, the debut of nylon in 1938 marked the dawn of an era of synthetic materials that were superior, in many respects, to their natural counterparts.

Another key discovery made by Du Pont in 1938 was Teflon™ fluoropolymer, a substance with applications ranging from the nonstick coatings used in industrial and consumer products to critical parts of space vehicles. Orlon™ acrylic and Dacron™ polyester followed in 1948 and 1950; since then many other synthetic fibers have been developed by Du Pont scientists, most notably Kevlar Aramid™, introduced in 1970, a fiber that is five times stronger than steel.

Du Pont's prominence in the field of polymer chemistry is legendary. Of the approximately 50 major polymer groups, Du Pont participates in more than half on a commercial basis and has developed 16 separate businesses based on polymers.

The company has become one of the largest suppliers of agricultural chemicals, such as fungicides, herbicides, and insecticides, with manufacturing facilities in nine countries on five continents. The firm also supplies coal. Consolidation Coal Company, a subsidiary since 1981, is Du Pont's coal-mining and marketing arm. Known in the industry as Consol, the organization is the second-largest producer of coal in the United States and has one of the largest coal reserves of any coal-mining company.

For years Du Pont has provided products for use in construction, ranging from home building to large-scale industrial projects. The company is the world's largest producer of titanium dioxide, a white pigment used in paints, textiles, paper, plastics, and other products. Other Du Pont products used in the construction industry are Corian™ countertops for bathrooms and kitchens and Stainmaster© carpets.

Du Pont is one of the largest suppliers of materials, components, subassemblies, and manufacturing processes and services to the electronics industry, with half of its business outside the United States.

Many of the fibers produced by Du Pont are household names. These include Lycra™ spandex, Dacron™ polyester, Orlon™ acrylic, and Antron™ nylon.

Du Pont is also involved with health care, from fundamental research to manufacturing products used for research, diagnosis, and treatment of disease; imaging systems, products and systems designed to capture, store, reproduce, and transmit information both on the printed page and electronically; leisure, from sports to personal comfort products; petroleum; and transportation.

The company has always been committed to discovery and technical innovation, the globalization of its markets and its manufacturing, as well as its research and development programs. It operates more than 100 research, technical support, and customer service facilities worldwide. Delaware's Experimental Station is one of the largest and most sophisticated industrial research centers in the world, and remains the hub of Du Pont's research and development effort. In fact, the organization

spends more on research each year than all but a handful of corporations.

The Du Pont Company is also committed to the safety of its employees, its neighbors, its customers, and the environment. Today Du Pont is building on the legacy of scientific, engineering, manufacturing, and marketing resources to respond quickly and effectively to the needs of its customers worldwide.

The Du Pont Seaford Nylon Plant

Du Pont's nylon plant in Seaford has provided a strong economic base for the local economy for more than a half-century. It is the largest plant in southern Delaware, and thousands of people in Seaford and Sussex County have derived both direct and indirect benefits from this major employer.

The Seaford plant's roots date back to 1938, when Du Pont was seeking a location for what would be the world's first facility to produce a revolutionary new product called nylon. The company needed a site with a good water supply, available transportation, and a reliable work force. Initially, 14 locations were considered. That number was pared down to three, and Seaford was the finalist.

At the time, Seaford was a typical rural farming community of 2,400 people. (The population today is 15,000.) It was feeling the effects of the Depression and subsequent farm and business recessions. Jobs were scarce. The primary industries were farming, poultry raising, fertilizer manufacturing, crate and basket

Top: The Hotel du Pont in Wilmington—since 1915, Delaware's prestige lodging facility.

Center: The Du Pont building in Wilmington serves as corporate headquarters for Du Pont Company.

Bottom: Du Pont's Seaford nylon manufacturing plant—southern Delaware's largest plant.

making, vegetable canning, watermelon and canteloupe growing, and oyster shucking. The 465-acre community consisted of 700 homes and 150 commercial buildings. Today there are 2,321 homes and 534 commercial buildings.

Du Pont decided on the Seaford site for a number of reasons, including its proximity to raw materials and markets, Sussex County's low tax base, an abundant labor market, and favorable freight rates. Adding to these factors is the nearby Nanticoke River, which provides good transportation for coal.

On October 19, 1939, Seaford learned that Du Pont had purchased 340 acres for construction of a plant there. When the news broke, the townspeople celebrated. The Du Pont plant would mean the creation of 1,000 jobs for Seaford's young people, plus a more stable income for farm families and an upswing in business.

Since that time, Seaford has continued to thrive. New housing projects have been developed, as have hotels, hospitals, recreational facilities, and shopping centers.

Du Pont's Seaford plant initially produced 2.6 million pounds of nylon per year. It had one product line, one end user, and two customers. Today the plant produces 500 million pounds of nylon annually. It has three major nylon product lines—BCF (bulked continuous filament), fine denier textile, and staple. These three lines produce a total of 250 different products with countless end uses, serving 225 customers. More than 2,300 people are employed at the plant, which has an annual payroll of $85 million.

The Hotel du Pont

Thousands of business executives consider a stay in the Wilmington area synonymous with a stay at the Hotel du Pont.

The elegant hotel on Rodney Square is owned by the Du Pont Company, but it is entirely self-

Du Pont's titanium dioxide is used as a whitener and opacifier in a wide variety of products. Its three major end-use areas are plastics, paper, and coatings.

supporting. Since it opened on January 15, 1913, the hotel has been Delaware's most prestigious lodging facility. Its reputation for service is impeccable, as are its standards and loyal, long-term employees. The ratio of employees to guest rooms—1.4 to one, or 375 full-time workers for 266 rooms—is the highest in the state.

During its first week of operation in 1913, 25,000 visitors toured the hotel. In 1919, 118 additional guest rooms were added to the original 150. That same year a new lobby was built, adding the intricately designed ceiling patterned after a Venetian palace.

Today the hotel's 266 guest rooms feature antique reproductions and original works of art. Original paintings by three generations of Wyeths are found throughout the lobbies and hallways of marble and hand-carved paneling.

The Green Room and the Brandywine Room restaurants are consistently rated best in the state by critics and customers. But the hotel is not content to rest on its well-deserved reputation. During the past few years an additional 40 guest rooms have opened. And to

meet Wilmington's needs as an emerging corporate center, a conference center was added, featuring state-of-the-art facilities. These include simultaneous translation capability, teleconferencing, computer terminals, telex machines, facsimile machines, and other high-technology necessities of contemporary business. The conference center also includes five rooms, seating up to 75 people each, for small meetings. Also available is the Gold Ballroom, which seats up to 500 people, and the du Barry Room, which seats up to 125.

The Hotel du Pont also houses the Playhouse Theatre, which opened in 1913. The 1,200-seat theater was built completely within the walls of the hotel, and today presents quality theater to Wilmington residents.

Today the Hotel du Pont continues to meet, and exceed, its original objective—"high-quality service with no compromise."

Townsends, Inc.

Townsends, Inc., could easily rest on its laurels as Delaware's largest poultry processor and its fastest-growing agribusiness. But that would not be consistent with the company's rich tradition of seizing opportunities for growth and expanding to meet new challenges. Throughout its 90-year history of agribusiness leadership in southern Delaware, Townsends has been in the forefront of innovation. Over the past few decades it has also become a leader in the highly competitive poultry industry.

The family-held business, one of the top 20 employers in Delaware, with annual sales of about $400 million, has experienced record-setting growth over the past few years. This

5 million eggs in the process of being hatched; each week it hatches in excess of 1.5 million eggs. In the past Townsends has focused on supplying retail supermarkets (where it assumes the store brand), fast-food restaurants, and food-service industries. Today it is also penetrating the retail market under its own name.

One key to Townsends' success is its management system of vertical integration. This pulls together all facets of producing broilers—from growing the grain for feed to breeding flocks to producing the finished product. It enables Townsends to oversee the process from start to finish, resulting in better quality control. The company was the first

send turned to apple and peach orchards, and by the middle of that decade, he had more than 5,000 acres in production—the second-largest orchard in the United States. In the early 1930s the entrepreneur and his son, Preston, saw promise in Delaware's emerging broiler industry and decided to become part of it.

Townsends, Inc., was incorporated in 1937, and a year later the company built its first hatchery at the Swan Creek Orchard near Millsboro. An innovative profit-sharing arrangement was made with local farmers to grow chickens, which were supplied by Townsends' hatchery. The firm also built a mill to produce nutritious poultry feed. By the end of World War II Townsends had become the nation's leading producer of commercial poultry.

By the 1950s the company had abandoned the orchard business entirely and had cleared thousands of acres of fruit trees to grow corn, soybeans, and other feed grains. A

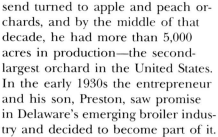

Left: Headquartered in Millsboro, Townsends, Inc., is the ninth-largest poultry company in the United States.

Below: The Millsboro hatchery is one of the largest in the nation, capable of setting 1.75 million eggs per week.

prosperity stems from an aggressive strategy of diversification, coupled with a commitment to develop new equipment and techniques to ensure that customers receive the highest-quality products at the most reasonable prices. Led by a team of top managers, Townsends' poultry production has jumped from 27th to eighth place nationally since 1984, and its payroll of skilled employees has increased from 700 to more than 3,600 (1,500 in Delaware).

Headquartered in Sussex County's Millsboro, Townsends' core business is chicken: It processes a half-billion pounds of chicken each year. Its Millsboro hatchery—one of the world's largest—has more than

broiler business nationwide to achieve full vertical integration.

Townsends' agri-products group supervises crop production, purchases feed ingredients, processes soybeans into a feed staple for chickens, and refines soybean oil into a high-quality salad oil. The corn, soybeans, and other feed grains are grown on more than 8,000 acres of company-owned farmland and are also purchased from local farmers.

The corporation was founded by John G. Townsend, Jr., a former U.S. senator and governor of Delaware. He began in the lumber business in the 1890s and later expanded into fresh produce, opening the area's first cannery. During the 1920s Town-

In addition to its poultry operations, Townsends farms more than 10,000 acres of corn, soybeans, and other feed grains, which are processed into a feed staple for the company's chickens.

soybean extraction plant was built in 1951. Townsends' evolution into a vertically integrated broiler business was completed in 1957 with the addition of a poultry-processing plant.

In the ensuing years Townsends experienced steady growth. A state-of-the-art hatchery was built during the late 1970s, and a new feed mill opened in 1982. A soybean oil refinery went into production in 1985, allowing Townsends to refine crude soybean oil into fresh salad oil. This product is now distributed overnight to manufacturers of mayonnaise, salad dressing, and margarine in the Northeast.

During the mid-1980s the company began expanding into other new areas—both geographically and by industry. In 1986 Townsends purchased a number of North Carolina and Arkansas processing plants, hatcheries, feed mills, farms, and a commercial egg-processing plant. These acquisitions are supported by a network of local broiler growers.

In 1988 the company purchased the former Dutch Pantry, an 80,000-square-foot commissary in Munroe Township, Pennsylvania. This facility will serve as a satellite to the Delaware packaging operation and will allow Townsends to expand into the "further processing"

of poultry, which is tailored to the fast-food market. The plant will employ between 500 and 1,000 people.

Townsends has also intensified its commitment to export. Since the early 1980s, 20 percent of the company's chickens—mostly frozen wings and legs—have been targeted for the Far East and Caribbean markets.

Still another new venture for the firm is real estate. In 1988 Townsends announced plans to convert 775 company-owned acres of low-production farmland along Indian River Bay, five miles east of Millsboro, into a planned community of 1,143 homes. This self-contained community will provide a balanced mix of housing for both year-round

and vacation living.

Townsends has also invested more than $8 million in a state-of-the-art wastewater-treatment plant. This will collect and recycle waste from all plant operations. The process has earned recognition from environmental authorities for its effectiveness in protecting nearby water resources while recycling nutrients through the crop chain.

Despite its diversification efforts, Townsends' mainstay continues to be poultry. The company is located at the center of one of the leading poultry production areas in the world: the Delmarva Peninsula, which provides enough broiler chickens to feed more than 28 million Americans. The industry has helped give the region a strong economic base.

Townsends, Inc., has had three presidents in its history—John G., his son, Preston, and Preston's son, P. Coleman. All three have made timely changes in the company's direction when new opportunities presented themselves. With this solid tradition behind it, the firm is now ready for even greater growth and diversification.

Processing more than 12 million bushels of soybeans per year, Townsends is Delaware's top soybean meal and soybean oil producer.

Atlantic Aviation Corporation

Atlantic Aviation Corporation, headquartered at the New Castle County Airport, is one of the nation's premier full-service companies dedicated to serving the needs of business aircraft operators. It is also the oldest company of its kind in the country.

It was founded in 1927 by Henry Belin du Pont, one of the first American businessmen to use aircraft for business transportation (he flew the aircraft himself). Atlantic's original facility was the du Pont Flying Field near Wilmington, which is now the site of the Du Pont Company's Barley Mill offices. Its original purpose was to provide fueling, storage, and maintenance services to business aviators. Among the well-known pioneer aviators who flew to Atlantic for service were Amelia Earhart, Wiley Post, Eddie Rickenbacker, and Jimmy Doolittle. Charles A. Lindbergh used Atlantic Aviation's services in 1927 during his U.S. tour with the *Spirit of St. Louis* after his world-record New York-to-Paris solo flight.

Atlantic has been under one family's guidance for its entire existence. Its chairman is Edward B. du Pont, son of the founder. The company has remained independent as a limited liability private stock corporation.

Virtually all of Delaware's major businesses, as well as many *Fortune* 500 national companies, have used all or some of Atlantic Aviation's services. Today the company employs 750 people at its subsidiaries and sites nationwide, including 500 in Wilmington. Approximately 10 percent of the employees have worked for the firm for at least 25 years.

Atlantic Aviation's major product and service areas are in maintenance and interior refurbishment, fueling and ground services, parts supply, flight services, insurance, and component overhaul. Here is an overview of each:

—Maintenance. Atlantic Aviation is one of only about a dozen North American companies involved in business aircraft major modification. Maintenance is provided for turbine-powered aircraft (including engine inspection and repair), airframe modification, repair and routine maintenance, custom interior refurbishment (including the

Right: Atlantic's chairman, Edward B. du Pont, takes a personal interest in the company's activities to ensure that its traditional standards of quality service and business integrity are faithfully maintained.

Above: Atlantic is well known and respected for its unlimited airframe repair capabilities as well as its interior refurbishment and paint work.

Right: Atlantic Aviation is a national company with operations from coast to coast. The latest addition to the company's growing number of fixed-base operations is this facility in Long Beach, California.

design and manufacture of interior furnishings), exterior paint, installation and repair of communication and navigation equipment, and specialty manufacturing. The latter refers to services using both conventional materials, such as wood and metal, and new lightweight composite materials. Specialty products include airline cabin class dividers and helicopter emergency medical services interior kits.

—Fueling and Ground Services. Atlantic has six fixed-base operations (FBOs) in the United States that act as service bases for business aircraft operators. They provide fuel, hangar space, rental cars, catering, lounges for pilots and passengers, weather briefing services, office space, conference rooms, and more. The FBOs are located at the following airports: Teterboro, New Jersey; Philadelphia International; Northeast Philadelphia; Houston; Los Angeles/Long Beach, California; and Wilmington. The company plans to expand its FBO sites to the Midwest and Southeast.

Atlantic also offers fueling service for commercial airlines in the United States. The company provides these services at Philadelphia International (where it services more than 90 percent of all airline flights), Long Beach, and San Jose, California.

—Parts Supply. Atlantic Aviation Supply Company, a subsidiary established in 1962, provides spare parts and supplies for aircraft operators. More than 23,000 different kinds of parts are stocked and are available for shipment 24 hours per day, seven days per week.

—Flight Services. Atlantic provides fleet management and aircraft charter services for businesses that use corporate aircraft. It will manage a company's entire flight operation, from training and hiring of pilots to scheduling the flights to maintaining the aircraft and handling administrative duties. Atlantic also provides aircraft charter services for domestic and international travel and can provide a jet and crew on a few hours notice.

—Insurance. Through a subsidiary, Berlow, Inc., founded in 1948 and acquired by Atlantic in 1972, the company offers insurance coverage for aircraft and aircraft operators, airlines, maintenance and service organizations, and flight schools.

Above: Into-plane fueling services for airlines represents a significant and growing segment of Atlantic's business.

—Component Overhaul. Established in 1988, Rotek, Inc., is a subsidiary engaged in the rebuilding of components used in business, commercial airline, and military aircraft. Components include hydraulics, instruments, brake assemblies, batteries, starter generators, and avionics.

Quality, craftsmanship, and customer service are the hallmarks of Atlantic Aviation. So confident is the company in its services that it backs all of its workmanship with a lifetime warranty. The only exception is its paint work, which carries a five-year or 3,000-flight-hour warranty. This is considered the best in the industry.

Atlantic Aviation offers its customers the newest materials and the latest technologies that are being introduced to the industry. This extends to both the ability to repair the new composites being used in aircraft and the installation and repair of the latest electronic instruments.

As for the future, Atlantic Aviation Corporation continues to innovate through providing new services while maintaining its tradition of quality and integrity. For more than 60 years it has sold and supported the industry's milestone aircraft, from yesterday's biplanes to today's sophisticated corporate business jets.

Below: Sophisticated electronic flight systems are installed and repaired by Atlantic technicians. The company invests generously in training programs to keep its employees up to date on the latest technology.

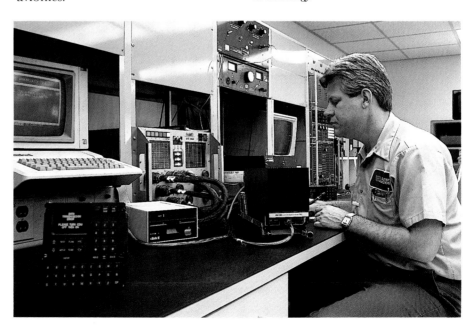

The Aqualon Group

Sales in excess of $500 million, products on the leading edge in the markets they serve, a global presence with several thousand customers worldwide, more than 3,000 employees: These are impressive credentials, to say the least. And they are even more so, considering that this particular company was formed as recently as 1987.

The company is Aqualon, and while it may be the new kid on the block, it has roots that date back to 1876.

The Aqualon Group is a leading worldwide manufacturer and supplier of water-soluble polymers and specialty chemicals to almost every

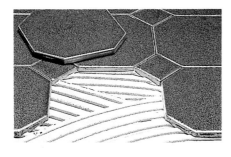

market in the chemical and coatings industries. It is, in fact, the only firm whose sole business is devoted to developing, manufacturing, and marketing these products. Sales in 1987 surpassed $300 million, and 1988 sales topped that at $356 million. By the year 2000 Aqualon is expected to be a billion-dollar enterprise.

Originally established as a joint venture of two corporate giants—Hercules, Incorporated, of Wilmington, Delaware, and Henkel KGaA of Düsseldorf, Federal Republic of Germany—Aqualon started with, and has since enhanced, the water-soluble products, services,

A leading supplier worldwide of water-soluble and organo-soluble polymers, Aqualon supplies the following industries (clockwise from top): pharmaceuticals, food, personal care items, petroleum, building products, and paint.

and technical expertise of its parent companies. In early 1989 Aqualon was acquired by Hercules Incorporated as an independent stand-alone company. Later the same year, as a result of the restructuring of Hercules Incorporated, Aqualon assumed the Hercules coatings products, including cellulosic polymers such as nitrocellulose. Aqualon has some of the finest water-soluble and

organo-soluble polymer research and manufacturing facilities in the world.

One of the Aqualon advantages concerns its product line. In addition to developing its own variations, the company has also inherited an established line of products—many of which have served as pacesetting standards in key industries for more than 75 years. It has a substantial market position in the building materials, paint, wood finishes, and ink industries, and is rapidly developing its presence in other areas as well.

For example, Natrosol®, a leading Aqualon product, is the world's

premier paint thickener. It has a 30-year tradition of excellence in coatings.

In the pharmaceutical industry, Aqualon polymers are used for the sustained release of tablets and caplets, tablet coating, and wet granulation. In the oil industry, the polymers provide essential properties for drilling, cementing, and fracturing. In personal care products, Aqualon is responsible for putting the gel in toothpastes and for thickening hair conditioners. The polymers give a smooth, rich appearance to foods such as table syrup and enhance the stability of other foods, such as ice

cream and cake mix. Wood furniture coated with Aqualon polymers has enhanced appearance and protection.

Prominently used in the building materials industry, Aqualon polymers control the flow of tape joint compounds, spray plasters, and tile cements. They also strengthen and enhance the printability of papers and paperboards. Inks for packaging and publication use Aqualon polymers as binders. Other industries making use of Aqualon polymers include textiles and ceramics.

Although Aqualon markets more than 20 products for specialized applications, a large majority of the polymers are derived from two sources: cellulose and guar.

From its home office in Wilmington, Aqualon's business extends worldwide. When Aqualon was established in 1987, it was organized into two distinct geographic regions: Aqualon East and Aqualon West. The former encompassed marketing and plant operations in Europe, South America, Africa, and the Middle East. The latter covered North America, Central America, and the Far East. These geographical lines have become increasingly blurred. Today, with a decidedly global approach to the business, all company units are interdependent and supportive of the entire enterprise.

Aqualon maintains a worldwide network of manufacturing, warehousing, research, and marketing

Aqualon's corporate headquarters is located at Little Falls Centre One in Wilmington (the building on the left).

facilities directed from multiple locations in the United States, Germany, France, Italy, the Netherlands, Spain, Belgium, Canada, the United Kingdom, and Brazil. Its state-of-the-art manufacturing sites in the United States are in Hopewell, Virginia; Parlin, New Jersey; Louisiana, Missouri; and Kenedy, Texas. The corporate research and development laboratory is located in Wilmington, which is also the site for a recently opened laboratory to develop prototypes for the pharmaceutical industry. The company also supports a technical sales and service staff trained in the latest developments in water-soluble and organo-soluble polymer technology and applications.

In early 1988 Aqualon moved its home office from downtown Wilmington to Little Falls Centre on Centerville Road. The new three-story, 52,000-square-foot headquarters office overlooks the Hercules Country Club. Aqualon employs more than 200 people at its headquarters office and research laboratory facilities in Wilmington.

What of Aqualon's future? It lies in a multifaceted approach that includes the development of new and complementary products; new applications for existing products—

especially in paint and surface coatings, personal care products, and food additives; acquisitions; and new market penetration. Through it all, Aqualon's vision will be to evolve from a growing specialty company into the world's premier manufacturer of water-soluble polymers and specialty chemicals.

Aqualon has established an innovative, worldwide quality management program. Called the Triangle of Excellence, the program revolves around people, products, and profits. The program is designed to maintain excellence in the current operations, while propelling Aqualon toward future growth. Fueled by open communication and without the constraints of traditional organizational barriers, the firm's quality management program relies on the team management concept, with an emphasis on full participation by all employees in developing and marketing high-value specialty products that set industry standards for quality and service.

Aqualon has also been a pacesetter in the area of employee relations and benefits. For example, it was the first major chemical concern in Delaware to institute a flexible benefits program. The team management philosophy places responsibility at the lowest appropriate organizational level and emphasizes open communication. Safety is another area where Aqualon has already earned a sterling reputation. The Chemical Manufacturers' Association has recognized the company with certificates of honor for the safety record of a number of its facilities.

"Bright" is the word for Aqualon's future—a future that includes quality, value, and service to its customers. This means the development of new and complementary products, new applications for existing products—especially in paints and surface coatings, personal care, and food additives—and penetrating new markets.

General Motors Corporation

It is no exaggeration to say that the General Motors Corporation's Boxwood Road assembly plant, located five miles southwest of Wilmington, is the future of the North American auto industry. The sprawling, modern facility is considered one of the most highly automated vehicle assembly plants in the world. Its state-of-the-art technology has served as a model for similar operations.

It is also no exaggeration to describe the General Motors plant as a major presence in Delaware's business and economic forecast, and one of the more prominent and vis-

renovation. The purpose was to gear up for the high-technology production of Chevrolet's new "L" cars—the Corsica and the Beretta. The Corsica is a four-door car, and the Beretta is the sportier, two-door model. The $311-million conversion program included the addition of another 602,329 square feet to General Motors' existing 2.7 million square feet of enclosed buildings.

The conversion also called for the installation of 294 robots, most of which were placed in the body assembly area, with others assigned to such functions as general assembly

tive, particularly in light of the foreign imports on the market.

Statistics convey part of the story: Each year for the past four years the plant has invested approximately 125,000 hours and more than $2.4 million in employee training and education.

The official start-up of regular, ongoing production of the "L" cars was October 1986. This culminated in the introduction of the Corsica and Beretta for the 1988 model year. The cars, which are now assembled at the Boxwood Road plant at the rate of 60 per hour, have

ible employers. The plant sits on 145 acres and employs approximately 4,100 workers. It has a payroll of $162 million and is one of 25 General Motors automotive assembly plants in the United States. Each year approximately 226,000 cars roll off the assembly lines. The plant also has had a sizable economic impact on other businesses in the region: It works closely with more than 425 local suppliers within a 50-mile radius of the facility.

During the past few years the Boxwood Road plant has undergone a monumental overhaul—one that involved extensive modernization and

and modular paint.

An integral part of the plant conversion was a GM history-making effort to train and educate all plant employees so they would be prepared to manage and work well with the new technology to produce a quality product. This training and education effort included a cooperative program with Delaware Technical and Community College, an emphasis on open communication and feedback from the employee ranks up to top management, and an overall philosophy of unity in accomplishing the goals of becoming more efficient, effective, and competi-

The General Motors Boxwood Road plant, situated five miles south of Wilmington, occupies 145 acres and employs a force of 4,100 workers.

since become the nation's top-selling automobiles.

The only other plant assembling Corsicas and Berettas is in nearby Linden, New Jersey. The Boxwood Road plant also makes the Pontiac Tempest and is the only General Motors plant to do so. The Tempest is a version of the Corsica that is sold only in Canada.

Constructed in 1947, General Motors' Boxwood Road plant began pro-

*Chevrolet prepares for the 1990s with its technolog-
ically advanced "L" cars—the Corsica (top),
Corsica Hatchback (center), and the high-
performance Beretta GT (bottom)—all assembled
at the General Motors Boxwood Road plant.*

output of Buicks.

In 1975 the plant began assembling the compact Chevrolet
Chevette. This continued for the
next nine years, with the production
rate of 70 cars per hour. In 1984
the plant had come full circle, and re-
tooled to resume production of the
larger-size Oldsmobile and Chevrolet models.

Also that year, as a result of a

duction with 800 employees. The
focus in those days was on Buicks,
Oldsmobiles, and Pontiacs. Production started at the rate of 40 cars
per hour. The first eight cars were
1947 black Pontiacs that were
shipped to Philadelphia dealers on
October 6, 1947. By 1952 there were
2,200 employees at the Boxwood
plant, and by 1955 the plant was
assembling 60 cars per hour. That
year a second shift was added to
increase production, and by mid-1955
there were 4,400 employees.

In 1968 the plant began producing Buicks, and by 1970 Boxwood Road was producing 20 percent of General Motors' national

companywide reorganization, the
Wilmington plant was assigned to
the Chevrolet-Pontiac-GM of Canada
group, now known as C-P-C
Wilmington.

Both top managers and other
employees of the Boxwood Road
plant are highly involved in civic
and charitable organizations and
causes. Just a few examples of this
include the Job Banks training and
placement program, the annual
loan of General Motors Corporation executives to United Way
organizations, and a companywide
canned food drive each year to
assist needy families in the Tri-
State area.

Slocomb Industries, Inc.

Slocomb Industries, Inc., is a recognized pioneer and one of the nation's leading manufacturers of vinyl window products. The Wilmington-based company designs, extrudes, and manufactures vinyl windows for homes, apartments, and many types of commercial buildings. It is one of the most successful small businesses in Delaware.

As a company, Slocomb is relatively young. It was established in 1955 by Leon F. Slocomb, Jr. (now president) to sell and install storm windows and doors. Within five years he became a manufacturer, one of the first in the country, in fact, to make vinyl storm windows and doors. The vinyl products, which Slocomb also marketed to dealers and retailers, rapidly became known for their white color, durability, and superior insulating properties. In 1962 the business was incorporated under Delaware law.

By 1967 there was renewed interest in the rehabilitation of older homes, which was spurred by the high cost of new construction and rising interest rates. In response to this trend, Slocomb began manufacturing replacement windows. Then, in 1974, again responding to shifts in the market (the emphasis on energy conservation), Slocomb entered the insulated glass business. Due to its limited manufacturing space and the rapid growth of insulated windows, the firm stopped production of its vinyl storm

Above: Window frames are extruded at Slocomb Industries' vinyl profile extrusion line. Plastic extrusion transformed the company from a small concern to a national presence in the industry.

Below: Awaiting shipment from Slocomb Industries' warehouse, windows of many shapes and sizes will soon be used throughout Delaware and beyond.

windows and doors in 1975.

Meanwhile, Slocomb had been studying new designs for a window that would have consumer appeal, yet would be easy and inexpensive to fabricate. The effort paid off, and a major turning point took place in 1979, when Slocomb formed Acro Extrusion Corporation to produce vinyl frames for windows. The move into the plastic extrusion field catapulted the company from a regional business into

one with a major national presence.

Today Acro is one of the top 10 producers of all vinyl replacement windows in the United States. Each year the company supplies frames for more than 300,000 windows to both Slocomb and about 30 other window manufacturers.

Slocomb Industries, the parent company, focuses on a regional market. It continues to manufacture about 50,000 insulated glass replacement windows each year, selling them to several hundred home improvement dealers within a 150-mile radius of Wilmington.

The steady growth of this family-owned business has resulted in a physical expansion. Today the company oversees a total of 120,000 square feet of manufacturing and warehouse space at three facilities: its headquarters at 900 East 30th Street and plants at 3015 Bellevue Avenue and 1601 Jessup Street. The extrusion plant at 30th Street runs 24 hours per day, seven days per week. A total of 190 people are employed.

Slocomb Industries, Inc., has grown about 30 percent each year over the past decade. This growth, in part, can be attributed to the popularity of vinyl windows, which provide energy efficiency when combined with insulating glass. But another major factor is the company itself and its philosophy of providing a quality product and reliable service.

Photo by Eric Crossan

Photo by Eric Crossan

9

Delaware State Chamber
of Commerce, 178

Mellon Bank (DE), 180

Bayard, Handelman &
Murdoch, 182

Skadden, Arps, Slate,
Meagher & Flom, 184

Young, Conaway, Stargatt
& Taylor, 186

Pepper, Hamilton &
Scheetz, 188

Delaware Development
Office, 189

Citicorp/Citibank, 190

Business and Professions

*Delaware's business and professional community
brings a wealth of ability and insight
to the area.*

Delaware State Chamber of Commerce

Origins of the Delaware State Chamber of Commerce date back to 1837, when prominent local businessmen formed the Wilmington Board of Trade. At that time Wilmington was a manufacturing hub, producing railroad cars, wheels, and sailing ships, as well as gunpowder and dynamite at the Du Pont Company Powder Works.

More than 153 years later the state's manufacturing climate still ranks high. A study released in 1989 put Delaware at the top of the list in terms of manufacturing, and second in the country in incentives for new business and growth in manufacturing industries.

The board of trade changed its name to the Wilmington Chamber of Commerce in 1913, which later, in 1953, became the Delaware State Chamber of Commerce, when the organization assumed a statewide role as an advocate for business.

While influential, the State Chamber remained small. Until 1979 membership lingered at around 500. Today under the leadership of president John M. Burris, the Delaware State Chamber of Commerce is considered the First State's largest business advocacy agency and offers a variety of publications, programs, and marketing opportunities to its 3,800 members.

The *State Chamber News,* founded in 1981, is a biweekly informational newsletter ranging from 24 to 64 pages in length. Nine out of its 26 issues per year feature special sections focusing on topics ranging from tourism, to real estate, to health care, to the environment. The paper boasts a circulation of nearly 10,000 and readership of 28,000.

Other publications include a *Delaware Directory of Commerce and Industry,* listing more than 5,000 companies alphabetically and by Standard Industrial Classification (SIC) code, a "Legislative Roster," with names, addresses, and photographs of all state and local government officials; board and staff directory; a business calendar; "Monday Morning," a listing

and status report of bills introduced in the General Assembly, when it's in session; and "What We Stand For," a legislative issues booklet.

The State Chamber's Meetings Division offers more than 100 programs throughout the state concentrating on a wide range of issues such as drug and substance abuse in the work place, presenting a winning image, stress management, and small business financing road shows.

There are monthly luncheons on employee relations topics, monthly dinners devoted to the discussion of business and economic development, and export seminars to acquaint members with the ins and outs of foreign markets and trade financing in preparation for Europe 1992.

Marketing opportunities are available at state chamber trade shows, held throughout the year at different locations. The State Chamber Showcase is geared to the home consumer, while Market Delaware, a business-to-business exposition, is aimed at both small and large companies. Some 40,000 to 50,000 individuals attend each of the two home shows and 6,000 to 10,000 business leaders the business shows, each year.

Networking after hours at a State Chamber Mix & Market has also become a popular event for Delaware's young and old alike. The State and Chamber's December Holiday Mix & Market attracts a sellout crowd annually.

The State Chamber represents its members at all levels of government through its Government Relations staff, which has been successful in a wide spectrum of

Above: John M. Burris, president.

Facing page: One Commerce Center, headquarters of the Delaware State Chamber of Commerce.

issues from personal income tax cuts to unemployment compensation reform, gross receipts tax law changes, and regulatory reform.

Economic development information and referrals are also handled. Out-of-state companies interested in moving to the First State may call the state chamber for labor and demographics information, and names of those who might offer assistance.

As Delaware begins the 1990s, the state chamber's focus has shifted slightly to include both economic development and livability issues, such as education and children at risk, water and the environment, employee drug and substance abuse, and transportation and infrastructure.

The Delaware State Chamber of Commerce will continue its mission—"To assure that Delaware's economic climate benefits all its citizens by keeping Delaware competitive"—while at the same time attending to those factors affecting the state's quality of life.

Mellon Bank (DE)

Mellon Bank (DE) has the longest and one of the most colorful histories of Mellon Bank Corporation's seven retail banking subsidiaries. The Delaware bank was organized by Henry Ridgely, its first president, and chartered as Farmers Bank in 1807, 20 years after Delaware became the first state to ratify the U.S. Constitution and only 26 years after the nation's first commercial bank was established.

While most banks of that era catered to wealthy landowners and merchants, Farmers Bank quickly established a different identity: It adopted the policy of granting six-month loans of up to $2,000 to "any farmer, mechanic, or manufacturer" in Delaware. Farmers was also a pioneer in other areas: It became the first bank in the nation to establish branches when it opened facilities in Georgetown and New Castle to supplement the primary office in Dover. A third branch was established in Wilmington in 1813. The Farmers Bank branching strategy created another industry first when the bank opened an office inside the John Wanamaker's department store in Wilmington.

During the 1950s Farmers Bank merged with or acquired seven other financial institutions. And, in 1981, Philadelphia's Girard Bank acquired Farmers and renamed it Girard Bank Delaware. When Girard merged with the Pittsburgh-based Mellon Bank Corporation in 1983, Girard Bank Delaware became part of the Mellon organization.

One year later it changed its official name to Mellon Bank (DE).

Mellon, a super-regional bank holding company headquartered in Pittsburgh, Pennsylvania, is one of the largest holding companies in the United States. Its

Harry Kephart, chairman, president, and chief executive officer of Mellon Bank (DE), convenes a meeting in the historic boardroom at the Dover community office. The painting is of Henry Ridgely, first president of Farmers Bank.

Trust and Investment Department is one of the largest in the nation, with more than $218 billion in assets under custody. The corporation maintains 565 domestic retail banking offices, including 335 community offices. The firm's banking subsidiaries are located in the central Atlantic states of Pennsylvania, Maryland, and Delaware, with additional locations in key domestic and international business centers.

Mellon Bank (DE) is one of the five largest banks in Delaware. Under the solid leadership of Harry Kephart, chairman, chief executive

Below and below right: A look at the old and the new. Office automation has simplified the recording of customer information, as illustrated by these two platform areas.

Airport Plaza office, Mellon Bank (DE)'s newest community office.

officer, and president, Mellon Bank (DE) continues its tradition of service to individuals and businesses of all sizes. Mellon currently operates 24 full-service branches statewide, including its headquarters office at 10th and Market streets in downtown Wilmington.

Mellon Bank (DE) is unique among Mellon Bank Corporation's retail banking subsidiaries. Primarily because of Delaware's favorable banking laws, Mellon Bank (DE) became the headquarters for Mellon's national credit card operations in 1985. Today more than 300 associates service nearly 900,000 credit card accounts for all of Mellon's retail banks.

Mellon Bank (DE)'s credit card department has become an industry leader in offering unique Visa and MasterCard services. These include an "affinity card" specifically tailored to organizations such as the World Wildlife Fund. This card offers special benefits to its users and generates donations that the fund uses for its conservation projects.

Mellon offers numerous services to businesses, all designed to streamline and simplify daily transactions and boost productivity. These include Bank-By-Phone, a touch-tone system available seven days per week that enables the caller to quickly review account balances, transfer funds, and pay bills. Mellon

also offers Business Investment Accounts—seven- and 28-day certificates that allow small businesses to manage their finances the way large companies do, with extra cash earning higher interest than regular business money market accounts. There is also a toll-free telephone hotline for businesses to ask questions on financial matters such as credit, cash management, and retirement plans. Always a champion of small business, Mellon has consistently been the largest processor of U.S. Small Business Administration loans in Delaware during the past

several years.

Mellon historically has been a leader in technology and continues to invest in technological innovations. In 1955 Mellon became one of the first banks in the nation to acquire and install its own computer. Three years later Mellon established the first clearinghouse for the overnight processing of checks from its correspondent banks. In Delaware, Bunker Ramo terminals have been installed at every customer service desk in Mellon's community offices. This platform automation system enhances customer service by, among other things, providing up-to-date product information and direct access to customer account information.

Mellon Bank (DE)'s commitment to Delaware is strong, and its reputation for outstanding customer service contributes to its leadership position among the state's financial institutions.

This set of drawers, on display at the Dover community office, once housed the entire Farmers Bank account filing system.

Bayard, Handelman & Murdoch

Delaware's dynamic growth is reflected in the aggressive forward vision of Bayard, Handelman & Murdoch. The general practice law firm has developed a strong organization tailored to meeting its clients' present and future needs.

A relatively young firm, but with solid roots, BH&M's formation is the result of a careful amalgamation of law specialties and talents. In 1984 the strongly entrenched litigation firm of Bayard, Brill & Handelman merged with the state's renowned tax boutique, Murdoch and

igation clients.

Today BH&M has 35 lawyers and a support staff of more than 70. Offices in Dover, Georgetown, Newark, and Washington, D.C., complement the Wilmington headquarters, and all five locations provide a full range of services throughout these areas. In addition to the specialized corporation law practice common to most of the larger Delaware firms, BH&M services its clients in such areas as litigation, commercial and environmental matters, land-use development, tax, estates and trusts, and

ers in rezoning applications and related land-use matters. Our practice includes Superfund and insurance coverage, litigation, practice before regulatory agencies, and the representation of parties to real estate transactions.

"In 1988 New Castle County approved a new comprehensive plan that will serve as a guide for zoning and other land-use decisions. This replaces an outdated document that was adopted 20 years ago and had not been updated. In the land-use field, implementation of the new com-

Robert C. O'Hara, land use/environmental

Robert Meyer, tax

Neil B. Glassman, transactional

Walsh. Shortly afterward, BH&M attracted Delaware's largest residential real estate law firm, and the synergistic growth began.

The firm's excellent reputation is borne out by the joinder of the Honorable Robert C. O'Hara after his 1987 retirement from Delaware's superior court. Judge O'Hara brought with him a background in the trial court's infrastructure that has proven invaluable to the firm's lit-

residential and commercial real estate. The firm's size allows it to maintain flexibility in responding to clients' needs promptly, effectively, and economically.

A few members of the firm were asked to describe their areas of practice and comment on past and future advances:

Robert C. O'Hara, land use/ environmental: "The firm represents land owners and real estate develop-

prehensive plan will be a challenge for local governments and those who practice law in this area."

Robert Meyer, tax: "We advise Delaware holding companies and give opinions on the impact of state taxes on transactions that have Delaware contacts. We also provide a full range of general tax services, such as the structuring of business organizations, the establishment and management of pension plans and other fringe benefit programs, and estate planning and estate administration.

"In the tax area, the most significant recent advancements have been in the reduction of both state and federal tax rates. Statewide, we have had a dramatic reduction in our personal income tax rates and a significant reduction in the gross receipts tax. Over the next three years the most positive advancement will be the continued prosperity of the state's economy, which should lead to even further tax reductions."

Neil B. Glassman, transactional:

William G. Campbell, regulatory

"We act as special Delaware counsel for out-of-state law firms, *Fortune* 500 companies, and other large entities regarding compliance with Delaware law. These transactions may involve financing, the acquisition of businesses, or the issuance of securities by Delaware corporations, limited partnerships, and business trusts. In the area of local practice, our firm is also actively involved in the financing, acquisition, and render-

ing of advice regarding ongoing operations of local business. We've been very active in the acquisitions of subsidiary companies for large insurers and in counseling both lender and borrower in financing transactions.

"In the area of commercial law, the most significant recent advancements have been in the developing sophistication of not only Delaware corporation law, but Delaware law relative to other entities, such as business trusts and limited partnerships, which are now commonly used in national transactions. Meanwhile, the

Peter J. Walsh, commercial litigation

growth of the state's financial industry has required Delaware lawyers to act as both special Delaware counsel on large, national transactions and to sharpen their general counsel skills so they can advise and represent the banks, consumer credit organizations, and insurance companies that are moving into the state. The most positive advancement in commercial law will most likely involve increased growth in the finan-

cial services industry and continued development of real industry in Delaware."

William G. Campbell, regulatory: "We're primarily involved in the insurance regulatory area, where we probably do more work than any other firm, as well as some other financial regulatory and some environmental regulatory work. The latter is a strong growth area for us.

"In the regulatory area, the tremendous growth is in the financial institutions' regulatory practice and in the local aspects of environmental regulatory practice. The most likely areas for strong future advancement are the changes that will occur in the structure of financial institutions nationally in the next few years. This in turn will lead to tremendous growth in local financial institutions' regulatory practice. The second item that will probably lead to growth is the extreme interest in Delaware environmental regulation, which should greatly enhance the needs of businesses for local environmental counsel in the next few years."

Peter J. Walsh, commercial litigation: "In our bankruptcy practice, we have a history of representing both debtors and creditors. Our involvement has covered almost all aspects of the practice. In general commercial litigation, we are actively involved in both the state and the federal courts. Commercial litigation has been increasing due to the growth of New Castle County's economy.

"Bankruptcy practice is one of the fastest growing areas of the law. This is the result of both the Bankruptcy Reform Act of 1978 and the fading stigma surrounding bankruptcy. Corporate reorganizations under the new act are no longer viewed as bankruptcies, but a legitimate form of debt adjustment. While this is a national trend, it is certainly experienced locally. With the growth of Delaware's commercial sector, the increase in bankruptcy practice is expected to surpass that of the rest of the country."

Skadden, Arps, Slate, Meagher & Flom

Skadden, Arps, Slate, Meagher & Flom was the first national law firm to establish an office in Wilmington. Its commitment to Delaware is strong, and Skadden's size, stability, and position on the cutting edge of legal developments will ensure continued growth.

The law firm's office opened in 1979 in downtown Wilmington. Its presence coincided with the start of a burgeoning economic growth that has since characterized the state. Opening a Delaware office was also a logical step for Skadden (which has long been considered the nation's premier mergers and acquisitions firm), as many business combinations spawn Delaware litigation.

Skadden's tremendous growth in just 10 years has mirrored the growth of Delaware. Today Skadden's Delaware office is among the fastest growing law firms in the state. In 1979 six lawyers worked in the Wilmington office; today there are 42. Of these, 10 are partners and two serve as special counsel.

A full-service, international law firm, Skadden was formed in 1948 as a practice largely dependent

Partners Steven J. Rothschild and Rodman Ward, Jr.

upon referrals. It has since evolved into the nation's top-grossing law firm, a firm that is always responding to the changing needs of its clients. It has 1,048 lawyers in 11 offices. In addition to the Wilmington office and its New York headquarters, Skadden maintains offices in Boston, Washington, Chicago, Los Angeles, San Francisco, London, Tokyo, Sydney, and Hong Kong.

While Skadden has established a solid reputation in mergers and acquisitions, its diverse practice extends from beyond this area. The original areas of practice Skadden offered its clients were corporate litigation, general corporate, securities, antitrust, tax and pensions, real estate, labor, and trusts and estates. During the past decade, the period when the firm has experienced its most rapid growth, Skadden has added a number of new practice areas led by recognized experts in each field. These areas include prod-

ucts liability, bankruptcy, financial services, energy, communications, environmental, mortgage-backed securities, and commodities, international commercial transactions, and financial futures.

The Wilmington office has emphasized corporate transactions and litigations, with added strength in financial services.

Leading the litigation practice locally is Rodman Ward, Jr., practice leader of the Wilmington office, and Steven J. Rothschild. The busi-

Below: Partner Richard Easton.

Below right: Partner Edward Welch.

Top: Attorneys Jean Kissane and Paul Regan review a case in the law library.

Bottom: Attorneys Kirk Jordan and Matt Boyer discuss a client's legal problem in the law library.

ness transactions section is supervised by Richard L. Easton and Irving S. Shapiro. Shapiro joined Skadden in 1981 after his retirement as chairman of the Du Pont Company. He was also chairman of the National Business Roundtable, of which he remains an honorary member.

Skadden represents 43 of the 250 largest industrial corporations in the United States—more major corporations than any other U.S. law firm. It is primarily a transactional firm: No single client accounts for more than 2.5 percent of Skadden's annual revenue of more than $400 million. This diversity of clients virtually guarantees a posture of professional independence.

Always innovative, Skadden has sought new ways to serve its clients. It became the first corporate law firm to establish "boutiques" of legal specialties, or nonroutine services, which are offered to existing clients.

Skadden has also been innovative in its encouragement and use of paralegals, both nationally and in Wilmington. This practice is cost effective to clients. In fact, the firm's nonlegal staff includes one of the largest groups of paralegals of any U.S. law firm. In the Wilmington office, the 12-person paralegal staff is supervised by Sarah Stiegler and Catherine Ledyard, former president of the Delaware Paralegal Association.

The firm's success and rapid growth has not precluded its awareness of fulfilling its social and professional responsibilities. Skadden attorneys are active in a wide spectrum of community, professional, and charitable endeavors. For example, Rodman Ward became president of the Delaware State Bar Association in June 1989.

Both nationally and locally, Skad-

den lawyers devote an average of 4 percent of all hours billed to pro bono work. One local example of this effort is a successful program to assist overburdened prosecutors in the state criminal courts. Nationally Skadden has created a special unit to handle death penalty appeals led by a full-time, nationally respected special counsel.

But the firm's social conscience is perhaps most vividly expressed through its newest and most ambitious pro bono project: the Skadden Fellowship program. The $2-million-per-year program will provide fellowships annually for the next five

years to up to 125 graduating law students nationwide. In return, the young lawyers will serve as staff attorneys for public interest organizations, legal aid offices, and other facilities that provide civil legal assistance to the poor and the disadvantaged. The program begins in 1989, and an independent committee, with only a minority of Skadden partners, will choose from among the applicants. In all, Skadden expects to spend roughly $10 million on this pro bono program over the next five years without reducing its commitment to pro bono in other areas.

Young, Conaway, Stargatt & Taylor

Although Young, Conaway, Stargatt & Taylor is relatively young among major Delaware law firms (it was established in 1959), it has grown consistently. It now has 45 attorneys, and its other 75 employees include 12 paralegals, ranking YCS&T among the five largest law firms in Delaware. The firm is also young with respect to the age of its members—nine of the 26 partners are under the age of 40, and only six partners are over 50.

The firm has a general, varied practice with an emphasis on litigation. A unique feature is the balance between the firm's vigorous and growing national corporate and commercial law practice and its diver-

The offices of Young, Conaway, Stargatt & Taylor are in the Wilmington Trust Center, located in the heart of Wilmington's financial and business district.

sified local work. Specific areas of practice include corporation law and litigation, plaintiffs' personal injury and insurance defense litigation, environmental law, commercial law and litigation, bankruptcy, real estate, labor and employment discrimination law, public utility work, estates and trusts, tax, patent, and family law.

With its knowledge of state and local governmental structures, full range of services, and quick adaptability, YCS&T is especially adept at assisting businesses that are relocating to the state. YCS&T attorneys try cases in all Delaware state courts and all federal courts. Its attorneys also appear frequently before many state and federal agencies.

The firm has four operating sections—corporate litigation and corporate transactions, personal injury and insurance litigation, labor and employment law, and commercial transactions and commercial litigation. The section concept is not based on rigid attorney specialization, and many attorneys participate in more than one section.

The corporate litigation and corporate transactions section works closely with the best and largest firms in other major cities, particularly New York. Among the cases litigated by the firm were those involving the acquisition or attempted acquisition of Getty Oil, Houston Natural Gas, Phillips Petroleum, Revlon, Continental Airlines,

MacMillan, and RJR Nabisco, Inc.

The corporate litigation practice also involves the defense and, on rare occasions, the prosecution, of stockholder class action and derivative suits. In addition, the firm's attorneys are frequently asked to render informal advice and formal opinions to both corporations and other law firms on Delaware corporate law issues.

The firm's personal injury and insurance litigation section represents those who are injured or killed as a result of product defect, professional negligence, equipment failure, vehicular collisions or construction, and maritime accidents. A full-time private investigator is available to assist in these cases. The firm also defends numerous liability and workers' compensation cases on behalf of insurance company clients and their insureds.

Before the labor and employment law section was established in 1981, local employers needing labor law advice were generally required to seek out attorneys in Philadelphia, Baltimore, or more remote locations. Today this section is considered the largest in Delaware. Attorneys counsel and represent private and public employers in matters ranging from contract negotiations, arbitrations, and NLRB unfair labor practice proceedings to employment discrimination, wrongful discharge, ERISA litigation in federal and state courts, and administrative proceedings before federal and state agencies.

Attorneys in the commercial transaction and commercial litigation section provide business organization and tax counseling to those starting, purchasing, or selling real estate or a business. They counsel ongoing business clients on contractual and collection matters, government regulatory issues, and financial planning. Attorneys also serve as local Delaware counsel to regional and national clients who conduct business in Delaware.

YCS&T's bankruptcy practice has increased dramatically in recent

Young, Conaway, Stargatt & Taylor's main conference room in Wilmington is one of eight available for meetings and depositions. The firm's Georgetown, Delaware, office has two conference rooms.

years. Today the firm plays a major role in most significant Delaware bankruptcy cases pending in the district, and it routinely represents creditor committees and shareholder groups in this and other jurisdictions.

YCS&T's growth is reflected in its physical facilities. The firm relocated in 1982 to new, spacious quarters in the Wilmington Trust Center, overlooking downtown Wilmington's historic Rodney Square. In 1985 it expanded again by opening an office in Georgetown (Sussex County). Today this office is staffed by four full-time attorneys (who live near Georgetown), and several Wilmington-based attorneys who are there on a part-time basis to service clients in southern Delaware.

The Wilmington office has recently undergone a major expansion. Recent innovations of direct benefit to clients include the installation of an in-house computer system that provides state-of-the-art word and data processing, litigation, and practice management support. The firm's two offices are linked by computer for word- and data-

The firm's offices on the 10th and 11th floors of the Wilmington Trust Center have been designed to create an atmosphere of beauty to assist its attorneys and staff in producing a legal product with speed and precision in a responsive, individualized, and personal manner.

processing purposes.

The firm's attorneys represent a cross section of law schools, including American University, Cornell, Dickinson, Georgetown, Harvard, Pennsylvania, Rutgers, Temple, Virginia, and Yale. The YCS&T staff participates in numerous bar and

public service activities: Present firm members include two past presidents of the Delaware State Bar Association, two former presidents of the Delaware Trial Lawyers' Association, a former president of the Delaware Chapter of the Federal Bar Association, and one director of Delaware Volunteer Legal Services, Inc.

The firm's flexible section structure exposes its attorneys to most aspects of legal practice, yet there is also ample opportunity to do substantial work in specialized areas. YCS&T provides an in-house continuing legal education program for associates that emphasizes the "nuts and bolts" practice of Delaware law, counseling, and litigation, and addresses timely issues arising before the courts. YCS&T also sponsors ongoing retreats involving the participation of all attorneys. These full-day sessions, held outside the office, are devoted to long-range planning.

This innovative, competitive, yet team-spirited environment has yielded a firm noted for its stability and low turnover, and this extends from the partners through the secretaries.

Pepper, Hamilton & Scheetz

Pepper, Hamilton & Scheetz, through its Wilmington office, has responded well to Delaware's burgeoning demand for specialized legal services. Local clients benefit from the resources of one of the 50 largest law firms in the nation, with roots dating back to the nineteenth century and a present-day complement of 300 lawyers.

With offices in the Manufacturers' Hanover Plaza downtown, Pepper, Hamilton & Scheetz established its Wilmington practice in 1983. The firm's Wilmington office has concentrated on representing management in employment labor law, with a growing practice in commercial law, litigation, and immigration law. While the firm's most visible presence has been in the public sector (state, county, city governments, and school districts), it also serves private employers, ranging from *Fortune* 200 companies to small entrepreneurs. Its client base increasingly reflects the state's economy; the banking, insurance, construction, and chemical industries are well represented.

In representing employers, PH&S practices in all aspects of labor and employment law, including labor negotiations, union organizing attempts, labor litigation, wrongful discharge litigation, employment discrimination, immigration law and litigation, occupational safety and health law, and environmental law.

The Wilmington office is headed by partners Alfred J. D'Angelo, Jr., and James J. Sullivan, Jr. D'Angelo graduated from Princeton in 1970 and received his J.D. from Villanova Law School, cum laude, in 1974. Sullivan graduated from Pennsylvania State University, cum laude, in 1977 and received his J.D. from Georgetown University. The partners are also active in community, professional, and civic affairs statewide.

PH&S' major strength has been its ability to provide clients with personal service, while simultaneously offering the resources and legal diversity of a large, national firm. Other PH&S offices are located in Philadelphia, Berwyn, and Harrisburg, Pennsylvania; Los Angeles, California; Detroit, Michigan; Washington, D.C.; and London. The Philadelphia office, which is also PH&S' headquarters, has more than 170 lawyers. Many of them participate in cases that originate in Delaware. Interaction between its Wilmington, Philadelphia, and Washington offices has afforded PH&S' Delaware clients with the highest level of legal specialization—essential for companies operating in Delaware's rapidly growing economy.

For example, the firm recently successfully represented the State of Delaware in the first fact-finding proceeding under Delaware public employment law. This representation has set the standard for future fact-finding procedures in the state. In the private sector, PH&S has represented many of Delaware's chemical and manufacturing plants.

The firm, which celebrates its 100th anniversary in 1990, has experienced impressive growth, particularly in the past decade. During this time Pepper, Hamilton & Scheetz more than doubled in size. This growth is largely attributed to the firm's commitment to excellence in representing its clients, and in crafting unique and creative solutions to problems arising in both existing and anticipated cases.

Wilmington office partners Alfred J. D'Angelo, Jr., (left), and James J. Sullivan, Jr., on the bow of a tugboat. The marine transportation industry represents one facet of the Wilmington office practice.

Delaware Development Office

Delaware's booming economy— the state has taken the lead in expanding opportunities and providing a favorable climate for business and industry—is no accident. Much of this effort has emanated from one organization, the Delaware Development Office, which, as part of the executive branch of the state government, reports directly to and works closely with the governor.

The DDO, which employs 51 people, was established in 1981 to encourage the expansion of existing businesses within the state, attract new businesses, and promote tourism. The DDO's purpose is to promote orderly statewide economic growth, leading to a healthy

Financial Center Development Act, which was aimed at diversifying the state's economic base. This landmark legislation invited out-of-state financial institutions to establish operations in Delaware. Together with subsequent legislation, this initiative created an internationally recognized responsive environment for the financial community.

Other initiatives include legislation allowing Delaware corporations to limit or eliminate directors' liability in certain instances. Most recently the state adopted what may be the nation's most favorable law governing hostile takeovers. The state has also expanded business tax incentives, created innovative financing

Above: Wilmington—and all of Delaware— enjoys an outstanding quality of life enhanced by balanced, well-managed growth.

Left: Delaware boasts many top tourists events, including the annual Rehoboth Beach sandcastle contest, held each August.

economy while enhancing the quality of life and protecting the environment.

The DDO philosophy is that this type of growth requires solid cooperation between the public and private sectors, through well-planned, coordinated, and aggressively marketed programs that are matched to community needs.

In its brief history the DDO has been involved with an impressive list of achievements. This begins with the 1981 passage of Delaware's

opportunities, and reduced business and personal tax rates. In the world trade realm, DDO has established an Exporter Assistance Program, an important component of which includes the Shared Foreign Sales Corporation Program. The Exporter Assistance Program was recently recognized for excellence and presented with the President's "E" Award.

The DDO has professional specialists on staff in the areas of business development, finance, research, education, training, recruit-

ment, tourism, external affairs, and international trade.

Among its responsibilities, the DDO recruits new business to Delaware and provides relocation and expansion assistance to existing companies. It helps small businesses obtain financing; collects, analyzes, and distributes statistical data on the state's economy and business climate; and provides education and training services to new and expanding businesses. It also develops and implements a regional, national, and international marketing and promotion plan for Delaware as a travel destination. Other responsibilities include administration of the Capital Budget and the Delaware State Housing Authority. Finally, the Delaware Development Office assists small and medium-size businesses wishing to take advantage of the state's world trade programs.

Citicorp/Citibank

Citibank Delaware, a subsidiary of Citicorp, began with the visionary idea of establishing a bank based on the concept of corporate cash management—a full-service financial institution for the exclusive use of corporate cash managers throughout the United States.

Citibank, one of the first out-of-state banks to locate in Delaware, moved to the state in 1982. The move was inspired by the state's favorable business climate and banking laws—specifically the Financial Center Development Act of 1981. Other factors included the active cooperation between the private and public sectors, the overall quality of life, and the state's central location in the Northeast.

Citibank was also the first major tenant in the New Castle Corporate Commons office park. In fact, its move there led to the further development of the park. Citibank's office opened October 6, 1982, with just 31 employees working in a 75,000-square-foot building. By the end of its first year the payroll had grown to 100. Today Citibank is the Corporate Commons' largest single tenant, with more than 500 employees. After outgrowing its original facility, it added another two buildings, so that it now occupies 220,000 square feet of office space. The company also recently purchased an additional six acres to accommodate future expansion.

The specialty of Citibank Delaware is corporate cash management—the rapid collection and controlled disbursement of funds for its corporate clients. As headquarters for this national operation, Citibank Delaware serves *Fortune* 500 firms and mid-range growth companies, including many Delaware clients. Thanks to the most advanced electronic cash-management system in the world, daily transaction volumes approaching one billion dollars are routine.

Citibank's Delaware facility is also national headquarters for Citicorp Banking Corporation (CBC),

which is the holding company for Citicorp's principal U.S. subsidiaries other than commercial banks. The primary function of CBC is to raise money in financial markets outside the United States. These funds are then used to finance the lending activities of CBC's various subsidiaries.

Citibank's energy is focused on tailoring emerging technology to meet the individual needs of its customers. But Citibank is also a good corporate citizen. Its employees are involved in a wide range of community activities, including the Boy Scouts, the Leukemia Society of America, and the Ronald McDonald House. The company has clearly given Delaware a long-term commitment.

A 220,000-square-foot building in the New Castle Corporate Commons is home to Citicorp in Delaware. Initially occupying the expansive headquarters with only 31 employees, the bank now is the office park's largest tenant, with more than 500 employees.

Citibank Delaware and Citicorp Banking Corporation are part of the global network of Citicorp, the nation's largest bank holding company and the largest credit card operation in the world, with approximately 89,000 employees, offices in 89 nations, and more than $200 billion in assets. An industry leader in banking, Citicorp offers a broad range of products and services worldwide.

Photo by Kevin Fleming

Jack Corrozi, Builder, 194   Krapfcandoit, 195   The Linpro Company, 196   Gilpin, Van Trump and   Wyman Electric Service   Wohlsen Construction
                                                                                 Montgomery, Inc., 198   Company, 199   Company, 200

The Healy Group, Inc.,   Emory Hill Development,   Stoltz Bros., Ltd., 206   James Julian, Inc., 208   Amato & Stella Associates,   Snyder, Crompton & Asso-
202   Inc., 204   211   ciates, 212

Petrillo Brothers, 214   Louis Capano & Sons,   The Commonwealth   Nanticoke Homes, 219   City Systems, Inc., 220
                           Inc., 216   Group, 218

From the Ground Up

A thriving building industry provides the
expertise to shape the Delaware
of tomorrow.

Jack Corrozi, Builder

Jack Corrozi, Builder: The name has become synonymous with outstanding quality and fine craftsmanship in single-family homes throughout New Castle County.

The Newark-based company—owned and operated by Wilmington native and former state trooper John A. Corrozi—currently builds and sells roughly 200 semi-custom homes per year, ranging in price from $200,000 to $500,000. Most are located within a five-mile radius of Hockessin. Although Corrozi homes tend to reflect the preference of Delaware buyers for the two-story colonial style, the homes are also distinctive in their attention to detail.

Today's successful enterprise is a far cry from Corrozi's beginnings. Corrozi left the state police force in the early 1970s and became a construction foreman for a national developer. This experience led to forming a residential remodeling and maintenance company, and it was during that time that Corrozi built his first house.

The builder established Corrozi Homes in 1978, but the business got off to a slow start: The first five years were troubled with high interest rates and the struggle of being an unknown entity. During those first years, for example, Corrozi built and sold a total of only 50 homes.

Major growth for the company has occurred during the past three years. Corrozi's 1986 single-family home sales topped $23 million. This

feat was recognized by the National Homebuilders Association, which noted that Corrozi was one of only three Delaware developers to report more than $20 million in single-family home sales. The company's 1987 sales were $28 million.

Corrozi is a conservative builder: He tends to sell his homes before building them. He prides himself not only on the excellence of his construction but also on his personal relationships with clients.

ment, some multifamily construction, and has also expanded, as of 1988, into commercial work with a 15,000-square-foot office complex in Pike Creek Valley.

Yet another outgrowth was the 1987 formation of Preferred Proper-

A Corrozi home in Ramsey Ridge. It includes a spacious deck, a soaring ceiling in the family room, and site placement that maximizes the view of mature trees.

Selective about his work, Corrozi may typically look at 30 to 40 developments, then choose to build in only five. He contends that home buyers must know and trust the company that is building their house. He remains personally involved with up to 90 percent of the sale and settlement contracts.

The builder-developer's success in residential construction has spurred other ventures. Corrozi now does a small amount of land develop-

ties, an independent residential and commercial real estate brokerage with its own sales staff.

Active in professional organizations, Corrozi has served as president of the Home Owners' Warranty Program of Delaware and as treasurer and vice-president of the Homebuilders' Association of Delaware. He is also the only builder to serve on the New Castle County Zoning Study Commission and was involved with the county's comprehensive planning group.

Krapfcandoit

The Krapf Construction Group, also known as Krapfcandoit, has been providing construction services to business and industry since 1917. Over the course of 70 years, this Wilmington construction family has built a reputation on quality, diversity, innovation, and service.

The firm was established by Frederic G. Krapf, Sr., a Wilmington carpenter whose parents emigrated from Germany. Krapf became a general contractor, specializing in residential and commercial alterations. Shortly after World War II, Fred Krapf, Jr., joined the firm and expanded the company's services to include the building of commercial and industrial facilities, as well as design-build projects. The third generation of Krapfs joined the organization in the 1970s and again expanded operations to include construction management and value engineering.

The firm's numerous list of clients includes organizations large and small throughout the East Coast. Primarily Krapf's clients are located in the Delaware,

Pennsylvania, Maryland, Washington, D.C., and New Jersey areas. It has occasional projects in Florida, North Carolina, Maine, Vermont, Illinois, Michigan, Tennessee, Ohio, and Louisiana—or, one could say, east of the Mississippi.

During the late 1970s The Krapf Construction Group made a commitment to the life care industry. Krapf has received national recognition for the construction of several life care facilities. The firm specializes in tailoring projects to an owner's needs and applies budget constraints. On many occasions the Krapf organization has reduced the project cost 25 percent through value engineering in order to make

a project feasible. The company has completed 16 major projects that provide housing for the elderly, from subsidized apartments to nursing homes and full-service life care facilities. Krapf's plans are to continue this commitment to the elderly into the 1990s as the country's population and the need for life care facilities continue to rise.

In addition to life care facilities, Krapf is presently building low- and high-rise hotels, utilities buildings, freezer warehouses, computer centers, marinas, and low-income housing. It has also expanded into athletic facilities, which includes one of the largest ice skating arenas in the world.

Whatever the project may be, Krapfcandoit is the logo and operat-

ing philosophy of the family, which is justified by their hands-on involvement in every project. The company's in-house staff excels in all aspects of construction, including site acquisition, value engineering, general construction, project management, building maintenance, and management.

These elements have resulted in The Krapf Construction Group's track record for on-time completion, cost guarantees, and a team approach to all projects. As the new decade begins, Krapf will continue to provide construction services for office, retail, commercial, residential, and life care industries.

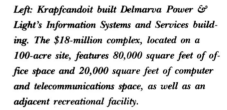

Left: Krapfcandoit built Delmarva Power & Light's Information Systems and Services building. The $18-million complex, located on a 100-acre site, features 80,000 square feet of office space and 20,000 square feet of computer and telecommunications space, as well as an adjacent recreational facility.

Below: The Quadrangle, located in Haverford, Pennsylvania, is an integrated life care community built for the Marriott Corporation. Built at a cost of $36 million, The Quadrangle features 309 residential units in seven three-story buildings. Also included are a health care building, a community building, and 67 acres of woodland.

The Linpro Company

The Linpro Company is a relative newcomer in Delaware's economic arena, but in just a few short years, it has established a significant presence.

The national real estate development firm, headquartered in Berwyn, on Pennsylvania's Main Line, provides a diverse and extensive portfolio of commercial, industrial, residential, and retail projects nationwide—from Connecticut and New Jersey to California and Texas.

Since the company was created in 1978, it has developed mid-rise and high-rise office buildings in downtown and suburban markets, as well as custom-built projects for numerous corporate clients. Linpro projects include warehouse and distribution buildings, offices and showrooms, and high-technology facilities. The company has also developed mixed-use suburban communities that include residential units, office buildings, shopping centers, and recreational facilities. The resi-

dential market has also been penetrated, with the development of apartments, condominium town houses, and single-family homes.

Today Linpro oversees the ownership, development, and management of millions of square feet of real estate nationwide. This includes at least 10 million square feet of office space valued at more than $1.3 billion. The company has 26 operating offices from coast to coast and is a major presence in 28 cities.

Unlike many other national developers, The Linpro Company's staff actively manages all of the firm's properties. In fact, its professional management services are so well received that they are utilized by other businesses, both institutional and private.

In Delaware, Linpro projects range from a major mixed-use development in the city of Wilmington to a sophisticated suburban office project to condominiums.

The company's first effort in Delaware was colossal in scope: the Christina Gateway—which has been called the largest mixed-use development in Delaware's history. The $250-million urban-renewal project is testimony to the state's booming economy and its optimism in attracting new businesses and residents.

Christina Gateway is being devel-

The sleek new 14-story Three Christina Centre, headquarters to First USA Bank, is a sign of Delaware's booming economic growth. The building is the first phase of the Christina Gateway, a 12-acre financial/retail complex that is revitalizing Wilmington. Marine Midland Bank (Delaware) is occupying an adjacent office tower. The project is being developed by the Christina Gateway Joint Venture of The Linpro Company and Delle Donne & Associates.

Landfall, *an outdoor sculpture designed by Ned Smythe for Christina Gateway Park in Wilmington, is a new urban amenity that welcomes visitors outside the city's train station. The park echoes Wilmington's cultural heritage. Smythe is known for similar works in Pittsburgh and in Battery Park in New York City.*

oped over a seven-year period. When completed, the project will consist of 12 acres along the Christina River in the heart of Wilmington. Together with the Wilmington firm of Delle Donne & Associates, Linpro has been charged by the city with redeveloping the seven city blocks into an attractive and inviting conglomeration of offices—more than 1.2 million square feet of office space alone is planned—which will include a financial district, retail stores, restaurants, a hotel and conference center, parking garages, parks, and promenades. The project is designed to serve as a focal point of the city, as both a vibrant riverside marketplace and a sophisticated business environment. It will cater to Delaware residents within a 20-mile radius, as well as serve as a magnet for visitors and business-people.

The Christina Gateway project is being constructed in five phases. Phases I and II are office space. Phase III is the marketplace and hotel, while Phase IV and V will be additional offices. Phase I construction began in October 1986 and included the completion of Three Christina Centre and Gateway Park. Phase II consists of One Christina Centre, a 17-story office building. Lead tenants in these two buildings are First USA Bank and Marine Midland Bank. The office facilities will include a 1,400-car on-site covered garage and an on-site day-care center, as well as concierge services.

Phase III will be the two-story

Above right and below: TowerSide, a festive waterfront mixed-use complex, will delight all with upscale dining and shopping, and will give Wilmington an exciting new hotel and conference center.

riverfront marketplace spanning seven acres. Called TowerSide, it will anchor the gateway project by providing 100,000 square feet of upscale retail shopping, cafes, and restaurants. Festive, vibrant, and inviting in tone, TowerSide will also include a major 200-room hotel and conference center. The most visible element of TowerSide will be a 120-foot clock tower, an attractive addition to the Wilmington skyline.

Linpro was attracted to the Christina Gateway concept by a number of factors. These included Wilmington's natural amenities, such as its riverfront, its nearby historically significant buildings, and on-site Amtrak station, which receives approximately 750,000 riders each year. Christina Gateway also offers easy access to major highways and is located midway between New York and Washington, D.C. These factors, plus Delaware's rosy economy, convinced the firm that the Gateway project would be successful.

While Christina Gateway is, by far, the largest and most visible undertaking by Linpro in Delaware, the company has also made inroads with other projects. These include the development of Three Little Falls Centre in suburban Wilmington. This 80,000-square-foot, three-story office building, which overlooks the Hercules Country Club Golf Course, is Linpro's first suburban office project in Delaware. It opened in January 1988 and now serves as corporate headquarters for Himont, Inc., a Wilmington-based operation that holds the distinction of being the world's largest producer of polypropylene-related products. Himont is leasing the entire Three Little Falls Centre facility.

Linpro's first project in Wilmington's residential market is the Ashton condominium complex. Ground breaking for the project, located south of the city on 16 landscaped acres, took place in the fall of 1987.

Linpro's presence in Delaware is long term. As joint developer of the largest building project in the state, Linpro has become an active supporter of civic and charitable causes in and around Wilmington. These include the March of Dimes, the Leukemia Society, and Delmarva Boy Scouts.

Other recent Linpro Company developments are 1919 Market Street in Philadelphia, Hickory Pointe in Plymouth Meeting, Berwyn Park in Berwyn, and One Penn Square West in Philadelphia.

Gilpin, Van Trump and Montgomery, Inc.

Gilpin, Van Trump and Montgomery, Inc., is one of the most diversified and most experienced real estate companies in Delaware.

The privately held firm is most visible to consumers through its Residential Sales Division. Gilpin was a pioneer in the post-World War II development in New Castle County, and has been involved in many suburban development projects of substantial size.

Gilpin is also Delaware's oldest and largest full-service mortgage banker. It serves as loan correspondent for many of the world's largest lending institutions and, since 1950, has been a leading mortgage originator for Metropolitan Life Insurance Company.

Other involvements include commercial sales, residential property management, and many other areas of service to the community. Since 1981 Gilpin's Relocation Center has coordinated out-of-state referrals and third-party property sales, and provided personnel relocation services to corporate individuals and families on the move to Delaware, Maryland, and Pennsylvania.

The company's impact is also seen through its development of commercial and industrial properties. There Gilpin pools its real estate, marketing, financial, and development know-how often in joint ventures. As a developer and investor in downtown Wilmington, Gilpin has played a major role in the revival of the city. Urban projects include the purchase of eight city blocks in the heart of Wilmington and the development of the Radisson Hotel Wilmington, the Kirk Building, and First Federal Plaza. A Gilpin joint venture, Custom House Square Associates, received the nation's first Urban Development Action Grant (UDAG) for the Radisson Hotel Wilmington project.

Gilpin's current residential sales market includes New Castle County, Delaware; parts of Cecil County, Maryland; and Chester and Delaware counties, Pennsylvania. Future plans

include regional expansion into Kent County, Delaware. In addition to its Wilmington headquarters and relocation center, the company has six residential sales offices and a mortgage banking office. More than 200 employees and sales associates work for Gilpin.

The firm's roots date back to 1865, when Edwin Van Trump formed an insurance agency in

Pictured are, from left: Ferdinand L. Gilpin, Edwin A. Van Trump, and John A. Montgomery.

The Gilpin Realtors' sign is a familiar sight in Delaware and surrounding areas in Maryland and Pennsylvania.

Wilmington. Six years later the insurance agency of Ferdinand Gilpin was organized. The successful Van Trump and Gilpin agencies merged with John A. Montgomery in 1904 to form Gilpin, Van Trump and Montgomery, Inc. Expansion has been steady since 1941, when Gilpin redirected its attention from insurance to begin specializing in real estate brokerage, mortgage banking, and development.

Gilpin's managers and other employees serve in key leadership positions in civic, cultural, and professional organizations. These include the Wilmington Economic Development Corporation, the YMCA, the Leukemia Society, Leadership Delaware, the Brandywine Arts Festival, the Greater Wilmington Convention and Visitors' Bureau, the chamber of commerce, the Grand Opera House, and many other community-based organizations.

Wyman Electric Service Company

The behind-the-scenes electrical work for many of the state's major buildings has been handled by the Wyman Electric Service Company, one of the largest electrical contractors and the largest merit shop in Delaware.

Wyman, headquartered in Elsmere, has become a recognized leader in commercial and industrial electrical construction, engineering, design, and estimating. With close to 100 clients throughout Delaware and in nearby Maryland and Pennsylvania, Wyman serves as general contractor in about half of its projects; in the rest, it is a subcontractor for large construction companies. Annual sales are approximately $10 million.

Recent projects have included the two-year-long major renovation of the electrical system at the University of Delaware's Morris Library, where Wyman also prepared the building for a new computer network, and supervising the electrical work for the new Christina Gateway marketplace. In addition, the firm has completed work for numerous public buildings.

James R. Gordon, president and chief executive officer of Wyman Electric, stands before two of the firm's most recent projects.

The privately owned family business has also become a leader in computerization. About 10 years ago Wyman became completely computerized, and this service has benefited customers through faster, more efficient cost projections, accounting, and project analysis. Daily reports provide updates on the status of each project. However, the firm's expertise in computers extends beyond its own offices: Clients now call on Wyman to handle hookups as they pertain to electrical systems.

Wyman was founded in 1968 and incorporated a year later by James R. Gordon, Sr., its president. During the next two years Gordon, a master electrician, hired Bill Greenplate, who now serves as chief field engineer, and Jim Brooks, the chief operations officer. John De Matteis, chief estimator, joined later.

The principles of quality workmanship and customer satisfaction have always guided the company. It is also known for the stability of

Mr. and Mrs. Jim Gordon overlook the skyline of Wilmington, which Wyman Electric helped to create.

its work force, with approximately half of its 110 employees on the payroll for at least 15 years. And Wyman emphasizes a safe, healthy, and pleasant working environment. For example, all employees are required to participate in company-sponsored safety and CPR courses (at least one worker on each project is familiar with CPR), and employees have access to a company-sponsored counselor for help with such issues as alcohol abuse or family problems.

Wyman actively recruits young people to the trade and promotes professionalism. Eight graduates from local vocational technical schools are chosen for apprenticeships each year, and five are eventually hired. The firm also offers weekly professional development classes to employees, and pays for their enrollment in courses offered by the Delaware Contractor Association.

Wyman Electric Service Company is active in the Delaware Contractors Association (Gordon has served as president of its merit shop division), Associated Builders and Contractors, and the Electrical Contractors Association of Delaware.

Wohlsen Construction Company

"It took Wohlsen 90 years to discover Delaware. Fortunately, it hasn't taken Delaware quite that long to discover Wohlsen."

Tom Wohlsen smiles broadly as he makes his point. He and his brother Bob represent the fourth generation of the family-owned and -operated firm bearing their name. Wohlsen Construction Company traces its origins back to 1890, when it was founded by an immigrant German carpenter who had settled in Lancaster, Pennsylvania.

However, it wasn't until the early 1980s that Wohlsen began building in Delaware. Since then, the firm has served as general contractor for a broad spectrum of Delaware projects. "We're making up for lost time," says Tom Wohlsen.

The more notable projects include the new Delaware Theater Company building, the 10-story American Life Insurance Company office building and three-story parking garage at Seventh and King in Wilmington, and the Avenue of the Arts Associates building, the first restoration in the Christina Gateway. Wohlsen also served as both general contractor and construction manager for ICI Americas' corporate headquarters expansion, which encompasses new offices, laboratories, and parking facilities.

Tom Wohlsen also points with pride to the new cafeteria at the Du Pont Company's Experimental Station, the Kamin retirement home in Ardentown, and numerous other industrial and commercial buildings. "I know they're not physically in Delaware," he says, "but I just can't omit the Brandywine River Museum addition and the Terrace Restaurant and Lily Ponds in Longwood Gardens."

Wohlsen's Delaware operation was established in late 1982, when it completed the concrete and interior work on The Du Pont Company's new Life Sciences Building. The following year Wohlsen opened its Wil-

mington Division office at Bancroft Mills. As business has grown, the company has moved to larger and larger quarters. After a few years in Centerville, the Wilmington Division expanded into Boulden Interstate Park—a Rouse Associate project built by Wohlsen in New Castle.

Since 1983 Wohlsen has served as general contractor and/or construction manager for at least five major Delaware projects each year. The First State has accounted for half of the company's sales volume.

According to Tom Wohlsen, the Delaware staff has doubled since 1983 and is expected to double again during the early 1990s. Today the local staff of 40 is supervised by five project managers. The firm's future lies in "industrial and commercial construction and planned expansion into the field of industrial maintenance."

Wohlsen's phenomenal growth in Delaware mirrors the company's success in Lancaster County, where it is the leading general contractor, and throughout the mid-Atlantic region, where it is the largest merit shop contractor. The corporation reports annual contracts in excess of $50 million; 1990 marks the third year of a three-year plan to increase sales to 50 percent. This would move Wohlsen up to the 250th-largest construction company in the country.

Wohlsen recently doubled the size of its Lancaster home office and has opened a branch office to serve the suburban Pennsylvania counties of Bucks, Montgomery, Delaware, and Chester.

"We've made a substantial commitment to our future," says Tom Wohlsen. He cites heavy investment in computerization and the creation of a nucleus of 10 key management staffers (Project 100) to creatively channel the organization's growth into the 1990s. The growth plan includes systematic, comprehensive training for the company's 200 employees in such areas as technical skills, computers, and communication. Wohlsen established an employee assistance program that includes one of the

Wohlsen began this Wilmington project with a 500-car parking garage featuring poured-in-place concrete columns and floor decks. Next, Wohlsen erected the 10-story ALICO building above the garage using matching architectural precast concrete.

most progressive substance abuse policies in the industry.

Wohlsen's work force is unusually stable for a company of its type, and 25-year anniversaries are not uncommon. Wohlsen is committed to keeping its employees

Above: Andrew Wyeth's paintings deserved a distinctive showplace. Instead of being stored in the artist's old mill, they now reside in the Wohlsen-built wing of the Brandywine River Museum. A special roof filters the light so none falls directly upon the masterpieces.

Below: Three Mill Road is a magnificent visual drama in glass and steel jutting out over the Brandywine River. Wohlsen's challenge was to build up and out from a small base between the river and a steep slope.

working, and layoffs are rare. In fact, the work force has not gone below 130 during the past five years.

The firm's visionary approach is grounded in a solid tradition of quality, practicality, and pride of workmanship. It is a tradition that has endured through four generations, and the Wohlsen family is diligent about remembering its roots.

It all began in 1876, when Herman Wohlsen came to the United States and settled in Lancaster. He specialized at first in small buildings for farms, stables, and homes, then began to build many of the city's famed row houses. It wasn't long before Wohlsen gained a reputation for sound, quality construction, and in 1890 he formed Wohlsen Construction Company. Over the years Wohlsen and his family erected some of the area's most memorable architectural landmarks, including the original Woolworth building, the original Hotel Brunswick, the Hager department store, and the YMCA.

The firm's portfolio is diverse: office complexes, industrial facilities, schools and colleges, plant additions, stores, churches, banks, homes, and historical renovations—in short, projects of every size, shape, construction material, and technique.

Wohlsen's expertise today lies in both general construction, design/construct, and construction management. In the latter case Wohlsen works closely with the owner in developing budgets, scheduling, and overall planning—often before the architect is hired. About 80 percent

of the company's work is now in the dynamic commercial and industrial arena. Wohlsen also performs concrete work, mill work, and carpentry at its projects and subcontracts the other trades.

Wohlsen Construction Company has evolved from a small business owned by an industrious German immigrant into an innovative, multimillion-dollar fully integrated corporation with a strong reputation for attention to detail, integrity, and economy gleaned from a century of experience. It has become a successful blend of tradition and technology.

Today the firm is headed by

When the Delaware Theater Company decided to build its new theater using the existing foundations of a razed building along the Christina River, it created an unusual challenge that Wohlsen met in time for the first play of the new season.

Robert S. Wohlsen, Sr., president and chief executive officer (and the grandson of the founder); Robert S. Wohlsen, Jr., vice-president/construction operations; J. Gary Langmuir, vice-president/finance and administration; and Thomas H. Wohlsen, assistant to the president and vice-president/marketing.

The Healy Group, Inc.

From the concrete foundations of Delaware's most prominent buildings to the intricate gingerbread window casement carvings in historic renovations to the full-scale design and construction management of major industrial properties, The Healy Group, Inc., offers its clients an impressive magnitude of expertise and experience.

Since 1891 four generations of this solid, family-owned and operated company have been in the forefront of Delaware's development and have helped shape the skyline of Wilmington. While the firm has completed literally hundreds of projects totaling millions of dollars, it is perhaps best known for its construction of large-scale industrial and commercial complexes, office buildings, and historic renovations.

Healy-built buildings are familiar sights throughout the area. They include Christiana Mall, Penn Plaza at New Castle Corporate Commons, Chase Manhattan's new office building, the restoration and renovation of Wilmington's Grand Opera House, restoration of Immanuel Church-on-the-Green in New Castle, the Du Pont Company's Life Sciences Buildings; Beebe Hospital, Christiana Hospital, Wilmington's city/county and state office complexes, Citibank Delaware's operations campus, the University of Delaware's field house, the Wilmington campus of Delaware Technical and Community College, the Brandywine Hilton and Sheraton, and the *Wilmington News-Journal*'s new office, printing, and distribution facility.

Healy was founded as a small residential construction firm in 1891 by Irish immigrant and carpenter John E. Healy, Sr. Active in public life,

Above: The Healy family, from left: Michael J. Healy, John E. Healy II, James V. Healy, and William K. Healy.

Left: Two Penn's Plaza, a Healy project designed by Design Collaborative, Inc., features a redbrick and glass exterior. Located in the New Castle Corporate Commons, a 128-acre site just north of the Greater Wilmington Airport, the building features 100,000 square feet of space.

Healy served in the state house of representatives and on the Wilmington City Council for many years, and was a major force in local Irish-American affairs.

From its downtown Tatnall Street headquarters, the company quickly developed a reputation for quality, dependability, and flexibility. Healy's initial focus was on schools and churches, and a major client was the Catholic Diocese of Wilmington. Early projects included the original St. Francis Hospital, St. Paul's and St. Hedwig's churches, St. Thomas Rectory and Convent, and Claymont Elementary and High School.

In 1915 the firm was incorporated under the name of John E. Healy & Sons. Since then it has been successfully managed by Healy's sons, grandsons, and great-grandsons.

The company is presently organizing into two operating subsidiaries: John E. Healy & Sons and Healy Management Services. John E. Healy & Sons is the construction subsidiary, handling all general contracting field work and specializing in concrete and carpentry. The concrete work began in 1904, and today Healy's reputation in this area is so strong that its competitors often call on it to handle the structural concrete of their projects.

Finish carpentry is another John E. Healy & Sons specialty. Company craftsmen have garnered a reputation for outstanding workmanship and attention to detail equal to that of an earlier era. This workmanship can be seen at historic restorations of the Old State House in Dover and Wilmington's Grand Opera House. Healy's carpentry expertise is also evident in such contemporary buildings as the Hercules Atrium in downtown Wilmington.

Healy Management Services was formed in 1984 to specialize in general construction and construction management. This includes predesign consulting and planning, scheduling, contract preparation, labor relations, and management of every phase of construction to bring each project in on time and within budget.

Both John E. Healy & Sons and Healy Management Services are linked under a parent corporation, The Healy Group, Inc. The latter was formed in May 1988.

The founder's sons, Thomas J. Healy and John E. Healy, Jr., have passed the business on to Tom's sons: James V. Healy is president of

The Healy Group, and John E. Healy II is its chairman and chief executive officer. Great-grandsons involved with the business are Michael J. Healy, president of Healy Management Services, and William K. Healy, president of John E. Healy & Sons.

Today Healy ranks as one of the largest construction firms in Delaware, with an annual sales volume in excess of $30 million. Repeat business from satisfied customers accounts for a large percentage of its volume.

Healy's strongest geographic market is Delaware, but the company has also established a presence throughout the mid-Atlantic region. Now headquartered in New Castle, Healy employs an administrative staff of 35 people, and a field work force that can number 500, depending upon work load. From five to 15 projects are under way at any given time. The work force is stable— many employees have been with Healy for 20 to 30 years.

One of the cornerstones of the corporation's business philosophy is a strong commitment to the future of the industry. In its efforts to upgrade the profession, the Healy family has been involved with local and nation-

Above: Built by the Healy Group, the Chase Manhattan Bank building features an impressive 445,000 square feet over 17 stories and has a 500-car parking garage. Dominating the Wilmington skyline, the building houses the bank's credit card operations center.

Left: John E. Healy and Sons played a major part in the complete restoration of Wilmington's Grand Opera House. Within one year the classic structure was restored to its century-old grandeur, inside and out.

al organizations such as the Associated General Contractors of America (AGC), which represents 40,000 contractors nationwide. John E. Healy II has served as the organization's national president, and other Healy managers are involved in AGC leadership positions. William K. Healy presently serves as national chairman of the manpower and training committees and often travels throughout the country to speak before schools and other groups, focusing on the need to train tomorrow's construction professionals.

Professionalism is a key Healy concept. Rather than serving in a limited role, the firm prefers a more visionary approach in its projects. More often than not, the company is involved from the beginning and works closely with the owners, architects, and financial planners to help convert specifications into a living, functioning building.

Emory Hill Development, Inc.

Emory Hill Development, Inc., has more than 70 major real estate projects in four states, totaling 6 million square feet of developed commercial real estate. The figures are projected to double before the mid-1990s, and all of this has been accomplished since 1983.

The above demonstrates what Emory Hill Development, Inc., is, not what it is about. The company is about such things as a commitment to quality and value, long-term ownership of projects, and innovative design and construction. It is about the ability, and, perhaps more important, the willingness to work on creative solutions to complex and intricate building or design problems utilizing a thorough knowledge of market trends. This willingness demonstrates the integrity required to create projects to fill the needs of the marketplace and also gives the impetus to provide excellent tenant services.

New additions to Emory Hill Development's large and diverse portfolio of properties in Delaware include Centerpoint Business Complex, an 85-acre business park in New Castle that will eventually have more than

850,000 square feet of space; Enterprise Business Park, a 100-acre site in Dover, Delaware; and 10 Corporate Circle, a three-story, 40,000-square-foot, class-A office building in New Castle Corporate Commons.

In Maryland, Emory Hill has recently completed 7250 Parkway Drive, a four-story, 80,000-square-foot office building; in New Jersey, the firm is developing Highland Business Park in Burlington County; and Westpark Business Center is Emory Hill's first development in Pennsylvania's Lehigh Valley.

Other properties in the four-state operating area range from build-to-suit projects to award-winning office buildings, research and development facilities, manufacturing and warehouse/distribution centers, banking operation units, office condominiums, and shopping centers, in addition to an apartment complex. The average project cost is $7 million.

It was these successful property management efforts that were instru-

Emory Hill's four general partners are (from left) J. Richard Latini, R. Clayton Emory, Robert H. Hill, and Carmen J. Facciolo, Jr.

mental in the Aqualon Group signing a lease to establish its world headquarters at One Little Falls Centre, a 99,000-square-foot, four-story corporate office building west of Wilmington; two 120,000-square-foot leases in the Interchange Industrial Park to The Du Pont Company and Morgan Products; and a 57,500-square-foot lease to Collated Products in the Pencader Corporate Center in Newark, Delaware.

Yet another facet of Emory Hill's successes can be attributed to the commitment to nurture long-term relationships with its clients. The firm's corporate policy of personal service is not merely lip service. One or more of the four senior partners is directly involved in every project, thus allowing easy and direct access to a decision maker at all times.

On another positive note, the senior partners, as well as the nine associate partners, are all part-owners of Emory Hill projects. This ensures a personal stake in the success of each project, in addition to providing a dynamic blend of development, construction, property management, and leasing expertise.

Along with this build-to-own policy, Emory Hill's success also stems from the integration of its services—from financing and site development to building design and construction to marketing, leasing property management, and maintenance. This teamwork approach allows the company to operate as a

closely knit unit, resulting in efficient utilization of manpower, and personal assurance of on-time, within-budget delivery for its clients.

The firm also serves as the general contractor or construction manager on its projects. On-site construction management means greater flexibility in meeting clients' specifications and deadlines, and offers timely solutions should

Top: The Courtyards at Pencader, a new concept in suburban office space, is an excellent example of Emory Hill's ability to develop projects that meet the needs of a changing commercial real estate marketplace.

Center: One of Emory Hill's recent developments is this warehouse/distribution building at Interchange Business Park in Newark, Delaware. Emory Hill is a full-service developer with construction, leasing, and asset/property management service.

Below: Centerpoint Business Complex in New Castle, Delaware, is one of Emory Hill's newest developments. The company has active projects in Maryland, New Jersey, and Pennsylvania in addition to Delaware.

problems arise. In addition, the company bids and negotiates as a general contractor for outside firms.

While Emory Hill's excellent construction practices assure quality projects and its leasing staff places the tenant, it is the property management and maintenance staffs that oversee the services that keep Emory Hill's tenant-loss ratio amount the lowest in the region. The firm currently has more than 300 tenants—from *Fortune* 500 companies to small, locally owned businesses—and provides asset-management services to many other building owners.

While it is easy to say Emory Hill believes in these philosophies, qualities, and ideals, it is another matter to substantiate it. And substantiate it the firm does, with numbers such as an average of 1.5 million square feet leased each year, one-third of it to existing tenants.

Statistics such as these have made Emory Hill one of the fastest growing, most successful real estate development companies in the mid-Atlantic region, with active projects and full-service offices in Delaware, Maryland, New Jersey, and Pennsylvania.

These projects may involve start- to-finish development of a large corporate operations center within six months or solving complex security problems of a small, high-tech research firm. Whatever the scope of work, Emory Hill responds quickly and intelligently to the special needs of its clients. It is these fresh ideas, innovative solutions, and versatility to tailor each project to meet the particular demands of the individual client that make up the cornerstone of the firm's philosophy.

The same approach applies to the commitment to maintaining long-term ownership of properties. Since 1983 Emory Hill Development, Inc., has planned, designed, built, and maintained ownership of more than 6 million square feet of commercial and industrial real estate, with another 3 million square feet in the planning stages.

Stoltz Bros., Ltd.

Superlatives such as "best," "first," and "top" are no exaggeration when describing Stoltz Bros., Ltd., and affiliate Stoltz Realty Company.

The family-owned and -operated holding company, through its Stoltz Realty Company affiliate, is Delaware's number-one commercial real estate broker and one of the largest diversified real estate organizations in the mid-Atlantic area. It is also the first commercial brokerage firm in the state to exceed $850 million in commercial sales, leasing, and financing production in a calendar year.

Through its affiliated companies, Stoltz Bros. handles commercial, industrial, and residential brokerage; property management; mortgage banking; investment syndication; and the development, construction, and ownership of income-producing properties. The company's market extends beyond Delaware into Pennsylvania, Maryland, New Jersey, and southeast Florida. Its clientele is scattered throughout the globe, including Europe and Japan.

A list of Stoltz Realty Company's sales is impressive. The firm has sold many, if not most, of the apartment complexes, major office buildings, and shopping centers in its trading area. In the 1960s Stoltz Realty Company sold Delaware's then-largest shopping center and, more recently, the largest office building in Wilmington, the 586,000-square-foot Delaware Trust Building.

Stoltz Bros.' current prosperity is a sharp contrast to its modest beginning in the mid-1950s. Today's diversified real estate holding company started with Stoltz Realty Company, founded by A. Archie Stoltz and his wife, Evelyn. Archie established a small real estate business from rented desk space in the Delaware Trust Building (a structure that was later sold and managed by Stoltz). Evelyn served as bookkeeper and secretary, and Archie was the president, salesman, and sole means of support for the company. This husband-and-wife team prospered

and soon moved to larger quarters on North Market Street, in a converted row house. At this point Evelyn and Archie's son, Jack, joined the business, at first as a residential salesman, and later as his father's right-hand man.

The turning point for the organization came in 1966, when Archie Stoltz negotiated the sale of the 500,000-square-foot Merchandise Mart, then the state's largest shopping center, together with the sale of the adjoining 1,200-unit Clifton Park apartment complex. Unfortunately, prior to the transaction being consummated, Archie passed away at the age of 53. At this point his son, Jack, only 26 years old, had to take over the reins of the family business and close on his own the Merchandise Mart/Clifton Park transaction.

With Evelyn in the background handling office affairs and providing encouragement, Jack not only closed that transaction, but made the decision to have Stoltz Realty Company concentrate and specialize in commercial and industrial sales and leasing. Jack's decision to specialize in commercial and industrial real estate proved fortuitous, and soon the firm moved to its current headquarters at 1600 Pennsylvania Avenue.

In 1978 Jack was joined by his brother, Skip, in the business. Skip had graduated from Dickinson School of Law and joined the Delaware firm of Morris, James, Hitchens & Williams. After three years with the Delaware law firm, Skip decided to expand his real estate background by becoming a vice-president and general counsel for a Florida public development company. With the combination of Jack's background in commercial real estate and marketing and Skip's

Rockwood Office Park is a 210,000-square-foot suburban office complex located in North Wilmington. The project is a joint venture with the major tenant, American Life Insurance Company.

in law development and construction, Stoltz Realty Company grew tenfold in the next 10 years, and the property management, development, and ownership of income-producing properties expanded dramatically.

In 1987 Skip and Jack formed Stoltz Bros., Ltd., as the holding company for Stoltz Realty Company and their other affiliated organizations. Jack serves as president and chief executive officer in charge of brokerage and marketing activities, while Skip, chairman and chief operating officer, is in charge of the investment, development, and property management aspects of the holding company.

Following the family tradition, another key family member is Keith, Jack's son, who serves as Stoltz Bros.' executive vice-president. He is responsible for financing Arbern Investment Co.'s portfolio. In addition, he is president and founder of Stoltz Mortgage Co. In August 1988 Jack's other son, Randy, another Dickinson School of Law graduate, and Morris, James alumnus, joined the firm as its in-house counsel.

The business is headquartered at 1600 Pennsylvania Avenue in Wilmington for its northern operations and at 301 Yamato Road, Boca Raton. It employs more than 250 associates, and the business has expanded so that Stoltz Bros. has become a holding company for several distinct businesses:

—Stoltz Realty/Stoltz Management Company. Over the past few years Stoltz Realty's brokerage sales have exceeded one billion dollars, and it has served as exclusive leasing agent for more than 3 million square feet of commercial real estate. This arm of the business is also the exclusive property manager for better than 2.5 million square feet of commercial properties and more than 3,000 apartment units. Its commercial leasing activity totals in excess of 3 million square feet. These transactions have involved major national and local clients.

—Stoltz Mortgage Company. Founded in 1986 by Keith Stoltz through this affiliate, the firm has placed loans in excess of $700 million with national lenders. Loans secured ranged from $2 million to more than $300 million, on properties in 10 states.

—Arbern Investment Company. Through Arbern and its affiliate, Stoltz Bros. owns or has converted to condominiums more than 3,500 apartment units. It also owns 2 million square feet of office space. In 1987 Arbern established a Southeast headquarters in Boca Raton, where it currently owns two major office buildings, 184 apartments, a 120-unit

Boca Bank Corporate Center is located in Boca Raton, Florida. The six-story, 130,000-square-foot building is owned by Arbern Investment Company, an affiliate of Stoltz Brothers, Inc.

town-house complex, and is soon to be breaking ground on a new 334-unit apartment development.

Among the Delaware projects, Arbern owns Rockwood Office Park, Brandywine Gateway Plaza, Presidential Towers, Riverview Gardens, Thomas West House, Arbor Pointe, the Plaza, 600 Market Street, and 504 Market Street. New projects will include a 380,000-square-foot office park in the Pike Creek Valley and a 300-unit garden apartment complex.

Stoltz has developed a reputation for taking under-utilized and under-managed buildings and properties and turning them around through strong management/leasing and renovation. For example, the

238-unit Plaza was acquired by Stoltz in 1983 when it was an FHA-subsidized project. Stoltz invested more than $1.5 million in renovation, and today the Plaza is considered Wilmington's premier rental luxury high-rise apartment building.

The experience gleaned in Dela-

Left: Delaware Trust Building, located in center city Wilmington, is leased and managed by Stoltz Realty Company. The 586,000-square-foot, 22-story building is the largest multitenant building in Wilmington.

Below: Arbor Pointe Apartments, owned and developed by Arbern Investment Company and Charles Evans Company, consists of 264 residential apartments.

ware with the Plaza was successfully employed in Philadelphia, where Stoltz owns, with Philadelphia partner Rittenhouse Management, more than 500 luxury apartments in the Rittenhouse Square area. These vintage buildings were totally renovated and are today considered some of Philadelphia's most luxurious.

The company has evolved in just 30 years from a small, family-owned real estate brokerage into today's giant enterprise with a reputation that extends far beyond Delaware. Stoltz Bros., Ltd., is known not only for its savvy in commercial real estate and development, but also for the service, experience, and knowledge it provides its many clients.

Boca Bank Corporate Centre

James Julian, Inc.

It would be difficult to drive anywhere within 100 miles north, south, or west of Wilmington and not travel on a road built by James Julian, Inc.

The Elsmere-based general contractor, which celebrated its 50th year in 1989, is a diversified company that has helped Delaware become the economic force it is today. JJI has been a predominant force in shaping the state's infrastructure. Although construction and rehabilitation of highways and roads are the mainstay of JJI's business, accounting for 80 percent of its volume, the company has also played a role in building and expanding sewage plants, airport facilities, and waterways. With annual sales in excess of $50 million, the firm is one of the largest general contractors in Delaware and has maintained a strong, vigorous presence throughout the mid-Atlantic area. JJI is among the 400 largest general contractors in America.

Although incorporated in 1953, the business has roots that go back almost three-quarters of a century. It was started by James Julian, an Italian immigrant who came to America in 1923 at the age of 15. In 1939, with a core of co-workers, he started the James Julian Company. That same year his operation won the first of three contracts—and began earning its reputation for integrity, innovation, and expertise in superior concrete paving and for community service. Today James Julian remains active with the company, but has transferred major responsibilities to Joseph R. Julian, who, after 30 years of overseeing operations with his father and brother, Frank, now serves as president.

A well-designed and expertly built infrastructure is essential to any economy's health: Quality transportation is vital in the efficient distribution of products and services.

JJI's specialty—highway contracting—is also its most visible and widely utilized contribution to the state's economy. From blazing new, more direct paths from one geographic point to another to rehabilitating or widening existing routes, JJI has placed more than one million square yards of concrete, plus approximately 500,000 tons of blacktop, in Delaware alone.

JJI's portfolio of highway and road projects includes the interstates I-495 and I-95. The company was the contractor on a great deal of I-495. JJI also handled the original clearing, earthwork, and grading on I-95 from Maryland to Route 72. Another original portion of I-95, from the Brandywine River to south of Chester, Pennsylvania, was largely constructed, from clearing to paving, by JJI. Since the original four-lane highway was built, JJI has also widened it to six, then eight, lanes in separate sections of the 25-mile road.

In Kent and Sussex counties, where agriculture and tourism reign, JJI has also made an impact. Roads essential for transporting everything from farm crops to beach goers have been built by JJI. These include U.S. 13, U.S. 113, Delaware

Above: The founder of James Julian, Inc., with the core of first-generation JJI staff. From the left are Sam Showell, Gus Griesbach, James Julian, Guy Marcozzi, Arch Hellen, and Gene Julian (the founder's brother).

Below: I-495, shown girding the city of Wilmington, is an example of JJI's expertise in concrete roads, ramps, and bridges.

Route 1, and the Seaford Bypass.

The construction of more than 200 bridges, in Delaware, Maryland, Pennsylvania, and Virginia, is credited to JJI. The Tyler McConnell Bridge, which spans the Brandywine River by the historic Hagley Museum, is a highlight. Built by JJI in 1954, the bridge is memorable because it presented challenges of both craft and speed. Since parts of the bridge are directly over the museum, it was essential to avoid a mistake, which could have destroyed 200 years of history. Completing the

work without mishap was testimony to JJI's competence, as well as its commitment to Delaware's community. When the bridge was redecked in 1982, the challenge of precision was again met, as well as another challenge: finish the project in six months or pay a $3,500-per-day fine. Again JJI surpassed all expectations, completing its work two months ahead of schedule.

JJI also constructed the Delaware Memorial Bridge's eight- to 16-lane, two-mile approaches (I-295) on the Delaware side, and was involved with building the nearby Christiana Interchange. This complex maze of

bridges and highways, incorporating the merger of I-95, I-495, and I-295, annually accommodates the 22.5 million vehicles that pass over the Delaware Memorial Bridge, as well as traffic en route to and from Wilmington and Philadelphia.

In addition to roads and bridges, water transportation is essential to economic growth. For the past 30 years JJI has had a working relationship with the U.S. Corps of Engineers, the agency responsible for keeping the nation's waterways navigable. In 1963 JJI completed a contract to maintain and widen a portion of the C&D Canal to accommodate the large ships destined for Wilmington, Philadelphia, and

Baltimore. During the past 15 years, in addition to work on other scattered waterways, JJI has also helped the corps maintain the dikes at the Port of Wilmington.

Still another transportation element is airport construction. JJI built the primary parking aprons for the massive Galaxy C-5A transport planes at the Dover Air Force Base, as well as the 10,000-foot-long main runway at Pittsburgh Airport.

During its half-century of service JJI has chalked up a number of firsts. Among these is the company's use of new waste-treatment techniques in sewage systems and

plants. One such method was employed in the Wilmington Interceptor System, a facility constructed in the early 1950s that prepared New Castle County for the growth explosion it has experienced over the past 25 years. Without this system, many contend the county would be unable to manage its present level of economic growth.

In its highway projects in particular, JJI has been an innovator, primarily in the use of emerging technologies. For example, JJI was the first Delaware contractor to use a portable high-yield concrete plant and a portable drum-mix plant for blacktop. JJI was also the first contractor to utilize the modern concrete slipform method in Delaware. Innovations such as these, which ultimately reduced costs for taxpayers, helped JJI become a leader in paving. Among JJI's myriad paving successes is national recognition earned in 1969 for paving one mile of concrete in one 10-hour day.

Left: James Julian, with back to camera, surveys an asphalt rehabilitation project in rural Delaware.

Below: This technologically advanced waste-water-treatment plant for the town of Delmar is an illustration of JJI's diversity.

Above: Among JJI's newest projects is Route 7, which transfers virgin ground to highway—linking I-95 to U.S. 13.

Below right: The Tyler McConnell Bridge safely carries motorists across the beautiful Brandywine River, a testament to JJI's efficiency and safety.

JJI has also served as a training ground of sorts for employees and associates who later established their own businesses. Among the JJI-associated companies are Tire Sales and Service, Eastern Shore Pipe, NEHMCO, the Mispillion Marina, Mardel Trucking, and Maryland Materials. These organizations, together with JJI, employ more than 1,200 people. JJI's family spirit manifests itself in the fact that JJI has numerous second-generation families among its work force, as well as some third-generation employees.

JJI has forged strong ties with the community. Company executives are active in a multitude of professional, community, and charitable organizations. James Julian has contributed equipment, labor, money, and time to Catholic Charities in the Wilmington Diocese. As a company, JJI has participated in many diverse charities, from the Mary Campbell Center and the East Side Boys' Club to the YWCA's Womanpower and the Delaware Safety Council.

With regard to professional ties,

James Julian serves on the Delaware River and Bay Authority Commission. He was also a national director of the Association of General Contractors, as well as president of AGC's state chapter. Both he and president Joseph Julian have served as trustees of the Wilmington Savings Fund Society. Joseph Julian continues to be involved with a number of professional groups, including the Delaware Utility Transportation Contractors' Association. He is also a national director of the American Road and Transportation Association.

With an emphasis on quality, innovation, integrity, and community, JJI has played an intrinsic role in building Delaware's infrastructure. Safe and efficient highways, bridges, airports, waterways, and sewage plants affect the state's ability to accommodate new residents, new busi-

nesses, and, subsequently, new traffic. Building on the foresight and principles of its founder, James Julian, Inc., with a new generational view and enthusiasm, looks forward to the challenges of the next 50 years. The end result: a stable infrastructure and prosperous economy now and for the future.

• • • • •

JJI was involved with the construction of the following roads and other projects in Delaware. In many instances, the company was responsible for building the entire project.

Limestone Road
Concord Pike
Stein Highway
Delaware Route 1
Elkton Road
Little Creek Bridge
Rehoboth Bypass
Third Street Bridge Substructure
Court Street Bridge
Petersburg
Delaware 404
Marsh Road
Shipley Road
Milford Bypass
New Castle Avenue
Churchman's Road
I-95 service area
Paper Mill Road
Kent County Treatment Plant
Roads and sewers in such communities as Hockessin, Selbyville, Milford, Fairfax, and Green Acres

Amato & Stella Associates

Although it is a relatively young company, Amato & Stella has, in less than two decades, positioned itself near the top of Delaware's commercial real estate ladder. Growth has been both consistent and phenomenal—about 50 percent per year for the past five years.

The company was established in 1975 by Italian immigrant Renato Stella and Joseph Amato, Sr. Today the family-owned business specializes in commercial real estate brokerage, counseling, leasing, and property management in Delaware, Pennsylvania, and southern New Jersey. Ninety-eight percent of Amato & Stella's work is commercial and industrial: office buildings, warehouses, shopping centers, and malls. Clients are local, out-of-state, and international, and range from *Fortune* 500 companies to small retail businesses.

Amato & Stella also provides equity partners for joint ventures on existing properties or proposed developments. Investment counseling is also available to clients as a separate service. Other services offered by the firm include sale, exchange or lease negotiations, investment property analysis, property management analysis, income and expense proformas, and cash-flow projections.

Amato & Stella's primary strength is its staff of 14 professionals. It has deliberately remained small to ensure personal attention and service to clients. The staff is headed by four partners: Renato Stella, Joseph Amato, Sr., Robert Stella, and Anthony Stella. At least one partner is involved in all major transactions. All four are experts in different aspects of real estate, from land development to leasing. Together they have a total of 50 years of professional experience.

The company's portfolio of expertise has been expanding in recent years. Most recently Amato & Stella Associates has been instrumental in commercial and residential land acquisition and development for its clients. Among the New Castle County residential subdivisions brought about by Amato & Stella are Sanford Ridge, Winding Bridge, Fox Hollow, and Kimberly Chase.

While the company is expanding its services and broadening its base to handle all facets of real estate, it has also been growing geographically. Most of its Delaware work has been focused in New Castle County, but Amato & Stella plans to move into the southern two counties in the near future.

Amato & Stella's headquarters has been at 1508 Pennsylvania Avenue in Wilmington since 1982. Its full-scale renovation of this building earned it a Cityside Award.

The company's innovative spirit has gone hand in hand with environmental and civic responsibility. Amato & Stella has a history of success with its clients' development plans, in part because it works closely with government planners and civic groups to ensure responsive growth.

Officers and staff of Amato & Stella participate in such organizations as the Industrial Development Research Council, the Delaware State Chamber of Commerce Business and Economic Development Committee, and the Committee of 100.

Amato & Stella Associates' renovation of its own headquarters at 1508 Pennsylvania Avenue in Wilmington earned the company a Cityside Award.

Snyder, Crompton & Associates

Snyder, Crompton & Associates is a custom residential and commercial contractor with a strong emphasis on quality workmanship, attention to detail, and an excellent track record of completing all of its projects on time and under budget.

Although its specialty is now in office and commercial construction, the Wilmington firm's heritage lies in the building of large, custom residential homes. Its president, C. David Murtagh, provides an impressive background—almost 30 years of architectural and construction experience. Today residential work is just a small part of the company's business—it builds only one or two custom homes each year in suburban Wilmington.

Snyder, Crompton & Associates is perhaps most widely known for its development, design, and construction of the Concord Plaza office complex located a few miles north of the city of Wilmington. Concord Plaza was the first project of its kind in suburban Wilmington and one of the first of its kind on the entire East Coast. Built in the mid-1970s, the $13-million project has become the prototype for numerous other suburban office complexes. Many builders have emulated its design and construction.

Concord Plaza sits on a 20-acre site on Silverside Road and could very well be a college campus. It blends in well with the landscaping, and its design and appearance are entirely functional. The project consists of 22 two-story buildings, arranged so that parking facilities surround each structure. Offices are provided for approximately 95 tenants, from large corporations to small businesses. They include The Du Pont Company and ICI Americas. Concord Plaza's primary design features are its T-shape buildings that are specifically tailored for multiple occupants. For example, all offices at Concord Plaza have access to windows. The buildings are energy efficient and economical to operate.

Du Pont Company's Medical Products Department at Barley Mill Plaza.

Snyder, Crompton & Associates has a varied history. The company was originally named George F. Snyder, Builder, Inc., and was formed in 1954 by George F. Snyder. In 1964 C. David Murtagh joined Snyder as designer and estimator, and two years later Murtagh became a full partner. The two originally built custom homes, but soon recognized the need for a more broad-based approach. While custom residential work remained an integral part of the business, Snyder and Murtagh soon expanded into the commercial and design markets.

In 1973 a merger took place with Pierce K. Crompton, Jr., and his Crompton Construction Company. The firm then changed its name and became known as Snyder, Crompton & Associates, Inc. It continued to grow, both in the number and the size of its projects.

In January 1978 Murtagh purchased Snyder, Crompton & Associates from his partners, and in 1983, after 12 years with the company, Steven K. Potts became a full partner. Potts now serves as

senior vice-president and treasurer of the firm, while Murtagh is president.

Snyder, Crompton & Associates today specializes in the turnkey construction of fast-track building projects, ranging in size of up to one million square feet. Approximately 80 percent of the company's work is performed on a negotiated contractual basis. Its primary job is to assist in the preliminary design and estimation of projects.

The firm's portfolio of projects includes office buildings, medical facilities, laboratories, churches, warehouses, and recreational facilities.

In Delaware alone, Snyder, Crompton & Associates has completed five office complexes, including Concord Plaza and Foulkstone Plaza, plus numerous buildings at Barley Mill Plaza and Chestnut Run. The firm's projects also include the Silverside Medical

Center in Wilmington; the Limestone Medical Center in Newark; office buildings for Hercules, Inc.; the Brandywine River Museum in nearby Chadds Ford, Pennsylvania; the Stonegates retirement com-

Du Pont Company's Chestnut Run Plaza executive area.

munity in Wilmington; The Du Pont Company's Agricultural Chemicals Department facility at Barley Mill Plaza; a warehouse for the Pepsi Company in West Chester, Pennsylvania; the Brandywine Country Club in Wilmington; and the new WPVI-Channel 6 building in Wilmington.

Other Snyder, Crompton & Associates projects include the ICI Ameri-

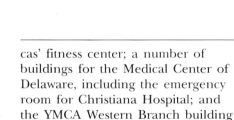

Du Pont Company's fibers department world headquarters at Chestnut Run Plaza.

cas' fitness center; a number of buildings for the Medical Center of Delaware, including the emergency room for Christiana Hospital; and the YMCA Western Branch building in Newark.

In all, Snyder, Crompton & Associates develops about 25 projects each year. Three-quarters are located in Delaware and the rest in southeastern Pennsylvania. The company employs a total of 75 people, including 60 in the field force.

The firm has deliberately remained relatively small, doing approximately $30 million in volume each year. Its major growth has been during the past decade, but this growth has been steady and consistent, rather than dramatic. Within five years the company anticipates an annual volume of approximately $40 million.

Snyder, Crompton & Associates' team approach enables the architect, builder, owner, and property manager to become involved from the conceptual planning stage to move-in day. This team approach fosters an emphasis on quality products, maintaining schedules, and meeting budget goals.

Petrillo Brothers

Petrillo Brothers is a family enterprise that spans three generations and more than a half-century of service. It was established in 1914 by Alexander "Billy" Petrillo, who started a stone quarry and hauling business and called it the A. Petrillo Company. Within 10 years, however, the organization had evolved into a road contracting firm, and in 1934 Billy opened his first concrete plant on the site of his quarry in Edgemoor.

During the 1940s the A. Petrillo Company expanded to include the first hot-mix plant in Delaware—a major venture that would ultimately pave the way for even more success. The company continued to grow, in both size and stature. In 1946, to supplement the business in Wilmington, Billy Petrillo built a sand and gravel processing plant and a second concrete plant in Minquadale.

Later that year Billy retired and left the business in the hands of his two sons, Charles and Denny. The name was then changed to Petrillo Brothers. Building on their father's expertise, Charles and Denny enlarged the operation, eventually making Petrillo one of the largest and most prominent material suppliers in northern Delaware. The brothers also established Certified Concrete and Newark Concrete.

Denny retired in 1970. Nine years later Charles retired, and the Petrillo Brothers tradition continued under the leadership of Charles' sons, John and Charles Jr., who now serve as vice-president and president, respectively.

All three generations of the Petrillo family have served as industry leaders by employing the latest technologies to benefit their customers. Petrillo Brothers, which employs 200 people, continues to be the first choice for general contractors, engineers, home builders, home owners, and commercial building owners. It is one of the most respected names in concrete, recycling, and transport services.

Petrillo encompasses six companies, with operations in Delaware, Maryland, and Pennsylvania. Its market stretches from the Susquehanna River in Cecil County to the Schuylkill River in Philadelphia. The company serves northern New Castle County; Cecil County, Maryland; and Chester, Delaware, and Philadelphia counties in Pennsylvania. It is one of the larger concrete suppliers in northern New Castle County and Cecil County.

The Petrillo companies are Newark Concrete, with plants in Newport, Newark, and Elkton, Maryland; Chester Materials, with plants in Philadelphia, Media, and Chester, Pennsylvania; Certified Concrete, in Minquadale, south of Wilmington; Transport Services, Inc., also in Minquadale, which is responsible for hauling dry cement, including sand, stone, and wood chips, to each of the Petrillo concrete companies; C&J Associates, a recycling company in Minquadale; and the Petrillo Brothers Sand and Gravel operation at the Petrillo Industrial Park.

Petrillo Brothers, as a network of several concrete companies, can accommodate jobs of all sizes, handling projects at different job sites simultaneously. Petrillo has been involved in the largest concrete jobs in the Delaware Valley. For example, in 1983 General Motors needed more than 3,400 cubic yards of concrete for its Boxwood paint facility. The project required 80 trucks and 12 hours of uninterrupted pouring.

Above: Alexander "Billy" Petrillo, founder.

Below: Charles (left) and Denny Petrillo, sons of the founder, took over the helm of the family business in 1946 and initiated an expansion program that brought the company statewide significance.

General Motors called upon Petrillo Brothers for what proved to be one of the largest single monolithic pours in Delaware's history.

In the summer of 1988 Chrysler needed a concrete company it could count on 24 hours per day for 57 consecutive days. It called upon Certified Concrete, which completed the job on time and within budget.

But size is only one component of Petrillo Brothers' success in the concrete industry. What makes the firm distinctive is the unique manner in which it develops and customizes its concrete mixes to meet customers' exact specifications. For example, the company developed the first high-strength concrete of its kind for the Blue Cross building in Philadelphia. The structure's architects had devised a new design to increase square footage for leasing. However, to use the design, they needed a stronger, denser concrete for support. The architects contacted Chester Materials, which then developed a custom mix.

For the Manufacturers Hanover building in Wilmington, Certified Concrete developed a lightweight concrete using solite. This mix allowed for larger spans without columns, thus increasing floor space. And Newark Concrete serves the needs of eight curb machine contractors who require a uniform low-slump mix. This allows concrete to be placed without using forms.

Other mixes developed by the Petrillo concrete companies in-

Above: The tradition continues—president Charles Petrillo, Jr. (left), and vice-president John Petrillo.

Right: The Petrillo companies pour more than 500,000 cubic yards of concrete annually.

clude concrete with steel slivers for increased strength, concrete with superplasticity for higher slumps, a densified concrete mix for the construction of indoor pools, concrete with antifreeze, concrete fibers to replace wire mesh, and the latest admixtures such as nonchloride accelerators to make concrete set harder and faster, which is especially useful during the winter months.

But Petrillo, even though it pours in excess of 500,000 cubic yards of concrete per year, is also flexible. It can adjust slumps, strength, size, durability, set time, color, and density—all to the customer's specifications.

Petrillo Brothers is committed to protecting the environment and

preserving natural resources. This commitment is borne out by the company's waste-management program at C&J Associates.

The firm recycles all demolition wood and tree stumps. After processing, this material is used as fuel by energy-generating facilities and large greenhouses and as mulch and sludge compost for nurseries.

At the recycling center, unlittered roads—not lines and building debris—greet customers. When they drive up to the scale house, a computerized weigh station weighs debris accurately and in seconds. Customers' in-

voices are processed by the time they step into the scale house. The main shredder shreds the inert demolition material, which C&J then recycles for other uses. The wood derived from the main shredder and the two auxiliary shredders is then sold for fuel.

Petrillo Brothers' trucking company, Transport Services, hauls an uninterrupted supply of cement, aggregate, and wood chips from the Lehigh Valley, Baltimore, and Philadelphia. The company's International tractors and cement tankers deliver 26-ton loads to all the Petrillo plants.

Louis Capano & Sons, Inc.

Diversification is both the formula for success and the key to growth for Louis Capano & Sons, Inc., one of the largest and among the most versatile development companies in Delaware.

The firm is involved in virtually all types of construction, from residential (single-family homes, apartment complexes, and condominiums) to commercial (shopping centers and office buildings).

Louis Capano & Sons, a family-owned company, was the fore-runner for many of today's development firms. It served as a training ground for those who later

From left: Thomas, Joseph, Louis Jr., and Gerard Capano are shown in the lobby of their Brandywine Plaza headquarters along with photographs of their father, Louis J. Capano, founder of Louis Capano & Sons, Inc.

established or joined other companies. Capano traces its roots to 1947. It was founded by Louis J. Capano, Sr., an Italian immigrant whose family settled in Wilmington when he was seven years old. In his teens, Capano became a carpenter, then a first-rate builder and developer. He specialized in residential construction, building single-family homes in Delaware and Pennsylvania. The company built, from start to finish, numerous developments as well as many custom homes in North Wilmington and Hockessin. In 1970 Capano diversified into multifamily housing, with the development and construction of the 744-unit Cavalier Country Club Apartments near Christiana.

Today Capano is headquartered in the Brandywine Office Plaza, a project it developed. It has more than 100 employees and comprises

numerous corporations and partnerships that build, own, and manage real estate. Most fall under the auspices of three companies, all established since 1975 when two of the elder Capano's four sons entered the family business.

Capano Development, Inc., specialized in single-family home developments. Among the projects to its credit are Shipley Woods, Rockwood I and II, The Woods, and Londonderry town homes. Related companies have recently ventured into commercial development. BC Development owns 30 acres on U.S. Route 202 proposed as the Brandywine Marketplace, a 220,000-square-foot retail complex. Capano Brothers Associates owns 62 acres of prime commercial property, called Center Point, adjacent to I-95 in Christiana. This will be developed into 500,000 square feet of commercial and retail space, hotels, and restaurants.

Capano Construction Company builds apartments and residential housing. Its developments include Drummond Hill apartments, Wood Creek single-family homes, Valley Stream Village single-family homes and apartments, and Walden town houses, all in either Pike Creek Valley or Christiana. The firm also completes construction for other Capano enterprises, including building additions and renovating the various shopping centers it owns.

Capano Properties Inc. assumes the management of properties, such as apartments and shopping centers, owned by all Capano businesses. Capano Properties is supervised by a full-time property manager, who heads a management staff of 35 people and has better than 10 years of experience in commercial and residential properties.

Other units in the Capano enterprise are Capano Investments and Capano Group L.P. They own several shopping centers, including Branmar, Midway, Brookside, Meadowood, and Plaza III. Branmar and Midway, two of the largest strip shopping centers in New Castle County, were completely rebuilt and renovated by Capano. The company has a commitment to the long-term ownership and management of its commercial properties.

Capano's latest commercial venture has been the purchase and conversion of the 200,000-square-foot John Wanamaker's department store, just north of Wilmington, into a major office complex. The project includes the construction of an additional 100,000 square feet of office space.

Still other elements of the Capano enterprise are a hotel, a bank, and resort land development. The company owns the 150-room Holiday Inn in Penns Grove, New Jersey, a property Louis Capano, Sr., invested in more than 20 years ago. The firm recently added 50 rooms and updated the hotel's exterior. It plans to build and operate more lodging facilities in the future. Two of the Capano brothers have also become major investors in First State Bank, a new financial institution that opened in Wilmington in late 1988. Capano is also involved in resort land development. It owns approximately $35 million of oceanfront real estate in Sussex County's Bethany Beach.

While residential construction has been and continues to be the mainstay of Capano's business—

it accounts for about 60 percent of its volume—the company's future will find even more activity in the commercial sector, a move that mirrors Delaware's burgeoning economic growth. The firm also plans to enter the industrial development area.

The senior Capano died at the age of 57 in 1980, but his business has been carried on admirably. At the time of his death, two of his four sons had already joined the company, learning the business, as he did, in their teen years. Today all four Capano sons are active in the corporation. Louis J. Capano, Jr., serves as president of Louis Capano & Sons, Inc., Capano Construction Company, and Capano Development. Joseph M. Capano is vice-president of all three companies. Entering the business in 1988 were Thomas J. Capano, a vice-president, and Gerard Capano, an

The four-story, 60,000-square-foot Core States Bank building exemplifies the excellence in constuction for which Capano-built commercial properties are known.

assistant vice-president.

Louis Capano & Sons, Inc., is a paradox of sorts. It is, on one hand, a stable business that has been around for more than 42 years, guided by strong family management and a reputation for reliability. It prides itself on the completion of all projects it has ever initiated. But Louis Capano & Sons is also a young and vigorous enterprise that thrives on diversity and maintains enough flexibility to take advantage of new opportunities. The paradox has proved successful: During the past 15 years the company has grown dramatically.

The Commonwealth Group

The Commonwealth Group is a fully integrated, diversified development company—and one of the largest enterprises of its kind in Delaware. The privately held, family-owned and -operated business provides a comprehensive portfolio of services to its clients. These services include real estate investment, development, leasing, property management, construction management, sales, and marketing. Projects are located throughout Delaware, Pennsylvania, and Maryland.

The company, more than 50 years old, has involved the expertise of three generations. It was established in 1936 by Benjamin Vinton, Sr., to oversee the investments of those who had financial interests in oil and gas properties in the West. Commonwealth received income from the oil and gas companies, then disbursed the funds to individual investors. In 1945, during its second generation of ownership and management, Commonwealth ventured into real estate and gradually developed a solid track record for innovative, cost-effective commercial projects.

Today Commonwealth is actively involved in more than $125 million in commercial, industrial, and residential projects. Another $50 million is planned through 1992. But Commonwealth's forte remains the office and light industrial sector, which accounts for at least 50 percent of its annual volume. Commonwealth has been in the forefront of office park development, not only in New Castle County, but also statewide. Some of its projects have been developed jointly with other companies.

Recent projects include Riveredge Business Park, a 40-acre light manufacturing and distribution center in New Castle. Other office/industrial parks developed by Commonwealth include the 31-acre Christiana Corporate Center, one of the largest complexes of its kind in the area; Fairview Corporate Center in Newark; Omega Professional Center office

condominium complex near Christiana; West Milford Business Center in Kent County; and Little Falls One and Two, west of Wilmington. Commonwealth was also the major developer of the Kent County Aero Park, a 115-acre industrial business park in Dover, adjacent to the Dover Air Force base.

One of Commonwealth's most ambitious projects has been the development of New Castle Corporate Commons, seven miles from downtown Wilmington. The 32-acre complex has 20 major tenants. Commonwealth, which has its headquarters there, became the first major developer to participate in the Commons in 1983. The company is

responsible for more than 400,000 square feet of office space in the Commons.

In multifamily housing, Commonwealth is the developer of Christiana Meadows in Bear and The Elms in Newark, both luxury apartment complexes that the firm owns and manages. So far, its single-family residential efforts have

been in Pennsylvania—specifically in West Grove, where two developments of 120 custom and semi-custom homes have been built. The Commonwealth Group is also involved in property management, with several million square feet of industrial, commercial, and residential property in three states under its supervision.

Above: Integral to the success of each Commonwealth venture are (from left) Edward L. Fioretti, property management; David Grayson, construction management; Natalie P. Freeman, finance and accounting; Andrew T. Panaccione, finance and accounting; president Brock J. Vinton; and Joseph R. Dugan, marketing and leasing.

Below: Located in Wilmington, Little Falls I and Little Falls II are examples of the office complexes that have brought The Commonwealth Group to the forefront of Delaware development.

Nanticoke Homes, Inc.

Nanticoke Homes, Inc., of Sussex County is among the top three sectional home builders in the country and the largest single-site home manufacturer.

With a market that extends throughout the Delmarva Peninsula, from the eastern shore of Virginia to New Castle County, Nanticoke is a model for success. The company was formed in 1971 by John and Peggy Mervine, who previously ran a chicken brokerage on the property where Mervine's father started the business in 1936. During Nanticoke Homes' first year of business, the Mervines built 17 sectional houses. The company expanded its facility four times during the first seven years. Since 1971 more than 9,500 homes have been built and sold to the consumer, developers, government agencies, and builders.

Today the $70-million corporation employs more than 750 employees and builds more than 1,000 homes per year. It is growing at the rate of 17 percent annually. Nanticoke produces five finished homes per day from its headquarters in Greenwood. There it has 400,000 square feet of manufacturing space in three separate facilities. There is also a model home, drafting department, cabinet shop, millwork operation, a prefinishing department, a molding shop, a truck maintenance facility, an interior door assembly operation, and corporate offices. On-site amenities for employees include a day-care center, a fitness center, and a cafeteria.

It takes Nanticoke only six days to build a home. By the time a Nanticoke home comes off the assembly line and leaves the plant, it is 85 percent finished. The homes are trucked to the owners' lots, set on foundations, and connected to utilities. The porches, garages, brickwork, driveway grading, and basements are handled by subcontractors at the home site.

Nanticoke works directly and closely with its customers, the prospective home owner. Although the firm provides 20 standard layouts, it also custom builds to a customer's specifications. Home prices begin in the upper $30,000 range, not including land, and can go up to $500,000. Fifty percent of all Nanticoke homes are ranchers; the rest are two-story colonials, Cape Cods, and saltboxes. The homes—from traditional to contemporary in design—range in size from under 1,000 to more than 8,000 square feet.

The firm uses only the highest grade of materials and the latest in plumbing fixtures, appliances, and windows. All homes are energy efficient. And because the homes are constructed in a controlled indoor environment, not dependent upon the weather and other causes of delay, costs are kept low, and quality control is enhanced. The low costs are passed on to the consumer.

About 95 percent of Nanticoke's current work is residential—mostly single-family homes with some town houses and multifamily units. But the commercial sector has become a growing part of the business.

Nanticoke Homes, Inc., has created a sales network on the Delmarva Peninsula, with offices in Delaware, Maryland, New Jersey, Pennsylvania, and Virginia.

Nanticoke Homes, Inc., has remained a family-owned business, with John Mervine serving as president and his three sons involved in some facet of the company, from marketing to operations. John Mervine also serves on the board of the Delmarva Homebuilders Association and is president of the National Association of Homebuilders' Modular Building Systems Council.

Homes built by Nanticoke are marked by quick construction, quality, up-to-date materials, and energy-efficient design.

City Systems, Inc.

A penchant for diversity, a unique style blending historic preservation with contemporary flair, and a commitment to urban living—this aptly describes City Systems, Inc., a full-service real estate development, construction, financing, and management company.

Only eight years old—the firm was established in 1981 by business and marital partners Selvino Cericola and Bonnie M. Sherr—City Systems has already established an enviable track record. Its specialty has been both long-term and short-term residential properties—with an emphasis on niche marketing for groups ranging from executives who need short-term housing to young professionals to empty nesters to business travelers. Whatever the project, City Systems has become known for its attention to detail, its emphasis on casual elegance, and its merging of yesterday's craftsmanship and charm with today's amenities.

During the past eight years the Wilmington-based company has been involved with projects ranging from renovated Victorian condominiums for young professionals to hotel suites to upscale apartments and town houses. The company manages more than 200 apartment and condominium units. With only a few exceptions, all City Systems projects have been located within city limits.

City Systems is perhaps best known for Christina House, Delaware's first all-suite hotel. Located in the heart of downtown Wilmington, the 39-suite facility opened in June 1987, and it has surpassed the company's expectations. Geared to the business traveler and thriving on repeat business, Christina House is characterized by personal service and individually styled suites. Its tone is that of a European inn. An atrium lobby, polished wood floors, a fireplace, concierge service, suites stocked with fresh flowers, a wet bar, full refrigerators, and three telephones per suite are just some of

the amenities tailored to the needs of the business traveler.

The hotel also offers state-of-the-art meeting rooms, as well as ready access to secretarial, computer and courier services; catering; and entertainment.

In addition to Christina House, City Systems has also completed Victorian Square, the Court of Delaware Avenue, and Delaview Apartments—these urban luxury apartments have all involved historic preservation and boast such features as crown moldings and original millwork. They have also been updated with new electrical and security systems.

The Guest House is a fully furnished apartment for executives planning to stay in town for a month or longer. Westhill is 42 upscale town houses in a large courtyard setting in Wilmington.

City Systems also built LeParc, a mid-rise, 76-unit luxury condominium complex on a six-acre site along the Delaware River, just north of the city. LeParc is the first development of its kind in this area in years.

Above: The executive office building of City Systems, Inc., typifies the firm's excellence in historic renovation projects.

Below: Downtown Wilmington offers the business traveler the elegant Christina House, a lavishly appointed all-suite hotel in the European tradition, developed completely by City Systems, Inc.

Photo by Robert J. Bennett

Photo by Robert J. Bennett

Grand Opera House, 224   Delaware Technical &
                         Community College, 225

Independent Higher Educa-   University of Delaware,
tion in Delaware, 226   227

Radisson Hotel, 228

Quality of Life

*Residents and visitors alike enjoy the quality of life
afforded by Delaware's culture, education,
and hospitality.*

Grand Opera House

Wilmington's Grand Opera House is Delaware's center for the performing arts. It is also nationally recognized for both the remarkable quality of its restoration and its outstanding programming.

Built in 1871 by a Masonic fraternity, the Grand quickly became one of the most popular variety halls on the East Coast. With one of the largest stages in the country, it hosted some of the most prestigious performers during its first 40 years. Edwin Booth, Ethel Barrymore, Buffalo Bill Cody, George M. Cohan, and John Philip Sousa were among the greats who appeared there.

When movies replaced the rich variety of live performances, the Grand declined into a second-rate, low-budget movie theater. It was marked for demolition in the late 1960s, but on its 100th birthday a group of concerned citizens launched a major effort to save the opera house, and it was reopened for its first live performance in 57 years. Eventually, $6.5 million was raised by businesses, individuals, and government to restore the Grand as a world-class performing arts center. By January 1973 the nonprofit Grand Opera House Inc. had been established, and live performances were once again held regularly.

Today the 1,100-seat Grand is in constant use and sponsors up to 60 programs per year. Generous community and business support has made the Grand's current level of excellence possible. The programming is a diverse mix of entertainment. Well known for its classical music performances, the Grand also features comedy, jazz, mime, dance, country music, and opera. The Grand also serves as home to OperaDelaware, the Delaware Symphony, and Chorale Delaware. In 1989 it established its own group of local musicians, the Grand Chamber Players.

The stability of its support (two-thirds of its income is earned and one-third comes from business, community, and government support) has enabled the Grand to periodically introduce emerging artists and those on the cutting edge of musical trends and avant-garde dance troupes. As a cultural resource for area schools, the Grand hosts approximately 8,000 students each year to attend performances.

A national landmark, the Grand was one of two theaters to receive the prestigious National Historic Preservation Award. It is one of the finest examples of cast-iron architecture remaining in the nation.

Its character distinctively preserved, the Grand nevertheless boasts the latest in multimedia technology. Its lighting and sound equipment are computer controlled and have been updated continuously since 1976. The Grand's superb acoustics, warm intimacy, and tasteful elegance have made it a favorite of many renowned performers. Beverly

Top: The 1,100-seat Grand Opera House plays host to a diverse mixture of musical and dance artists and entertainers with a blend of old-world elegance and modern technology. Photo by John Jenkins, Image Source, Inc.

Bottom: A national landmark, the Grand Opera House is one of the finest examples of cast-iron architecture remaining in the country. Photo by John Lewis

Sills calls the Grand "one of the three best concert halls for voice in the world." Marcel Marceau considered it one of his personal favorite theaters.

Over the next decade and beyond, the Grand Opera House expects to play an increasingly important role in improving the quality of life in Delaware.

Delaware Technical & Community College

Since its creation by the state legislature in 1966, Delaware Technical & Community College has been responding not only to the needs of the communities it serves, but also to the businesses that have shaped the state's economy. The college has played a central role in Delaware's educational, economic, civic, and cultural life.

The two-year, tax-supported institution provides academic, technical, and continuing education programs at four locations: Wilmington and Stanton in New Castle County, Dover in Kent County, and Georgetown in Sussex. The first campus opened in Georgetown in 1967 with 367 students. Since then, more than 10,000 associate degrees have been awarded, and enrollment keeps breaking records, with an average of 14,000 students each year. There are 566 full-time employees, including 342 faculty members.

For more than two decades Delaware Tech has earned an outstanding reputation through the success of its graduates. Nine out of 10 find jobs almost immediately upon graduation, and many students are employed even before they graduate.

Programs leading to a two-year associate's degree include business administration, public service, allied health and nursing, engineering technology, construction management, electronics, aeronautics, security administration, data processing, and secretarial studies. The curriculum reflects the economic climate of the state as well as that of each of the three counties. For example, programs in heavy equipment and automotive technology are strong at the Georgetown site, while mechanical engineering technology is popular at Stanton. Delaware Tech is the only college in the state to offer training in dental hygiene and the only

one to offer a fire protection technology program, complete with a nationally recognized burn laboratory. A program in hotel and motel management similar to the one under way in Sussex County is also offered at the Wilmington Campus.

Delaware Tech also serves as a resource for business. Through its Industrial Training Program, a statewide network of technical specialists work with industry to design courses that will meet its particular needs. This might include start-up training for newly located businesses or technical training to upgrade the skills of existing employees. Through this program, in conjunction with the American Institute of Banking, short-term training and personal computer courses have been offered specifically for employees in the local banking industry. Another example is the automotive service education program, a collaborative effort with General Motors Corporation.

The Industrial Training Program's growth has been phenomenal: Delaware Tech currently has about 270 contracts with businesses and industries involving the participation of more than 5,000 employees—twice the number of four years ago.

Delaware Tech has also earned an international reputation. Teachers attend the college to learn new teaching methods that they can take back to their own countries. In fact, Delaware Tech is one of only 14 community colleges nationwide that belongs to the Community Colleges for International Development, Inc.

Most of the students at Delaware Technical & Community College are Delawareans and remain in the state after graduation. They become the people whose expertise plays a major role in translating the vision for Delaware's future into reality.

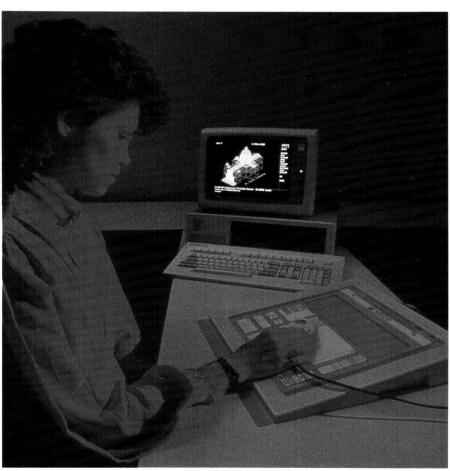

Computer science courses help Delaware Tech students build successful careers in today's technical work place. Photo by Mike Biggs

Independent Higher Education in Delaware

Goldey-Beacom College

Goldey-Beacom College is a fully accredited four-year, coeducational, teaching-oriented institution. The college is committed to enriching the community through quality education, technological progress, and equal opportunity. Baccalaureate and associate degrees lead to successful business careers in many fields.

The comprehensive education offered prepares students for success in the business community and provides an excellent foundation for higher-level training in a wide variety of fields. Programs focus on

Independent higher education in Delaware is a vital part of the state's economy.

conceptual and critical thinking skills in humanities and social sciences, and on major business skills in accounting, marketing, office technologies, computer information systems, and international business management.

Computer and word-processing labs include an IBM 4361 mainframe and IBM Personal System II/ Model 50s.

Goldey-Beacom College operates a Business Training Center in Wilmington and a Southern Campus in Milford.

Widener University

The Delaware Campus of Widener

University is the second largest of its three campuses. The main campus in Chester, Pennsylvania, and the Harrisburg Campus in Pennsylvania's capital are similar to the Delaware Campus in their beautiful, suburban settings and reputations for personal attention to student needs.

Of the university's eight colleges, the School of Management, School of Nursing, University College, the Law School, and the Brandywine College offer programs in Delaware. The Widener University School of Law, which has a branch

in Harrisburg, is headquartered in Delaware.

The one component of the university that operates solely on the Delaware Campus is Brandywine College, a two-year residential school emphasizing personal achievement and offering career-oriented and transfer programs with a liberal arts base.

Wesley College

The oldest private college in America's First State, Wesley College offers

ca's First State, Wesley College offers modern facilities, a central location, and quality education. A hallmark of its 117-year history is individual attention.

A fully accredited, coeducational, liberal arts institution, Wesley offers more than 20 baccalaureate degrees, including accounting, applied communications, computer information systems, computer science, education, environmental sciences, fashion marketing, history, marketing, management, medical technology, physical education, political science, and psychology. The college also offers associate degree programs in a variety of career directions.

Wesley offers daily lunchtime and twilight classes and special programs at Dover Air Force Base, as well as late afternoon and evening classes on campus. Classes at both locations are available during fall, spring, and summer semesters.

Wilmington College

Wilmington College, founded in 1967, is a private career-oriented institution offering undergraduate and graduate degrees.

The educational programs are designed to help students achieve their potential by providing a personal approach to career education. The primary goal of Wilmington College is to provide academic and personal growth through the integration of theory with practical experience.

To serve the educational needs of Delaware, Wilmington College offers programs at five sites statewide—the main campus in New Castle, Dover Air Force Base, Silver Lake Complex, Georgetown, and the Wilmington Graduate Center.

The personalized education and a well-trained faculty give students the skills that will make them competitive in the job market. Wilmington College accommodates the working adult through flexible scheduling, a liberal transfer-credit policy, and small class size.

University of Delaware

The University of Delaware has more than 17,000 graduate and undergraduate students, with more than 3,500 full-time employees on its payroll. Based in Newark, the university also has facilities statewide. Its faculty includes internationally known scientists, authors, and teachers, of whom 80 percent hold doctorates.

The university has strong ties to the state's business community. The College of Business and Economics, with 2,200 graduate and undergraduate students, is fully accredited by the American Assembly of Collegiate Schools of Business. In response to the demand by working Delawareans for high-quality graduate accounting and business programs, both the M.B.A. course and the recently created master of science degree in accounting schedule all required classes after 4 p.m., with all offerings taught by full-time faculty.

The Financial Center Development Act has led Delaware to become an internationally recog-nized location for banking and financial service activities. The new Financial Institutions Research and Education (FIRE) Center is committed to research on issues relevant to financial institutions and to education and public service. The American Bankers' Association's prestigious Stonier School of Banking, held at the university each year, brings about 1,200 students from across the nation to attend this intense, two-week session.

In 1982 the Small Business Development Center was established to provide training for entrepreneurs. The center also provides consulting services to more than 600 small business owners each year.

The Center for Information Systems Management, Education, and Research (CISMER) was established in 1985. The university is also a leader in the development of instructional programs that use sophisticated computer technology. Other university-related organizations serving the business community are the Center for Economic Education and the Bureau of Economic and Business Research.

With more than 1.8 million volumes of books and periodicals, the university library is the largest comprehensive research collection in the state. DELCAT, the library's

Graduates of the University of Delaware's Master of Business Administration program are in great demand by employers who want the best. Photo by Robert Cohen

on-line catalog, is accessible via off-campus modems statewide.

The university has also developed an outstanding reputation for research in cooperation with industry, including composite materials, information science, natural science, biotechnology, energy, virology, and agri-genetics. The Delaware Research Partnership, a fund established at the university by the state in 1984, provides matching moneys for new technological investigations with industry. The University Research Park at Lewes offers sites for corporate tenants to interact with university researchers.

The university's Division of Continuing Education provides professional development seminars, short courses, and certificate programs to enhance careers.

Through its 10 colleges, its institutes, and centers, the University of Delaware has helped foster growth and development in the chemical, computer, energy, food, agricultural, and marine sciences industries. It has truly served as a major force in Delaware's economy.

DELCAT, the University of Delaware Library's on-line catalog system, is accessible throughout the campus and, via modem, throughout the state. Photo by Jack Buxbaum

Radisson Hotel

A good barometer of any state's economic health is its success in attracting conventions and meetings. Judging from the thriving business at the Radisson Hotel Wilmington, Delaware is in top form.

The nine-story hotel, one of the state's largest convention complexes, has been hosting events for groups as large as 1,350 people since its 1979 opening. With a prime downtown location at 700 King Street, the Radisson offers versatility in planning, pricing, and presentations. The hotel's staff of 150, particularly those involved with planning and catering, responds efficiently and creatively to the ever-growing demand for corporate meeting space and first-class accommodations.

While the hotel attracts a diverse clientele—including vacationing families, tour groups, and out-of-town guests of area residents—the staple of its business is the corporate traveler, both individuals and groups. The hotel has more than 600 active accounts.

Right: Executive-level service is featured in 40 guest rooms on the Radisson's eighth and ninth floors.

Below: The Radisson caters to the business traveler with such amenities as conference facilities and guest rooms that provide comfort, service, and privacy.

Among the advantages Radisson offers this market are two floors of meeting space; the largest ballroom in the state, spanning just under 10,000 square feet, which seats 850 for dinner and 1,350 for theater-style meetings; and a conference center with three executive boardrooms.

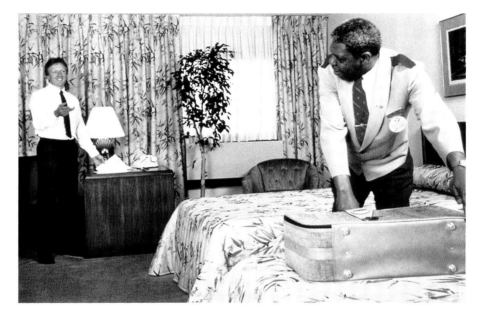

On the hotel's eighth and ninth floors, 40 guest rooms feature executive-level service. This includes complimentary daily newspapers, automatic drip coffee makers with a supply of coffee, milk and freshly baked cookies, and other deluxe in-room amenities.

During 1988 the Radisson completed a $3-million renovation program resulting in a refurbishing of all 217 guest rooms and suites and all meeting space, and the creation of a new, 200-seat restaurant, The American Bar and Grill. With its diverse menu and extensive wine list, the restaurant draws both

hotel guests and the downtown business lunch-goers.

The Radisson features an indoor hotel swimming pool, indoor garden court, exercise room and whirlpool, and underground parking. All rooms are accessible to the handicapped. There are also designated rooms for nonsmokers.

To ensure that it maintains its reputation for world-class service, the Radisson makes a special effort to communicate with its guests. Each month guests are invited to a two-hour reception where they meet and converse with the hotel manager about hotel services, operations, and policies.

The Radisson Wilmington is one of 165 hotels, inns, and resorts in the United States and 10 other countries under the auspices of Radisson Hotels International. Based in Minneapolis and one of the fastest growing hospitality companies in the nation, Radisson prides itself on operating not a chain of look-alike hotels but rather a collection of properties that reflect the character of the markets they serve.

The Wilmington hotel is a partnership of Carlson Companies and Gilpin Wilmington Inc.

Patrons

The following individuals, companies, and organizations have made a valuable commitment to the quality of this publication. Windsor Publications and the Delaware State Chamber of Commerce gratefully acknowledge their participation in *Delaware: First Place.*

Amato & Stella Associates*
Artesian Resources Corporation*
Atlantic Aviation Corporation*
The Aqualon Group*
Bayard, Handelman & Murdoch*
Canada Dry Dist. Co. of Wilmington
Louis Capano & Sons, Inc.*
Caulk Dentsply
Chesapeake Utilities Corporation*
Chrysler Motors Corporation*
CIBA-GEIGY Corporation*
Citicorp/Citibank*
City Systems, Inc.*
The Commonwealth Group*
Jack Corrozi, Builder*
Delaware Development Office*
Delaware Technical & Community
   College*

Delmarva Power*
Diamond State Telephone Company*
The Du Pont Company*
Emory Hill Development, Inc.*
First Atlanta Bank
FMC Corporation*
General Chemical Corporation*
General Foods USA*
General Motors Corporation*
Gilpin, Van Trump and Montgomery,
   Inc.*
Grand Opera House*
The Healy Group, Inc.*
ICI Americas Inc.*
Independent Higher Education in
   Delaware*
James Julian, Inc.*
Kaumagraph Corporation*
Keen Compressed Gas Company*
Krapfcandoit*
The Linpro Company*
Marine Midland Bank
Mellon Bank (DE)*
Nanticoke Homes*
NOR-AM Chemical Company*
C.C. Oliphant & Son, Inc.

Peninsula Oil Company, Inc.
Pepper, Hamilton & Scheetz*
Petrillo Brothers*
Plastic Materials Company, Inc.
Radisson Hotel*
Skadden, Arps, Slate, Meagher &
   Flom*
Slocomb Industries, Inc.*
Snyder, Crompton & Associates*
Stoltz Bros., Ltd.*
Sussex Trust
Take-A-Break, Inc.
Townsends, Inc.*
University of Delaware*
Wilmington Finishing Company*
WILM NEWSRADIO*
Wohlsen Construction Company*
Wyman Electric Service Company*
Young, Conaway, Stargatt & Taylor*
Harry David Zutz Insurance, Inc.

*Participants in Part 2, "Delaware's Enterprises." The profiles of these companies and organizations appear in chapters 7 through 11, beginning on page 131.

Bibliography

"A Delaware Almanac, Newcomers' Guide." *Sunday News-Journal,* 1988.
Baldwin, William C., ed. *Historic Brandywine Guide Book.* Kennett Square, Pennsylvania: Kennett News and Advertiser, 1962.
Balick, Lillian. *The Delaware Symphony: Origins and the First Fifty Years.* Wilmington: Delaware Symphony Association, 1984.
Brochures and maps supplied by Delaware Development Office and by local Delaware chambers of commerce.
Carter, Annette. *Exploring from Chesapeake Bay to the Poconos.* Philadelphia: J.B. Lippincott Co., 1975.
Delware: A Bicentennial History. New York: W.W. Norton and Co., 1977.
Delaware DataBook. Delaware Development Office, March 1989.
Ferriss, Benjamin. *Original Settlements on the Delaware/History of Wilmington.* Gateway Press, 1987. (Originally published 1846. Compiled by members of the Delaware Geneological Society.)

Fleming, Kevin and Jane Vessels. *Delaware, Small Wonder.* State of Delaware, 1984.
History of the Delaware State Chamber of Commerce. 1988.
"Insiders' Guide to Delaware." *Delaware Today,* April 1989.
Vessels, Jane "Delaware: Who Needs To Be Big?" *National Geographic,* August 1983, 171-197.
Eagan, James Michael. *Beautiful Delaware.* Beaverton, Oregon: Beautiful America Publishing Company, 1981.
Eberlin, Harold Donaldson and Cortlandt V.D. Hubbard. *Historic Houses and Buildings of Delaware.* Dover: Public Archives Foundation, 1962.
Federal Writer's Project of the Works Progress Administration. *Delaware: A Guide to the First State.* New York: Hastings House, 1938.
Fleming, Lorraine M. *Delaware's Outstanding Natural Areas and Their Preservation.* Hockessin, Delaware: Delaware Nature Education Society, Inc., 1978.
Hoffecker, Carol E. *Corporate Capitol,*

Wilmington in the 20th Century. Temple University Press, 1983.
Hoffecker, Carol E. *Delaware: A Bicentennial History.* New York: W.W. Norton and Co., 1977.
Miller, Jim. *Start the Presses.* Delaware State News.
Munroe, John A. *History of Delaware.* University of Delaware Press, 1979.
Newark Center for Creative Learning. *Fun in the First State.* Newark: Newark Center for Creative Learning, 1975.
Pitz, Henry C. *The Brandywine Tradition.* Boston: Houghton Mifflin Co., 1969.
Stauss, Tom. *Discovering Delaware's Coast.* Georgetown, Delaware: Sussex Prints, Inc., 1980.
Weslager, C.A. *Dutch Explorers, Traders and Settlements in the Delaware Valley, 1609-1664.* Philadelphia: University of Pennsylvania Press, 1961.
Young, Toni. *The Grand Experience.* Watkins Glen, New York: The American Life Foundation & Study Institute, 1976.

Index